Engaging Children and Youth in Africa
Methodological and Phenomenological Issues

Edited by
Mwenda Ntarangwi &
Guy Massart

Langaa Research & Publishing CIG
Mankon, Bamenda

CODESRIA
Council for the Development of Social Science Research in Africa
Conseil pour le développement de la recherche en sciences sociales en Afrique
Dakar, Senegal

Publisher:
Langaa RPCIG
Langaa Research & Publishing Common Initiative Group
P.O. Box 902 Mankon
Bamenda
North West Region
Cameroon
Langaagrp@gmail.com
www.langaa-rpcig.net

Distributed in and outside N. America by African Books Collective
orders@africanbookscollective.com
www.africanbookscollective.com

ISBN: 9956-762-74-1

Notes on Contributors

Patricia Henderson

Henderson holds a doctoral degree in anthropology and is currently a senior lecturer at Rhodes University in the Department of Anthropology. Her research interests include medical anthropology, the anthropology of children and youth and the anthropology of performance and creativity as social critique. Her theoretical interests include phenomenology and embodiment. Henderson's most recent publication is a monograph entitled *A Kinship of Bones: AIDS, Intimacy and Care in Rural KwaZulu-Natal* (2012, University of KwaZulu-Natal Press; 2011, Amsterdam University Press).

Ollo Pépin Hien

Hien is a political scientist and a researcher at the Department of *Sciences Juridiques et Politologie de l'Institut des Sciences des Sociétés (INSS)*, at the *Centre National de Recherche Scientifique et Technologique (CNRST)* in Ouagadougou, Burkina Faso. Hien is writing a PhD thesis in political sociology at the University of Ouagadougou and the *Université Catholique de Louvain* in Mons, Belgium. He is studying the social, political and historical conditions of the emergence of political opinions in Burkina Faso, the way those opinions are expressed and their impact on contemporary social and political transformations. He teaches at the *Ecole des Cadres Supérieurs de l'Institut National de Formation en Travail Social (INFTS)*, Burkina Faso, where he is also associated researcher with the *Laboratoire Pluri* of the Sociology Department at the University of Ouagadougou.

Jeremy L. Jones

Jones is Assistant Professor of Anthropology at College of the Holy Cross in Worcester, Massachusetts in the United States of America. He holds a doctoral degree in anthropology from the University of Chicago. His fieldwork in Zimbabwe (2006-2009) focused on young urban men, and their strategies for making ends meet amid severe economic crisis. Prior to taking up the position at Holy Cross, he worked as a part-time lecturer at the University of Pretoria and Eugene Lang College (The New School).

Guy Massart

Massart is a Belgian social anthropologist. He holds a PhD in Communication Sciences from the *Ecole Normale Supérieure de Lettres et Sciences Humaines de Lyon* (ENS-LSH). He is currently a consultant and professor of anthropology at the M_EIA - *Instituto Universitário de Arte, Tecnologia e Cultura*, based in Cape Verde, and active member of the Belgian NGO, Songes. Massart's anthropological work focuses on ethnography that avails opportunities for empowering collaborative practices for working with children and artists and as a communicative activity drawing on multimedia potential (multimedia, website, arts, events). His research interests focus on the transformations of masculinities in Africa, the relations between childhood and public knowledge and on contemporary popular cultures in West Africa.

Flavius Mayoa Mokake

Mokake is currently pursuing an Interdisciplinary PhD in Public Health, Social Medicine and Health Communication at Ohio University. He holds M.A. degrees in History (University of Buea) and International Affairs with a concentration in African Studies (Ohio University). His research focuses on disease and healthcare, media and governance, peace, youth criminality and socialization. His recent publications include articles in *Tropical Focus* (2011), *African Conflict & Peacebuilding Review* (2012), a chapter (with Dr Henry K. Kah) in *Germany and Its West African Colonies: "Excavations" of German Colonialism in Post-Colonial Times* (2013) and *Representations and Perceptions of the "Other" in Cameroon Popular Culture: The Journey across the Mungo River* (2013).

Mwenda Ntarangwi

Ntarangwi holds a doctorate in cultural anthropology from the University of Illinois at Urbana-Champaign and teaches at Calvin College in Michigan, USA. His research and teaching mainly focus on cross-cultural education and the intersection between culture and performance, especially as experienced and expressed by youth. He is the author of *Reversed Gaze: an African Ethnography of American Anthropology* (Illinois, 2010), *East African Hip Hop: Youth Culture and Globalization* (Illinois, 2009), *Gender Identity and Performance: Understanding Swahili Cultural Realities Through Song* (Africa World Press, 2003), editor of *Jesus and Ubuntu: Exploring the Social Impact of Christianity in Africa* (Africa World Press, 2011), co-editor of *African Anthropologies: History, Critique and Practice* (Zed, 2006), and guest editor of a Special Issue of *Africa Development* (Vol. 37 No. 3) focusing on *Parent's Involvement in Children's Lives in Africa* (2012, CODESRIA Books).

Silué Oumar

Oumar holds a Ph.D. in Political Sociology from the University of Bouaké and is currently in the Department of anthropology and sociology at the Alassane Outtara University in Bouaké. His work and research focus on youth interaction with politics, political parties, gender, and conflict. He is an expert in conflict management and development aid as well as a scientist, science journalist, political analyst and a member of the African Council for the Development of Social Science Research (CODESRIA).

Natéwindé Sawadogo

Sawadogo is a sociologist and holds a doctoral degree in Science and Technology Studies from the University of Nottingham (United Kingdom). He is a founding member of the *Laboratoire de Recherche Interdisciplinaire en Science Sociales et Santé* (LARISS) in the department of sociology at the University of Ouagadougou (Burkina Faso). His research interests include the history of social sciences in Africa, higher education, public policy, professions, markets and the public interest, and science, technology and innovation in contemporary Africa. He is a contributor to the *Encyclopaedia of Global Human Migration* (Blackwell, 2012, and author of *A Global History of the Sociology of Professions* (Lambert Academic Publishing, 2012).

Table of Contents

i

Introduction

Mwenda Ntarangwi and Guy Massart

Context

Since 1994, CODESRIA has dedicated resources to supporting research and the study of youth and children in Africa with the underlying belief that as the largest segment of Africa's population, children and youth should be at the centre of any understanding of and planning for Africa's contemporary social, economic, and political realities. Nestled within CODESRIA's larger umbrella of Child and Youth Programme this focus has had different tangents of research, including the Child and Youth Institute, established in 2002, a symposium held in 2006 to set the tone for engaged research and policy making in the field, and the Multinational Working Groups that focus on various aspects of this research topic. This volume follows in this same vein, comprising chapters developed from papers presented at a conference titled "New Frontiers of Child and Youth Research in Africa," held in Douala, Cameroon, on 26 and 27 August 2009. Prior to meeting at this conference, many of the contributors to this volume were also part of a Multinational Working Group on Youth and Identity in Africa through which some of the ideas presented here were developed and expanded. Fortunately, both editors of this volume participated in these last two programs and thus bring experience and perspectives gathered there.

Given the expanded field of childhood and youth studies in the world and its accelerated growth in Africa, this volume emerges within a context of conceptual, methodological, and phenomenological debates regarding children and youth

1

identities, agency, and discursive practices that specifically involve the processes by which cultural meanings of childhood and youth are produced and understood in today's globalised world. A general review of contemporary work on childhood and youth, for instance, reveals three types or categories of children and youth that inform some of the thinking expressed in this volume. First is the elusive nature of the categories of childhood, children, and child. Bluebond-Langner & Korbin (2007) see childhood as a social and discursive space and as such an object of dispute and power; children are regarded as a more or less homogenous sociological group; a child is an individual interacting with other individuals and a source of experiences. Secondly, critiques of representation coming out of recent scholarship and especially the "linguistic turn" in social science now recognizes childhood and youth as constructed concepts, as being in permanent and emerging construction in the social structure; a construction in which the "agents" so objectivised participate (Diouf, 2003). Thirdly, an old/new perspective is making a comeback on the front stage. Ideas about the relationship between an individual and his/her culture developed within the "culture & personality" school are emerging in scholars' attempts to connect individual personality with socialization (Quinn, 2005).

The current volume emerges from a specific academic context that also reflects these trends, albeit in a more nuanced way. Whereas earlier studies of children and youth in Africa tended to portray them as objects of adult activity, De Boeck and Honwana (2002) show children and youth in Africa as active and independent individuals who carry a great deal of agency that makes them both "makers" and "breakers" of social life in its multiple manifestations. Indeed, in our current volume, we follow De Boeck and Honwana's (2002) insistence on seeing African childhood and youth beyond the often constraining Western notions of vulnerability and innocence (especially for children) and instead show how recent advances in technology, the intensification of global processes and the continued weakening of the nation-state, while contributing to new and complex ways of being children and youth in Africa, also provide a valuable lens through which to study social change. Moreover as we gradually move away from Western notions of humanity and dignity that are predicated on the individual as the most viable platform for defining children and youth and embrace one that promotes social relations and obligations often mobilised in many African contexts, we are becoming cognisant of the limited ways in which scholars record children's and youth's own perceptions and practices of self-definition.

Studying Children and Youth

Three conferences organised by CODESRIA over a period of three years (2007-2010) in order to evaluate the results produced by the Child and Youth Programme, as well as contemporary debates and research in Africa, have showed the value and relevance of treating children and the youth as a contemporary agency and not like passive actors simply produced by society. This notwithstanding, youth and children have not been treated as autonomous and independent actors in much of research in Africa (as some of the contributors to this volume show). Research and writing about children and youth in Africa has been shaped by the same cultural assumptions and practices that often regard children and youth as adults in the making and almost always as individuals in need of adult guidance and supervision. This view of children and youth is not limited to Africa because much of the literature regarding Western societies also reveals similar trends, but with more positive changes being made to perceive, treat, and engage youth and children as participants in the production and structuring of society (Shanahan, 2007).

In the wake of the work produced by a few great African researchers (including but not limited to Reynolds, Biaya, Diouf, Mbembe and Honwana), there are new ways of regarding children and youth, particularly from cultural, political, sociological, economic, and spatial points of view. These works urge us to go beyond constructions of children and youth as victims and see them as actors, even if constrained, within different power relations and therefore, with disputed agency (Bordonaro, 2012). Comparatively, however, children have been less studied than youth. This dearth of research on children may simply be a consequence of cultural assumptions about children's lack of agency or could be a consequence of inadequate methods of research. As Amy Best has asked when considering methodological issues regarding representing youth, "how can investigators successfully negotiate the role of adult researcher as they work to gain access to youth worlds…and develop meaningful rapport? How can adults interpret and write about youth realities given the distance that exists between their worlds and our own?" (2007:8). Answers to these questions may lead us to a better approach to studies of children and youth in Africa.

Despite the many demonstrations of youth agency (see, for example, Biaya, 2000), conferences, articles and proposals by African researchers time and again present children and youth like objects forged by imported cultural products and as passive receptors and reproducers of the values, languages and behaviours conveyed through these cultural products. The theoretical challenge of contemporary social science research and especially anthropology is still, and always, in establishing a linkage between daily experiences and broader historic processes. But a number of research productions too often seem to project general postcolonial inequality relations over the individuals themselves and remain silent about or unaware of ways in which individuals and communities engage with such powers and structures in creative and complex ways. While this rhetorical process has a powerful political charge, it clearly jeopardises our efforts at knowledge production and support to the individuals concerned, that is, children and youth. We ought to observe power at play and its effects at all

4

levels, and, especially, that of the subjects' experiences as they feed social science research.

Cultural Theories, Politics and Dynamics

As the chapters in this volume ultimately reveal, many researchers are conscious of and concerned with the alienation of youth from their traditional African cultures and rootedness as a result of adopting and valorising behaviours, styles and consumptions which are not produced in Africa, including the diasporic Africa, by Africans. In other words, there is a very widespread concern, both personal and scientific, among young African researchers regarding relations of power in cultural production and consumption in contemporary Africa as they continue to witness the replacement of African cultural practices by foreign ones. Central to this notion of cultural imperialism are issues of power and inequality where values, practices, and even material products are not locally derived. The music, language, clothes, hairstyles, food, ways of relating to others, as well as larger identity issues that are embodied by majority of Africans today, all seem to be framed and derived from non-African sources and especially Western ones.

The inequalities that emerge from such cultural "take-over" are not only in the capacity to produce and disseminate cultural content, but also in the reduced accessibility that African youth and children have to cultural content in its larger sense. Moreover, even when they do have such access, the cultural objects that are involved in that access are often derived from elsewhere, despite African youth invention and creativity. We must note, however, that while the cultural dynamics are framed within a global phenomenon, the self of those concerns remains generically defined as "African" and at times there are specific choices made by the Africans who prefer these non-African cultural products. It is not unusual, for instance, to witness that the larger percentage of popular music that is aired on many FM radio stations in Africa is non-African even

5

though there is enough local African music to be played on these radio stations. We can think here of such nations as Zimbabwe, Kenya, Malawi and Ghana. Although cultural forms produced by Africans and Africa's diasporas have greatly influenced and continue to influence cultural forms all over the world, the perceived imbalance of cultural influence and presence on the global scenes is pervasive. The perceived "violence" emanating from these and other contemporary cultural and political relations calls for great intellectual caution and tools to analyse the emerging dynamics. What are the underlying factors that would explain such an imbalance of cultural consumption? What effects does such a practice portend for African youth and children's cultural productivity? From this observation, it appears that theory, as a disciplined imagination of social reality – considered as a process – is central to a dialogue with the conditions, motivation, concern and relevance of African researchers in youth and childhood studies.

Put bluntly, for better or for worse, youth and children are, as Deborah Durham (2000) would call them, "indexes", that continue to perform two tasks central to the imaginings of contemporary social reality in Africa. Firstly, children and youth are the products of socialisation, reflecting what our society is and has become. Hence the great concern with their getting away from mainstream adult and male norms. More than the results of proximity education, they are the "results" of contemporary relations which obviously overtake the local. Their sociality, their dreams, their music, their ways of marrying, of learning, etc. are products of relations that are largely beyond the local scene and as a result new spaces are constantly being created. We cannot, therefore, understand contemporary African youth and children's realities by just looking at the local. Secondly, youth and children often crystallise collective anxiety about the future. It is as if youth and childhood as categories whose frontiers are limited by time appear to be time containers and create a point from which

6

one can contemplate the future. This helps understand why children and youth become threats (see, Henderson and Silué, this volume; De Boeck & Honwana, 2005; Bordonaro, 2012), not only by what they reveal, but also by what they do.

Because children and youth are in these fluid conditions of formation, being, becoming, socialisation, and education, that make them cultural subjects or even turn them into convenient cultural boards on which global, neo-liberal and neo-colonial capitalism relations project, they can no longer be contained or understood by locally-generated sociocultural frames. This reality of uncontrollable youth and children's sociability creates anxiety even among researchers (let alone among adult kinsmen and African socio-economic elites). From this position, we can see youth and children not only as merely imbibing Western-derived cultural products, but rather as creating new cultural frames that may be inspired by Western sensibilities but which also reflect an ingenuity and risk-taking of their own that is unprecedented and often threatening to the status-quo (Honwana, 2012).

Particularly exposed to the question of the cultural dynamics of the contemporary world, researchers in youth and children studies are obviously more sensitive to contemporary experiences of youth than they are of childhood. As pointed above, there may be conceptual and methodological explanations for this research imbalance where researchers are unable to access the world of children because of various power dynamics as well as individual perceptions of children's viability as sources of information about their own lived experiences. Various CODESRIA selection report committees have pointed out that in this specific domain of cultural dynamics, one often reads simple straightforward communication models (Winkin 2000), a reception model that emphasises the power discrepancies in the cultural domain between Africa (receptor) and global businesses and international organisations (transmitter). Chapters analysing the pragmatics of popular practices (Ntarangwi, Mokake, and

7

Jones) show everyday creative practices and their effects on youth as well as on larger social relations with other social categories. They show what constraints orient their performance and what effects these performances have on the individuals and their communities. Studies considering actual cultural dynamics through time allow for the analysis of not only the symbolic relations captured, but also, through the practices and narratives of the subjects, an understanding of how youth and children imagine the social relations they encounter and are embedded in daily.

Theories, Narratives and Social Order

In fact, one might ask with the authors in this volume: how is society imagined among youth and children? What kind of folk sociology, or better still, sociologies, circulate? What is it concerned with? Which entities do those folk sociologies convoke? We do not have enough systematic empirically grounded research on this very imagination. For now, we would subscribe to Jeremy Jones' suggestion (this volume) that folk sociologies about youth are often normative, characterised by a reification of cultural processes and interpretations in terms of social crisis. The model prevailing in these folk sociologies, is positivist, structuro-functionalist, à la Durkheim and synchronic. Such a model will not capture the dynamism that regards children and youth as producers, rather than mere consumers, of culture. The model only sees them as deviating from "normal" culture and seeks to find ways to align youth with the traditions and "acceptable" practices, that is, a prevailing imagined social order obstructive to change.

The essentialisation of cultural encounters (a defective theoretical rendering of the reception of cultural products), places the researchers and all subjects in the impossible position of having to ideologically purify and Africanise cultural products, only to be reminded of the long-lasting colonial relations and the continuous power imbalances that

8

have produced what may be considered African today. To counter this reified notion of culture, it is much more promising to concentrate on the mechanisms of inventiveness and on the power struggles from the actors' points of view. As anthropologists, we recommend concentrating on the ways in which people, the actual youth and children being studied, deal with the various cultural flows and mediators of those flows and the specific practices and results of such dealings. Such observations should help researchers structure new theories of cultural dynamics in a much more interactionist perspective. The imaginings of social realities in such a locus of power allows researchers to play a central role in opening new horizons of interpretation. All contributions to this volume attest to the invention and creativity of youth demonstrated by Cameroonian girls creating new interpersonal spaces through cell phones and by so doing, placing themselves in more advantageous positions in daily interactions with families, friends and lovers (see Mokake, this volume). A simple gadget such as the cell phone transforms young women from mere subjects of culture who await direction from their parents or male guardians to agents of power and autonomy that allow them to decide how to engage with parents and even male friends. New ways of dressing, listening to and making music, marrying, loving, making a living, communicating, learning, praying, circulating, and socialising, are described here (see especially Jones, Hien and Silué, this volume), pointing to important sites for cultural production and at times subversion, and its consequential stigmatisation as a censure of their very inventions. Another discursive formation (besides the normative one discussed above) that has constrained the smooth conduct of research in contemporary Africa lies in the power nexus that consultancies have over researchers' activities.

Given the limited resources available for academic institutions in Africa to carry out regular research that is shaped by the basic desire to advance intellectual knowledge, many

African researchers have turned to consultancies. It is quite clear that in the essential dimensions of the intellectual activity involved in analysing the social world, research and consultancies are distinct in many ways, including in the responsibility of the definition of the problematic and methods (researcher or commissioner), the research time, the actual empirical work, the type of documentation referred to, the debates, rhetoric, norms related to quotations and other works, the use and aim of the knowledge produced, the freedom of expression and the way the works are evaluated and published (de Sardan, 2009). In this process, the financial, cultural and intellectual independence of researchers is threatened (Nyamnjoh, 2010) as researchers act as mere implementers of specific research agendas created by the funding agency to meet their specific internal goals. We have here another social arena of knowledge production, orientating and framing actual practices and discourses. These tensions but describe the capacity of those that commission research to constrain the activities of the researchers by imposing questions, methods, conceptual frames and values that shape both the research process and outcomes (see Henderson and Sawadogo, this volume). The importance of this private demand for knowledge production would not be very significant if it were not for the difficulties African Universities or other public institutions of research have in creating lasting conditions of work for researchers, to be poles of valued knowledge production and of much needed-sites and occasions for debate.

There is another phenomenon that has emerged following the presentation of new ways of dressing, of listening to and making music, of marrying, loving, of making a living, of communicating, of learning, praying, circulating and socialising. Because all those new ways are often associated with the influence of other cultures and thus regarded from a normative perspective, culture becomes reified, indeed an invention of fixed cultural entity (tradition) that in turn stigmatises the youth that are at the centre of creating these new ways. This logically

10

leads to an interpretation of social reality in terms of social crisis, showing clearly enough that the model prevailing in these folk sociologies, as Jones shows (in this volume), is a positivist one, despite the recognition by many of the extraordinary rapidity of social and cultural innovations going on in Africa today. This shows well enough how theory has a role to play in orienting the analysis of contemporary phenomena and in articulating visions of contemporary African social life.

We have pointed out the probable constraints stemming from a specific theoretical frame, based on an elementary model of contemporary cultural dynamics, rooted in personal experience and consciousness of inequalities, in the desire for order, meaning and closure, a narrative of a close system, achieved through forces, norms and values. To understand the pervasiveness of this narrative implies a need to know its pragmatics and an analysis of power relations in contemporary African realities. An analysis in terms of functions, (such a structural view of society produces strong moral discourses and is sustained by it), based on essentialised identities and symbols, will not do. As appears clearly in Oumar Silué's chapter (this volume), the ideology guiding relationships with actors of the formal political arena has long been understood by the youth of the *"grins de thé"* (Hien, in this volume), to be the gap between belief and pretence (Godelier 1999). Beyond ideology, youth are conscious that their practices are in specific times and spaces constrained by a more specific dimension of power. These gaps are numerous in the everyday life of contemporary African youth.

Interest in those gaps is not to construct an anomic figure, but rather a privileged way to analyse power relations in daily interactions and how constrained youth create new spaces and sociabilities (Honwana, 2012). Consequently, various forms of imaginings co-exists and we can only heed the call from Henderson, Sawadogo and Jones (this volume) to embrace other key notions for our theorising, focusing on provisionality, improvisation and dexterity, innovation, and code-switching. The youth do not constitute in this aspect a category, but rather embody many different forms of youths and of authorities that can be distinguished and analysed.

A second constraint leans on research activities with and about children and youth in all their aspects. These constraints stem from the institutional setting, the characteristics of the research arena on youth and children and its main actors. The difficulties in the universities and of the education systems and the pressing information and knowledge needs of international development agencies promoting specific ideas of development as well as of children, youth, family, education, protection and needs are but two elements shaping the overall research frame. Besides the actual effects of this situation on research and theories (which for the most part are not produced in Africa), one faces again the unequal power relations inherent in the cultural content (see Ntarangwi, Henderson, and Sawadogo, this volume; de Sardan, 2009; and Nyamnjoh, 2010).

Ricoeur reminds us that social order rests on the legitimation of a dominant system (Ricoeur, 1997: 31-2), that is, social order implies specific power relations. Normality and vulnerability do not seem to be central notions of narratives able to open up horizons and new imaginings of society which, we believe, African social scientists should participate in shaping. It is crucial to forge other explanations, remaining true to the daily experiences and challenges facing young Africans. This is best guaranteed by the proximity and debates with subjects and peers whereby the ethnographer enters in dialogue with subjects, popular musicians and amateurs about interpretations of contemporary African social realities; another creates moments when "habitual forms of interactions (are) suspended" to access children's voices (Ntarangwi, this volume). Those dialogues are key in studies concerned with cultural dynamics of contemporary Africa and some of their essential dimensions include the capacity of researchers to establish respectful dialogue with, listen to and take seriously

12

the perceptions and experiences of children and youth. Such an approach will allow the researcher to work within a research framework that is dictated by the child and youth agenda and priorities rather than by the researcher's own agenda and notion of what is important. But it also appears that between researchers and children and youth of different conditions, distance must be vanquished and performing conditions must be established. The analysis of the very selection of study interests, of the uses and effect of knowledge produced by scientists, should help us conceive new approaches, just as Sawadogo suggests in his chapter on the problematisation of youth and knowledge production in Africa.

So, being an infant, a toddler, or a young child seems to be a real frontier in childhood studies in Africa, even though certain categories of sociocultural identities need to be keenly scrutinised. Girls have, for instance, received some focus but are not much better off. It is as if researchers were urgently drawn to their referent lot, without much attention left to categories of other distinct identities with the noticeable exception of seminal work such as Lyn Thomas's (2004), where it appears that comparison and historical depth are crucial to the exploration of African gender relations, including dialogic forms of masculinities. If women are more involved in the anthropology of childhood (as books and scholarly papers authored by women indicate), and if time and experiential methods are to be supported, one can understand the challenges of such research, especially given cultural and institutional settings in which African social research is conducted, including the theories, methodologies and global and local politics that all shape knowledge production.

Doing Social Research: Youth

Doing social research within the post-colony is obviously faced with the theoretical challenges of connecting and linking the inequalities of the global capitalist cultural market that are

13

rooted in colonial relations to actual experiences of research subjects and the unequal relations that they have with those that conduct the research. This challenge not only requires imagining new forms of social order, but also new strategies for social research. If the frame of explanation is a normative model of society, as Jones points out, that society will surely be deemed to be non-functional at all, in crisis, pathological, requiring all kinds of fixing and compliance of categories. This frame and within it, this failure, implies (as is to be automatically expected) conflicts between social groups, a sort of impossibility to cooperate, to establish reciprocal relations, limiting the interactions and communication between those groups. This is only in part what is observed today. The difficulties and framing effect stemming from a normative theoretical approach are echoed by the difficulty to conceive of what society is, which is obviously a theoretical question.

A disputed social order also implies fundamental difficulties in reconciling individuals and groups with societal aspirations. It is in this light that one interprets the pursuit of particular social intents associated with the social space that is childhood and youth, as a treason, a loss of identity, as the destruction of an entity already under threat (our culture). We believe it is this quagmire that characterises the recurring questioning about new African social actors, persons, and selves that are torn between collective and individual identification (Janin, 2003) between individuals, families and ethnicity, or religion, and even nation. There is a blurring of the lines between theoretical difficulties on the one hand and experiential perceptions and political debates on the other. The post-colony, as we look at it from these constraints, is a challenge in the imaginings of social reality to researchers as well as to other social groups (Godelier, 1999). From this point of view, one can look at the new frontiers of childhood research, trying to reconcile different constraints weighing on social research as an activity in Africa, through two questions relative to relevant theoretical and political challenges: How to

14

question normative, synchronic and functionalist views which blind the researcher to the dynamics of social creativity?

Ricoeur suggested that utopias in their corresponding relationship with ideology (understood as a form of imagination, and with three performances: dissimulation, legitimacy and integration) create a *"décalage"* – a gap through which critique can flourish. Just as many moralising discourses of young contemporary artists create spaces for social critique, they also create spaces for the production of meaning and actions. How will researchers produce alternative scientifically grounded imaginings? Laplantine told us long ago about other *"voies de l'imaginaire"* [pathways of imagination], such as messianism, utopia and trance. How do we characterise the *"voies de l'imaginaire"* of contemporary youth in Africa? How are those imaginary pathways developed? What kind of effects do they have?

How do we participate in challenging contemporary power relations through our professional research activities? Obviously, by communicating researchers' analyses and by provoking debates at all levels, local and international. This communication supposes a certain kind of analysis: an analysis of contemporary power relations in Africa from the point of view of younger generations. The authors in this volume offer some answers, some weapons, and encouragements based on their practices and analyses.

Pathways to Theoretical Creativity

The first indication is to concentrate more on the actual practices of youth and children in contemporary Africa and/or to build upon interrogations, analyses, and observations from other social scientists. It is the observation of practices and the debating of those practices with the subjects and peers that can renew and create a relevant conceptual apparatus. Authors in this volume propose provisionality, creativity, innovation, invention, improvisation and dexterity, and code-switching.

15

Scientifically, this turning and attention to actual practices is a departure from both popular and development discourses and as such implies a conceptualisation of behaviours that establish different power relations. How subjects do things, be they in marriage, learning, working or in interpreting the world, should be a source of theoretical creativity (see Ntarangwi, this volume). In fact, practices feed into the actual production of knowledge faithful to the experience of subjects.

Sawadogo's chapter opens up, as he himself states, a new field of research in youth studies in Africa. It concentrates on the analysis of the production and effects of knowledge about childhood and youth. Understanding the power games at work in the production of knowledge is to analyse the circumstances in which the broad models highlighted above actually come to lean on individuals and collectives lives. This line of thinking confronts us with powerful institutions active in the control and production of knowledge; they are institutions that more or less affirmatively claim the capacity of creating and implementing policies, norms, rituals and a great capacity to disseminate images and narratives.

Both the structuro-functionalist view as well as the "universalist" development perspective rest on institutions' ability to guarantee norms, to dispute them in various spaces leading us to the occupation of the political sphere and to questions of legitimacy, relevance and applicability of norms and, more broadly, to the issue of the State, international development actors and religions. In other words, there is a whole field of investigation to develop in terms of institutional dynamics and their roles in the governmentality of youth and children in Africa and their mediation processes. This type of study requires a creative combination of text analysis, institutional dynamics, policy study and analysis of actual experiences.

It appears from this collection of chapters that the opening and exploration of new spaces are central in all processes in which youth are described to gain negotiation strength, the capacity to engage in political relations and the ability to form and participate in various social organisations. Firstly, through their uses of new technologies of information and communications, youth engage in new communication and virtual spaces that literally open up the world to them. They appear as points in a network, able to participate in larger movements or create other spaces where to negotiate exchanges and participation. The cellular phone, for its part, is one key device of these new spaces. Moreover, it is also a crucial support of music; it is a multifunction device that is central to the circulation of music and images. Musical activities continue to be a very vivid cultural world, widely disseminated through events, radio, TV and personal devices. They too open spaces of expression for youth, through political analyses, reflections and critiques (see Ntarangwi, this volume). The "street corners" that male youth occupy with peers as they construct interesting points of view and redefine the relevant political spaces allow them to participate in the development of spaces where differentiated citizenships meet. Those spaces are structured, as described to us by Hien and Silué (this volume), by geographies, social affinities, gender, family and ethnic bounds, as well as by a shared social condition. How the individual parts of those groups evolve and participate in different circles remains to be further investigated. The capacity of researchers to participate, observe and debate the carving out of new relevant spaces is crucial in the capacity to analyse these topographies of youth of different gender and conditions.

This leads us to methodological considerations and actual conditions of doing research. Time, finances, stability, documentation and debates often lack and/or are spread out. Long empirical works continue to be an essential requirement in the process of theoretical imaginings and research production in the world in general and in Africa specifically. This is well developed in Henderson's chapter and appears in others as well. Imaginative and adapted methods of work with

17

children, but also a combination of methods; all require continuity and means. Another continuity that is linked to this recommendation, a real frontier of innovation in the African studies of childhood, is the capacity for researchers to maintain an enduring interest in childhood and youth. Very few researchers have the possibility of articulating a long-term research programme based on an actual diagnosis of the field in Africa. This explains the phenomenological "blanks" in so far as the most easily reachable subjects are those investigated. As pointed out previously, young children are nearly absent in the research production, where young male cultural consumption and production is analysed, girl practices remain under-researched, translating the specific problematisation of young girls in societies as a field of dispute and power. Moreover, with so many research projects in Africa emerging from specific consultancy projects generated and shaped by specific needs of the commissioning agencies, a truly longitudinal research agenda on youth and childhood is a tall order.

The study of cultural dynamics in which youth and children are central actors deserves specific attention. Several reasons justify the relevance and importance of the study of cultural performances as a way of understanding youth and children in Africa today, because performances are social interactions looked at in their making, in their creating and enacting local conditions. Such study opens great spaces in the investigation of contemporary cultural dynamics, beyond a symbolic analysis. It opens access to imaginary dynamics, content, narratives, overtaking the straightforward alienation conundrum. Despite these inroads into youth and childhood studies brought by the attention given to performances, most researchers remains limited their interest to music, hip-hop movements and a focus on boys. Other popular expressions, such as theatre, soap operas, jewellery and hair and body grooming, deserve to be studied for the same reason, for their potential theoretical creativity. The pursuit of efforts in the multiple forms of popular culture should allow the production of complex reception models, and then to approach in nuanced terms the lingering issue of young Africans as consumers of low-quality imported goods. In this field, as in many others, girls and infants are close to being ignored, as they seem to be given consideration insofar as they are the central objects of "a-normality". It probably takes more female researchers to take these persons into consideration.

Another framing effect, a homogenising effect of the very notions of childhood and youth as they are circulated in their different meanings in Africa today, translates into the lack of social distinctions existing today among children and youth. It is imperative to work on social distinctions in this cultural field. Multiplying the evidence from different points of view will help analyse the narratives of contemporary cultural dynamics. In the studies of cultural dynamics, the researcher ends up debating with, and recognizing, the collaboration of the actors (musician, listeners, dancers, etc.) in making sense of their social reality. This potential for collaboration between researchers, artists and consumers is to be explored because it reasserts the theoretical interest and the necessity to pursue the analysis of actual performances.

The critical analysis of the very notion of "African" experience of youth and childhood can be tackled through multisited research and comparison, as shared in this volume. A comparative endeavour to tackle the Africanness of youth and children experiences certainly contributes greatly to the study of contemporary postcolonial conditions, but we still have lingering challenges. What do African youth and children have in common, and according to whom? What specific analyses would this construction avoid taking into account? What variations in youth's and children's lives and experiences are overlooked? Why? How do we relate different imaginings of Africa from political, academic and subject perspectives? These are important research areas for others to pursue as they build on the work presented in this volume. Some of the contributors have already provided this kind of comparative analysis without necessarily setting out expressly to do so.

In concentrating on a very specific urban scene in Ouagadougou and a clearly circumscribed empirical object, young men sharing tea on street corners – *grins de thé* – -Hien ties specific observed practices to social conditions, dynamics, political process and relations, and the creation of social and topographical spaces in the city. This study draws the reader to Oumar's and Jones's analyses and calls for a comparative and diachronic approach/follow up, to understand the role of those youth creations in context. It appears that the uses of those new spaces and their capacity to generate capital for their participants depends on the larger political situations where youth identity fluctuates according to their users' social positions.

The two last chapters by Silué and Hien dwell on the relations of youth with the public sphere, calling for comparisons between them and with other situations. The relations youth have with the public sphere are to be understood sociologically (the social conditions of the integration of youth as a generational identity into the political field) as well as conceptually (how these relations participate in the construction and reproduction of a specific notion of youth). As observed through both chapters, the phenomenon is referred to in francophone Africa (Mali, Burkina Faso, Côte d'Ivoire, Senegal and the DRC are cited). The comparison could be based on the very sociological, institutional, and historical conditions of integration of youth into the formal field through their action in public spaces. If, besides Silué and Hien's analyses present in this volume, we consider the analysis of the emergence of a revolutionary youth in France by Delplanche (2011), as was kindly suggested by one of our reviewers, we can distinguish the following significant elements from those cases; each of which open up further research perspectives.

The first trait to be underlined is the existence of a new definition of generational identities in all three settings, linked to the pedagogical innovations of the Enlightenment in pre-revolutionary France and to mechanisms related to the institutionalisation of formal schooling systems and the pervading notion of specific generational rights. (See Sawadogo and Henderson, this volume). Among all those youth political activists, students and their organisations play a determinant role. They are students who have bleak perspectives of professional integration, or consider such integration to be inadequate. The skills of those students in terms of communication and organisation are key to their empowerment. Contrary to what is observed in the *"grins"* of Ouagadougou analysed by Silué, both in French revolutionary as well as Ivorian SDS analysed by Hien, the members of those "youth" movements are in their (late) twenties and these movements have demonstrated their capacity to mobilise and use physical force. They act in institutional settings where political oppositions are clear-cut and exacerbated by the general political and military situations, with historically constructed social antagonisms (ideological, ethnic, regional, national, relative to the French "orders").

Although the authors seem often to present the youth as aligning with political positions they are excluded from and dependent on these forces, it is clear that youth action structures the political field. Both in the Ivorian and French cases, some youth leaders do access political positions and play a crucial role in the redefinition of the political structures following their coming to power. The question is therefore to analyse the threshold at which the occupation of public spaces by youth groups defined by experienced marginalisation, bleak perspectives and significant analytical and communicational skills switch from cultural innovations to open public political action.

The strength and pervasiveness of cultural innovation by youth and the social relevance of the youth identity both spur the authors to refer to the notion of "sub-culture". In this sense, we see how the nature of the actions of those youth groups is part of a larger social, cultural and political dynamic (see Ntarangwi, this volume; Honwana, 2012). Their presence in the public spaces is crucial in all instances. Per se, this calls for an analysis of the relations of younger generations to social, political, and cultural spaces in Africa. Those spaces are linked to communication skills (namely through popular arts) and are scenes of debates and tensions even though female youth seems to be largely absent from those youth groups. As the cultural agency of young women in Africa is gaining recognition (Thomas, 2004; Chitando and Chitando, 2004), their political roles deserve specific attention in contemporary research as no clear exploration of presence/absence and political ways of women are suggested. Allusions to the traditional monopoly of public violence by men have been made, but that is far from being a satisfying explanation.

In France, the revolutionary period awakened after more than a century of absolutism, followed by the opening up of the political space (the convocation of the Estates General by King Louis XVI in 1789), a sequence that echoes distinctively the situation in Cote d'Ivoire and Burkina Faso in the last decade. In their research, Hien and Silué were able to interact directly with youth and therefore to put to the fore youth motivations and to underline their ironic stance (they sell their work to politicians, they do not offer their militancy out of belief or adhesion to the political message). This allows the authors then to enhance youth behaviours as personal tactics or strategies to access employment. The French data does not allow that conclusion, and one wonders whether this personal motivation to play an active political role to gain integration into the power, or more prosaically the economic, structures of their society is specific to contemporary young Africans. This is in doubt, as Delplanche underlines that youth movements originated from university students with bleak professional perspectives and that in the negotiations with revolutionary

22

leaders they showed both submission and wit. The insistence on this ironic stance could also be a kind of moral bias in the researchers' perspective. Anyway, this ironic stance must also be considered as the result of the contemporary historical conditions in which young Africans live. The French revolution is old, lots of messianic ideologies have flown by in Africa, with their lots of disillusions. Comparison has its limits.

Nevertheless, the consideration of the consciousness of one's own interest through a group makes it possible to consider the interactions of youth groups and associations with other (non-youth) political actors as a relation of exchange where access to resources controlled by the latter are traded for social (and hence) political capital, the voices, presence, networks, potential violence mobilisation being a specific symbols of youth and social force traded for power and income. This utilitarian approach must not lead us to underestimate how those youth as a category and as agents in fact transform the structures of their society. With this, we still are considering the youth from a conflictual perspective. Finally, their irony and reflexivity as implied in this exchange are indicative of contemporary young African (and not only that) imaginings, typical multi-constrained conditions, fragmentised conditions and double (multi)-bound conditions which reminds us of Gilroy's (1993) endeavour to capture such a modern condition in an attempt to combine cultural and political perspectives in a truly phenomenological framework as they relate to contemporary young African experiences. Let us explore, the innovations, the constraints, the gaps, the contradictions, the irony and convictions that underlie youth identities.

One can see how these atypical youth in specific historical and political settings produce a peculiar category of "youth", a "breaker" youth, a significant political force and means of leverage, eager to carve out spaces for their becoming integrated youth, or rather persons, rather than able to upset the contemporary patrimonialism of contemporary political systems. Further research should reconnect these movements with the larger youth experiences in Africa.

The Chapters

The organisation of this volume reflects the emerging realisation of a need for African and Africanist scholars and researchers to insist on a more nuanced approach to understanding childhood and youth realities in Africa. The way we formulate research questions, the meanings we impose on specific categories of identity marking, the actual tools of research we employ, the role played by children and youth in shaping research questions, methodologies, and processes, and the analyses we make of data collected on children and youth in Africa ought to be informed by the concrete and yet complex realities of what it means to be a child or youth in a specific place and at a specific time in Africa. These issues are addressed in this book under three related parts: firstly, a framing of the theoretical and conceptual issues in child and youth studies in Africa; secondly, a focus on popular expressions; and thirdly, relations with the public sphere.

As mentioned above, Sawadogo's chapter sets the pace for the book with an exploration of new areas of research on childhood and youth in Africa, from two perspectives. The first is concerned with the processes through which sociological discourse on the professions in modern States has formed and transformed over time. In this case the role of the professions within the context of modern States has been ambivalent, revolving around collectivity-orientation and self-interest. Yet, the scientific basis of their knowledge makes them the State's privileged mediators for social control. The second focuses on scientific knowledge as the basis of professional power. Almost all the different theoretical orientations reviewed, in the sociology of sciences, share a view about the social construction of scientific knowledge. In relating the two perspectives, the questions of critical importance in future

24

research might be: as objects of scientific knowledge, have African children and young people been subject to distinctive constructions, which are sensitive to their historicity, by childhood and youth professionals in Africa? Since the collectivity-orientation of professions cannot be taken for granted, how do professions' own processes affect the understanding of, and acting upon, childhood and youth in Africa?

Henderson's chapter follows the trajectory taken by Sawadogo and lays out a critical analysis of research on youth and children in Africa, focusing on three major issues: the construction of Africa as a monolithic research Other, the transposing of (mostly) Western notions of youth and childhood on research on youth and children in Africa, and the assumed status of deviance for children who do not conform to linear conceptions of sociability tied to the nuclear family (as a basic social unit of a stable, endogenous, but reified social order). Henderson argues convincingly for a need to be sceptical about the universalising language of "HIV/AIDs orphan" and "child soldier" that often assumes that for children to be autonomous and have adult-like agency is a clear reflection of social disintegration. Using two case studies of research in Southern Africa, Henderson provides a model for research with and on children and youth that demonstrates a desirable new direction for African research on children and youth. Here she shows how longitudinal ethnographic studies that centre youth and children as narrators of their own life experiences provide the best accounts of their lives, projections, and aspirations.

Jones's chapter completes this set of three chapters that seek to theorise and problematise youth and childhood studies in Africa. Jones starts by problematising the terms "Africa" and "youth", arguing that youth have become an important element of research focus because of their numbers and also because of their assumed social deviance or disconnect. As Jones posits, how else would we explain the lack of analyses of, say seventy year olds and focus on their elderly status as we study young people and focus on their youth? To further push assumptions about youth, Jones focuses on Zimbabwean urban youth who get married and live in their own households but do not fit the conventional definitions or assumptions about social maturity expected of youth who "settle down" into marriage and head a household. Does getting married and having a household qualify one to be a socially recognized adult or does one still maintain youth status?

Questioning this Durkheimian social theory that expects social reproduction to mechanically follow a clear linear processes of childhood to adulthood, Jones shows how youth can follow the set steps of becoming social adults (through marriage and having a household) but fail to attain that social status. Using data from his ethnographic research in densely populated suburbs of Zimbabwe's capital city, Harare, Jones challenges scholarly assumptions of a societal stability that is assumed to be achievable when youth marry and keep a household. He instead shows how some youth continue to sustain a very truncated and unstable married life. Being married and having a household is not the answer to the social "instability" associated with youth. A new theorising is necessary and African youth will be at the centre of this paradigm shift.

In his chapter on "Children's Lives and Children's Voices", Ntarangwi uses music as a window through which to move scholarship on African children from being represented as passive and as victims to children representing their own social realities. While there are not many avenues through which children can represent their own lived experiences, Ntarangwi shows how critical expressive culture is in availing insights into children's lives that are not dominated by passivity and victimhood. What avenues can provide us with glimpses of complex children's lives and also avail to children opportunities to tell their own stories? Ntarangwi thinks that music is the answer to this question and shows, with examples from Kenya,

26

Uganda and Tanzania, how children's lives are represented by some musicians and by some children themselves. Young people are no longer just passive consumers of adult-sanctioned culture but are also very much producers and shapers of public culture.

Mokake's study examines the impact of mobile phones on teenage girls in the Molyko neighbourhood of Buea in Cameroon. It argues that to a number of girls that frequent the neighbourhood, a cell phone represents, among other things, a technology of contradiction, connectivity, identity, safety, status and above all a gadget to express personal autonomy. This has an empowering effect on girls to the extent that with just a beep a girl can influence relations she has with her male friends – especially a *mboma* (married male friend) – as well as evade parental control. Mokake argues that the introduction of mobile phones in Molyko has produced social consequences with far-reaching ramifications, reconfiguring social relations and power. Data for the study were collected primarily through participant-observation, random sampling of perceptions and a close reading of images of mobile phone advertisements publicly available at the research site.

In his chapter on youth in public spaces in urban Ivory Coast, Silué shows that with increased political and economic marginalisation of youth, a political culture has emerged through the use of certain street spaces as sites for dialogue and discussion of vexing political issues. These discussion spaces are organised in formats that reflect practices associated with parliamentary procedures, university lectures or public rallies, wherein participants not only recognize and follow certain protocols but also consider the exercise as an important means of accessing political power and influence. Indeed, as Silué reports, numerous participants have used these street spaces as avenues to larger political roles in the Ivorian government. Using the power of oratory, mobilisation, new technologies, and sheer numbers, youth in Abidjan's suburbs have created a culture of entrepreneurship and political power that many youth have had no access to in an increasingly globalising context. Silué uses data gathered through observations and interviews to show how young people reinvent their role in politics through self-education, taking advantage of new technologies that are often uncontrollable by the state, and building mob solidarity. As a result, many participants in these social spaces access jobs, income, and political power. The appropriation of some of the youth by politicians, however, shows the continued vulnerability of youth in many African countries where economic opportunities remain limited. That notwithstanding, Silué provides an intriguing discussion of how youth "social clubs" generate enough political clout to shape national political practices.

References

Best, Amy. L. 2007, "Introduction," in Representing Youth: Methodological Issues in Critical Youth Studies, ed. Amy L. Best. New York: New York University Press. Pp 1-36.

Biaya, T., 2000, 'Jeunes et culture de la rue en Afrique urbaine', Politique Africaine, N° 80, pp.12-31

Bluebond-Langner, M. & Korbin, J., 2007, 'Challenges and Opportunities in the Anthropology of Childhoods: An Introduction to Children, Childhoods, and Childhood Studies', American Anthropologist, Vol. 109, No. 2, pp. 241-246.

Bordonaro, L., 2012, 'Agency does not mean freedom. Cape Verdean street Children and the Politics of Children's Agency', Children's Geographies, Vol. 10, N°4, pp. 413-426.

Chitando, E. & Chitando, A., 2004, 'Black Female Identities in Harare: The Case of Young Women with Dreadlocks', Zambezia, XXXI (i/ii), pp. 1-21.

De Boeck F. & Honwana, A. (eds.), 2005, Makers and Breakers. Child and Youth in Postcolonial Africa, Trenton, NJ: Africa World Press.

Déplanche, N., 2011, 'From Young People to Young Citizens: The Emergence of a Revolutionary Youth in France, 1788-1790', Journal of Social History 45 (1), pp. 225-237.

Diouf, M. 2003, 'Engaging Postcolonial Cultures: African Youth and Public Space', African Studies Review, Vol. 46, No. 2, pp. 1-12.

Durham, D. 2000. 'Youth and Social Imagination in Africa: Introduction to Part 1 and 2,' Anthropological Quarterly, Vol. 73, No. 3, pp. 113-120.

Gilroy, P. 1993. The Black Atlantic. Modernity and Double Consciousness. Cambridge, Massachusetts: Harvard University Press.

Godelier, M. 1999, The Enigma of the Gift, trans. Nora Scott, Chicago, IL: University of Chicago Press.

Hastrup, K., 2005, 'Social Anthropology. Towards a Pragmatic Enlightment?' Social Anthropology, 13, 2, pp. 133-149.

Honwana, A., 2012, The Time of Youth: Work, Social Change, and Politics in Africa. Sterling, VA: Kumarian Press.

Janin, P., 2003, *'Vivre ensemble ou la douleur d'être "en grande famille"*. Politique Africaine, 3/2003, N°91, pp.33-50.

Jenks, C., 2005, Childhood (Key ideas). 2nd Edition, London: Routledge.

Levine, R., 2007, 'Ethnographic studies of Childhood: An Historical Overview', American Anthropologist, Vol. 109, Issue 2, pp. 247–260.

Quinn, N., 2005, 'Universals of Child Rearing', Anthropological Theory. Vol. 5(4). pp. 477-516.

Shanahan, S., 2007, 'Lost and found: The Sociological Ambivalence Toward Childhood'. The Annual Review of Sociology, 33. pp. 407-428.

Thomas, L. 2006, 'The Modern Girl and Racial Respectability in 1930s South Africa', The Journal of African History 47 (03), pp. 461-490.

Winkin, Y. 2000, 'Baltasound as the Symbolic Capital of Social Interaction', in Fine, Gary Alan, Smith, Gregory eds., Erving Goffman, Londres, Sage Publications, pp. 193-212.

The Professional Constructions of Childhood and Youth in Africa: New Directions for Research

Natéwindé Sawadogo

Introduction

Applying the perspective of the sociology of science and the sociology of professions to the study of the practices of childhood and youth in Africa can stimulate some original questions for future research in the continent. Clergymen, monarchs and modern statesmen have shaped the functions of the professions throughout different periods, because their technologies of government and their lives have partly meshed with the application of expert knowledge (Sawadogo, 2008). Professions and States developed together (Durkheim 1947, 1992; Parsons 1951; Spencer 1896). The history of their relations exhibits alternating conflicts, but their function for each other has been vital, particularly in modern societies (Halliday, 1987). Yet, as Halliday observes, "notions of professional civility have been jettisoned as completely as earlier functionalist interpretations have been repudiated" (Halliday, 1987:3). However, subsequent studies reassert the significant, though ambivalent, role of professions in the changing modern State (Dingwall, 2008; Freidson, 1970, 1986, 1994; Halliday, 1987). It is obvious that African States show quite different patterns (Medard, 1991; Ouédraogo and Sall, 2008) and their relation to formal knowledge are not always comparable to those of Western States. But these contingencies in the development of African States do not invalidate the central status of professions in government processes. The role of the professions in modern States has been ambivalent, revolving around collectivity-orientation and self-interest. Yet, the scientific basis of their knowledge makes them privileged mediators of social control.

This chapter discusses, from a sociological perspective, how the professions can shape children and youth identities as well as their lives. The aim is to pave the way for an alternative approach to the anthropological perspective. Moreover, it is not an empirical study of scientists and related interested actors of the construction of childhood and youth in a specific African country. Rather, the chapter highlights the relevance and the theoretical foundation for such empirical studies, from a sociological perspective.

The chapter is organized into four sections. The first section addresses key methodological issues. The second and third sections describe the character and dynamics of science and the professions respectively. They are both of general character. In the fourth section, the concepts described in the second and third sections are brought together to problematize some relevant sociological treatments worthy of further empirical research.

Methodology

This section describes the methodological foundation of the present research. The institutional dominance of anthropology in African social sciences has been an obstacle to perspectives which attempt to contribute to the "sociology" (Elias, 1978) of African societies (Omobowale et al., 2013; Ouedraogo and Sall, 2010). Although anthropologists have been attempting to blur this boundary, it is clear that such claims so far concern jurisdictional strategy (Abbott, 1988; Abbott, 2001; Terray, 1992). Sociology still exhibits a clear distinctive approach to social facts (Blumer, 1969; Durkheim, 1982; Elias, 1978; Parsons, 1951, 1971; Ouédraogo and Bouda,

2011) and anthropology is still far from demonstrating that its claim to the same object as sociology is consistently reflected in its methods, and even its actual research practices (Ouédraogo, 2010; Sawadogo, 2008).

This chapter therefore adopts a sociological perspective. It is not anthropological – this does not mean that anthropology is irrelevant. As is known, sociology, as a scientific discipline, was born in Europe in the nineteenth century to study law-like regularities governing the social world, in the same way the natural sciences study the laws governing natural world (Elias, 1978). It was born just around the period corresponding to the birth of the modern State (Elias, 1983, 2000). The main characteristics of the modern State are widely known (Elias, 1983, 2000; Weber, 1978). In general, a State emerged when a central authority obtained a monopoly of physical violence and fiscal authority over a relatively large territory. Other secondary monopolies came to be formed around these two main monopolies. Specialised apparatuses emerged for the administration of these monopolies (Elias, 1998, 2000; Weber, 1978). The modern State corresponds, therefore, to a level of development in which the use of these monopolies became relatively impersonal, and devolved to specialists groups (Elias, 1998; Weber, 1978).

As can be seen, the emergence of the modern State is the result of "an entire comprehensive transformation" (Foucault, 2008:13). But, here, to paraphrase Foucault, I want to stress the "the intellectual instrument, the form of rationality that made possible the self-limitation of governmental reason as a *de facto*, general self-regulation which is intrinsic to the operations of government and can be the object of indefinite transactions" (Foucault, 2010:13). The distinctive character of the knowledge of these specialists, to whom the monopolies are devolved, is its "scientific" character. This form of the State emerged in Africa at the end of the nineteenth century as a result of European colonization (Amin, 1981; Ki-Zerbo 1978). This is not to say that African States emerged with colonization

33

(Amin, 1981; Ki-Zerbo, 1978), or that the role of science, or knowledge, in general, was not known in pre-colonial African social formations (Diop, 2006; Keita, 2007; Ki-Zerbo, 1978). Moreover, to paraphrase Foucault, I do not mean that with the advent of this social formation in Africa in the nineteenth century, "politics or the art of government finally becomes rational [in Africa]. I do not mean that at this moment a sort of epistemological threshold is reached on the basis of which the art of government became scientific" (Foucault, 2010:18). Obviously, the facts contradict such an argument (Bayart, 1993, 1996; Bayart *et al.*, 1999; Chazan *et al.* 1999; Suret-Canal 1971; Ouedraogo et Sall 2008). Similarly, in pre-colonial African social formations, diverse specialists were necessary to rulers.

With regard to the political systems which emerged with European colonisation, to paraphrase Foucault again, "I mean that [this moment] is marked by the articulation of a particular type of discourse and a set of practices, a discourse that, on the one hand, constitutes these practices as a set bound together by an intelligible connection and, on the other hand, legislates and can legislate on these practices in terms of true and false" (Foucault, 2010:18). Social sciences of childhood and youth in Africa, which is dominated by the anthropological literature – whether done by anthropologists (Abeles and Collard, 1985; Erny, 1968, 1999; Eschlimann, 1982; Fortes, 1945, 1949; Rabin, 1979; Paulme, 1969; Pritchard, 1994; Turner, 1975, 1969) or researchers from other social science disciplines (d'Almeida-Topor *et al.*, 1992; Mignon, 1984; Ly, 1979; Ly, 1992; UNESCO, 1979; UNSDRI, 1984) developed in significant disconnection from this social formation and its correlative intellectual instruments.

This is not to say that, in Africa, this scientific knowledge flows down through all the social structure without any contingency. Nowhere has this level of integration been fully accomplished. The diffusion is gradual, more or less extended, but never uniform in a society (Elias, 1998). As Elias beautifully put it, with regard to European societies, "People cannot remember, and are not taught, how difficult it was for their own society to develop scientific modes of thought out of prescientific ones, and for the scientific modes to achieve ascendancy in all social strata" (Elias, 1978:44). The fact that this integration remains low in contemporary Africa must not confine research on childhood and youth, as in any area of social life, to selected networks of relationships dominated by prescientific or other non-scientific forms of thought and practice enjoyed, until now, by anthropology in particular. The current patterns of ascendancy of scientific modes of thought in contemporary Africa just reflects the fact that "the development of thought structures in a certain direction is itself seen as an aspect of the development of social structures" (Elias, 1978:44). Thus, what is required from the researcher is only to take note that the study of the "rationalisation" of childhood and youth must take into account the distinctive character of this "development of social structures" Elias points out.

Therefore, studying the specialists, whose most developed form is the professions, and scientific knowledge, becomes a key to understanding the dynamics of such rationalisation, in political practice, of childhood and youth or else. It is for this reason that the conceptual description in the two following sections, before outlining the relevant directions for future sociological studies of childhood and youth, is necessary. Both areas of research are yet to be established in social sciences in Africa (Omobowale *et al.,* 2013; Sawadogo, 2008, 2012).

The sections on science and professions are not therefore just literature reviews. African social scientists have had little interest in the study of professions. And the sociology of science and technology is yet to emerge in sociological teaching and scholarly publications. The aim is to make the key literature on the dynamic of professions and science accessible to the reader, in order to clarify the connections made between professions and science on the one hand, and childhood and youth, on the other hand, as much as possible to the reader.

Therefore, the discussion concerns the key approaches in each area with a view to stating the underlying assumption of each, and drawing the implications for the understanding of a specific 'rationalisation' of policy practices such as those related to childhood and youth in Africa. Although the scientific past of Africa cannot be denied, it is nevertheless currently secure to argue that this 'rationalisation' primarily started, in most part of Africa, from the late 19th century with European colonial expansion. It is for this reason that it is also important to know what African societies later made of it after independence.

The references to Foucault should not suggest that this chapter is about the history or philosophy of childhood and youth, using a Foucauldian perspective. When studying "governmentality", Foucault is not concerned with "real governmental practice" (Foucault, 2010:2), but with "the rationalization of governmental practice" (Foucault, 2010:2). Therefore, what this chapter suggests is the opposite of what Foucault did. Using the methodological resources provided by sociology, particularly those resources available in the sociology of science and the sociology of the professions, the chapter is seeks to help lay down the theoretical framework for the study of rationalisation (of childhood and youth) as it is actually carried out by interested actors in specific social contexts.

The following section deals with some of these resources in the sociology of science.

Science in Society: The Social Shaping of Scientific Knowledge

The argument of this section is that scientific activity is a social activity and is therefore more or less subject to the same social determinations prevalent in all human activities. It can be anticipated that the "rationalisation" of childhood and youth in Africa will reflect the dynamics of this historical context. The aim of this section is to document the socially constructed character of scientific knowledge. In this respect, it has a general content. This can help understand, in the third section,

36

the relevance of inquiring into how practices about childhood and youth show specific patterns in specific historical contexts of Africa (Omobowale *et al.*, 2013; Ouédraogo, 2010; Ouédraogo and Bouda, 2011; Ouedraogo and Sall, 2010; Sawadogo, 2008).

Indeed, classical epistemology in philosophy claims that scientific knowledge escapes from social determinations. It sees scientific truth as something outside its subjective construction through human social activity. Sociology, on the contrary, postulates that scientific activity is a social activity and is therefore more or less subject to the same social determinations prevalent in all human activities. The institutionalisation of scientific knowledge results not only from its internal dynamics but also from the social conditions within which it is produced and disseminated. How then do social scientists address the status of scientific knowledge and the conditions of its production in society? This chapter argues that we need to understand these processes in order to understand how a specific practice comes to dominate the organisation of childhood and youth realities in contemporary Africa, because the status of scientific knowledge and the conditions of its production are shaped by the historical conditions of African societies.

Many authors have been interested in the understanding human beings have of the development process in general (classical examples are Hegel, Marx and Comte). In particular, Durkheim's (1915) work sought to address the issue within a wider debate about social action as part of his larger project to make sociology a scientific discipline. Although he contributed to the development of sociology of knowledge, his legacy does not help much as far as debates on the basis of disciplines are concerned. A more specialised and recent approach comes from Bourdieu (2004), who developed sound arguments about the relative autonomy of scientific practice. According to this theory, all thoughts, perceptions, and actions derive their meaning from a specific social universe in which the social agents who produce them are located. That social universe constitutes a "field". It has its own specific logic, more or less formalised, which reflects its specific ends and the particular nature of the games that are played within it.

The internalisation of such a logic that enables the coordination of individual members of the field constitutes the "habitus". Since the scientific field displays hierarchical relationships, this incorporated disposition replicates the symbolic and material characteristics (scientific capital) of each individual member. The scientific field itself is in interaction with other social universes, that is, universes of power. The integrity of the scientific field depends on its capacity to refract external values, which enter the field through its members' networks of relationships. As a result, the study of scientific products becomes a study of the logic of the specific field and its relative independence from its environment; for the field "[...] function[s] as a system of censorship, excluding some directions and means of research *de facto* without even stating any restrictions" (Bourdieu, 2004: 60).

This approach to scientific products is a significant move away, not only from the old enchanted vision of science traditionally addressed in epistemology, but also and above all from three competing approaches, which can be described here. The first, and most classical approaches, is structural-functionalism. It was represented by Merton (1973), and has been remarkably illustrated by Cole and Cole (1967) and Cole and Zuckerman (1975). Its core assumption is that the scientific world is a "community" that develops for itself, fair and legitimate regulatory institutions, ascribing to scientific work, in so doing, a contingent status. The "reward system", as a mechanism of measurement of the degree of recognition from scientists belonging to the same community also functions as a system for the production and maintenance of the scientific community. Yet, this approach has been seen as objectivist and realistic, from a process sociology viewpoint. Given that sociology was institutionalising at that time, such an approach was giving an official account of science. Then insisting on the reward mechanism as regulatory system, Bourdieu (2004) criticised it for reducing science to a consensual "collective finalism".

The second approach that Bourdieu's proposal attempts to recast is the Kuhnian (1962) perspective, which introduced the notions of "normal science" and "scientific revolution". Scientific development is regarded as a discontinuous process, with a series of breaks, where periods of normal science and revolution alternate. The concept of "paradigm" or "disciplinary matrix" as an open framework acquired in the course of professional socialisation served to account for the internal dynamics of the scientific community. Yet by emphasising the normative frame of science, Kuhn reintroduced a mere internal change to science, and therefore overlooked its social environment.

The third trend which is related to the Bourdieusian discussion encompasses distinctive but convergent approaches under what it is commonly known as the "new sociology of science", summed up in the "strong programme" (Bloor, 1983). One of these distinctive insights is from the Edinburgh School, represented by David Bloor and Barry Barnes (1974). Drawing from Wittgenstein, Bloor (1983) developed a theory of science which attributes rationality, objectivity and truth to local legitimacy in relation to the contingent sociocultural norms and conventions of the particular group which produces them. Nevertheless, with Harry Collins (1981) and the Bath School, the formation of preferences within the particular group defined by the Edinburgh School is apprehended through an interpretation of the scientific community with a focus on hierarchies. The directions of the shifts of paradigms have been correlated with the quality of their producers and those of their receivers. This refers to the structure and the logic of the scientific field that is developed in the historical sociology of science. But, even so, from a historical sociology perspective, Collins "remains enclosed within an interactionist

39

vision", and for this reason "he does not at all consider the structural conditions of the production of belief [...]" (Bourdieu, 2004:21).

Other studies attentive to everyday scientific practices come from laboratory studies (Knorr-Cetina, 1992; Grmek, 1973; Holmes, 1974; Medawar, 1964; and Latour and Woolgar,1979). Their distinctive problematic rests on their radical realism, reflected in their suggestion regarding the generalised symmetry between human and non-human. But, as far as historical sociology is concerned, their emphasis on the permanent construction of scientific knowledge has led them to a highly sceptical conception of scientific knowledge. Unlike this approach, Gilbert and Mulkay (1984) ground their relativistic view on the very nature of scientific work. However, this approach leaves little place for external contingencies that would, as the pressure from peers does, influence the process of construction.

Bourdieu's approach attempts to balance this gap while incorporating the literature on science studies. From this sociological perspective, as noted in the first section of this chapter, Foucault's influential approach to knowledge production needs recasting (Foucault, 1971, 1972, 1970). An approach which situates itself at the level of broader systems of thoughts, like that of Foucault, has different implications for understanding everyday scientists' practices and the contingencies they are subject to as part of the nature of their work, of any work (Bourdieu, 1993, 1996, 2003; Elias, 1998). The knowledge of the implications of these contingencies in African scientists' practices about childhood and youth are, though, important.

Overall, two significant conclusions emerge from this analysis of the key literature. On the one hand, despite their difference of orientations in addressing scientific knowledge, there is a clearly shared interpretation of the constructed character of formal knowledge. On the other hand, as boundary-work, jurisdictional conflicts among disciplines are not only necessary for reflexivity and knowledge advancement, but can in some circumstances lead to dogmatism almost, when self-interest takes over the status of the object of study in knowledge production. Showing, through these key literatures, that scientific knowledge is socially constructed – which does not means that they are simple illusions – was the objective of this section. For example, the few empirical sociological studies of scientific practices in social sciences in Africa demonstrate their tendency to extraversion (Hountondji, 1992; Omobowale *et al.*, 2013; Ouédraogo, 2010; Ouédraogo and Bouda, 2011; Sall and Ouédraogo, 2010; Sawadogo, 2008). One might ask: what would be the implications of extraverted knowledge about African children and youth for a comprehensive understanding and efficient policy actions about childhood and youth in Africa? What would be the implications for the children and young people's self-definitions? These are not meaningless theoretical questions. Addressing these processes, as applied to childhood and youth, is necessary for a better understanding of children and young people's conditions in contemporary Africa. However, because these processes are occurring within the context of States monopolies, in which experts play authoritative roles, their mechanisms come more into focus when considered within the framework of the dynamics of the professions. This highlights the relevance of exploring the key sociological assumptions about the professions.

Professions and Social Order

Like the second section, this section examines the key assumptions in the sociology of the professions. Similarly to the second section, it is not about the application of the literature on the professions on childhood and youth in Africa or elsewhere. Here, it is just to familiarise the reader with the dynamics of the professions, as authoritative specialists of the modern State's social structure. As said in the first section, the use of experts is not intrinsic to modern States. The focus on the processes in States only relates to the purposive option of this chapter to move away from perspectives which take their starting point from traditional political systems. The fact that social sciences in Africa have neglected the professions as object of study justifies the need for this theoretical analysis. Besides, scientific knowledge is produced within professional contexts and governmental practice involves professions alongside other actors (specialists or not). The possible applications to childhood and youth of this literature, together with that on science, are addressed in the next section.

Indeed, formal knowledge embodied in science is critical to occupational hierarchy. Since the modern State has typically built its foundations and its technology of government on such a hierarchy, the role of the professions as alternative bonds of modernity consists in the control of that knowledge. For a State's control is at the same time a control over some configuration of reality, and this makes professions a significant actor of modern society. Yet scholars have been ambivalent about the role of the professions, interpreting them either as pursuing their own interest or as organising themselves to provide their services disinterestedly. This is why an inquiry into the agency of children and youth in African States must leave a place of choice for the inquiry into the dynamics of the professions which shape their lives, although such influences are exercised through transactions with other interested parties (individuals or organisations).

This literature is largely developed from the studies of professions in Western societies. However, this fact should not surprise because anthropology, which institutionally dominates social sciences in Africa, has showed little interest in the professions (Sawadogo, 2012). This is why it is necessary to know the existing literature, in order to depart from it and reveal, through future empirical research, what distinctive features the professions display in African contexts.

Chronologically, four types of discourse dominated the sociological approach to profession – starting with the functional, then the monopolist, before shifting to a relational approach with two periods of development. Firstly, the founding scientific literature on the professions was functional, with the main focus on the instrumental role of the professions against the asymmetric expert-client relationship. Professionalisation appeared as a logical effect of the evolution of structural guarantees for the expert-client mediation. Here, professions were simply alternative regulatory institutions to the disintegrating traditional social institutions in developing modern society. What was distinctive in them, and their actual function in the social system, were the major subjects of theorising. With regard to their attributes, Flexner (1915) has been regularly identified as the first scholar to have tried a systematic account. He stressed the central significance of the "professional spirit" as a distinctive disposition of the professional, with six core attributes: cognitive (intellectual and learned), moral and affective (personal responsibility and altruism), organisational (institutionalise body of knowledge and mechanism of transmission through education and internal organisation), and the finality of professional expertise (practical problem-solving oriented). Flexner's work, like that of others, is nonetheless a precursor to a sociology of the professions. As Dingwall reminds us, "[...] these have, for the most part, been treated as of mainly antiquarian interest" (Dingwall 1983:1).

Modern serious inquiry into the professions began with Parsons (1939, 1951, 1968) and Hughes (1958, 1971). Two core features emerge from Parsons' interest in professions in modern society. Firstly, he was concerned with the conditions and mechanisms of the maintenance of the social order in the changing social context. The functional specialisation of the family in modern societies was leaving niches in the social system. The emergence of professions resulted, therefore, from a structural need as an alternative regulatory mechanism to the

43

disintegrating traditional social institutions. The balance of power between client and professional was analysed within the framework of the role system, with dominant authority granted to the professional. As Abbott comments, "[f]or Parsons a professional's power over that of clients was necessary for successful treatment [...] It was grounded in expertise, guaranteed by professional control, and offset by the trust between professional and client" (Abbott 1988:86-87). Secondly, Parsons was seriously discontented with the universalism and abstraction of the utilitarian principle given economic motivations. Referring to Weber on the structure of action process, he argued for a historically grounded moral order that had been disregarded by utilitarian theory. The study of the professions, as non-profit occupations, was a means to this theoretical confrontation of utilitarianism. He placed the distinctive collectivity-orientation of the professional within the institutional framework which made it possible. In this view, he argued that, "[w]hatever difference there may be from a psychological point of view between the typical motives of physicians and businessmen must be analyzed with this in mind, taking it as a starting point" (Parsons [1951] 1991:473).

In fact, the functional approach to social order was influential in early writings (Durkheim, 1947; Simmel, 1971; Spencer, 1896, 1968; Tönnies, 1955; Weber, 1947). But, in general, the question that was crucial to Spencer, Durkheim, and Parsons, like the precursors of sociology, was: how should the new social relations brought about by the industrial revolution be ordered, and what are the alternative institutions to that end? All had seen in the professions the gate-keepers of the "absolute values" of the developing modern society and the guarantees of the public good. They were aware of the fragility of human motives, but treated irregular behaviour of the professions as reflections of dysfunctional institutions. In general they were not interested in conceptualising the professions as separate from the social system they were analysing.

Carr-Saunders (1928), Carr-Saunders and Wilson (1933) and Marshall (1939) contributed significantly to an attribute-oriented inquiry into the professions, with a clear delineation of their character of a social fact worth of specialised investigation. As Abbott and many others observe, the properties which they identified became the core of the later definitions of a profession. Basically, they observed the increasing number and varied types of professionals, with Marshal particularly stressing the changing patterns of professionals' relationships with the welfare State. Yet, in the early 1960s, the scope of the discourse about the professions shifted toward a more naturalistic approach, with a focus not on their function, but more on the structural transformation which led them to relatively full self-control. "Professionalisation" was portrayed in terms of an explanatory category about the ongoing processes of self-governance, as an indicator of accomplishment of some occupations (Millerson, 1964; Wlenski, 1964). Even though this approach was criticised for being linear (Abbott, 1988), "the explicit focus on structure and its evolution led to theories about the historical forces driving the structure, and hence the structuralists developed the explicit models of professionalisation [...]" (Abbott 1988:15).

Sociological discourse about professions significantly changed by the 1970s. The previous studies seemed to have provided basic details, leaving scholars to focus their attention on theorising. What was conspicuously changing was the explanatory framework of such processes. From its functionalist approach, the discourse moved to a monopolist one in which structural developments were considered instrumental to professional dominance. Their service orientation has been replaced by self-interested motivations, making professionalisation a collective endeavour for mobility.

The first decisive move came from Eliot Freidson, who considered illness as socially constructed, and held that the physician owed his exclusive right over illness and health management to the state. Professional dominance was initially interpreted as resulting from the State's demand, but through his further works he questioned professionals' claim over all the components of their work (Freidson, 1970b, 1975, 1983, 1986). Similarly, Johnson (1972, 1973a, 1973b) argued about the impressive character of professionals' claim to public service, supporting the manipulative character of medical knowledge, not only for being historically embedded, but in how it also generated clients' needs. Johnson's work clearly showed that professional autonomy appeared as contingent and always negotiated, since professions have never escaped the patronage of a third party (Johnson 1973b). His suggestion about "professionalism" and "third party control" in the professional-client relationship provided a framework for the classification and analysis of professional occupations (Freidson 1994, 2001). Scholars such as Larson (1977) followed this line of thought.

However, this view was also about to change in the 1990s, but before that a cultural approach to professional dominance (Bledstein, 1976; Haskell, 1984) emerged with a focus on the cognitive power of the professions. Comparative studies supported some insights of Parsons, and Hughes' effort to demystify the professions received supporting evidence. Freidson (1986, 1988, 1994, 2001) then reasserted the centrality of professional expertise in contemporary societies, but argued against a total occupational control over all the dimensions of its work, for some evaluative aspects could not be exclusively addressed by the mere professionals (Freidson 1978). Professions are institutionally distinctive, and professionals form their identities around them (Freidson 1994, Johnson 1972). Besides, the influence of third parties in the situations of professions was becoming apparent (Freidson 1970a, 1970b, 1973). From the 1990s, the argument was established in his writing, and his collected works were a product of permanent reflexive theorising (Freidson 1994, 2004), where professionalism is approached as a scale within which different occupations, according to their state of professionalisation, interact.

The ambivalent status and the character of the professions clearly come out from this analysis. The idea of professionalisation indicates that the professions' monopoly over a problem area and the expertise corresponding to it is subject to potential contestations either from other competing occupations or actors in their situations (state administrative authorities, peers, users of their expertise, etc.). The question of ambivalence of their status points to the interpretations that professions are sometimes preoccupied with pecuniary interests and are committed to the protection of their economic domains; often enamoured by the pursuit of upward collective mobility and consolidation of class interests. In these processes, the state appears only as benefactor of these privileges. However, despite their authority, the professions remain also vulnerable because of their increasing dependence (technically and socio-economically), on other people for the performance of their work. The control of these conditions (technical and socio-economic) varies with the social contexts. In Africa, this dependence is stronger.

Given that scientific knowledge is produced within the context of professions and that the professions' situation is that of increasing (inter)dependence, one can see how relevant it is to explore these processes as applied to the construction of childhood and youth in African contexts. The complex relationships of these processes cannot be adequately understood, as suggested in the next section, without the extended theoretical descriptions of the dynamics of science and the professions provided in the second and in this section. Only if the reader can make sense of the dynamic of science and the profession can she appreciates the sociological problematisation in the following section.

The Professional Constructions of Childhood and Youth in Africa: New Directions for Future Research

The above two theoretical discussions, when brought together, suggest a number of questions, which show how theories in the sociology of science and in the sociology of the professions can pave new ways to understanding childhood and youth in Africa. The following three strands form an integrated framework. However each strand can be explored separately depending on the interests of the researcher.

The Ecology of Childhood and Youth Collectives in Africa: Configurations and Transformations.

Description: This part has a descriptive character. It consists in mapping the network of actors interested in the problem area of childhood and youth. The fact that nowadays this problem area mobilises various actors locally and internationally should not make us lose sight of the fact that it is an historical product (Turmel, 2008). The emergence and structure of this network can be traced. The identification of the actors of the network enables the researcher to know their characteristics, including the kind of their expertise and professional status. The kind of professional status, which reflects the kind of expertise, is a key in the interactions between the actors in processes related to childhood and youth. Some potential sources can be identified.

Sources: Mapping the network of actors involved in the problem area of childhood and youth will involve exploration of the following potential sources. Firstly there are directories of government departments (law, police, education, social services, health, etc.), university departments (medicine, psychology, sociology, anthropology, population studies, psychiatry, etc.). Secondly, there are non-governmental organisations, directories of non-government organisations

48

institutions, families, civil society organisations, newspapers, academic journal articles in medicine, social sciences and biology, various reports, from different periods since colonisation, etc. Sources depend on the place where research is carried out. Therefore, these suggestions are not exhaustive. Depending on the stage of development of the network, their interactions can be marked by more or less disputant relations, for a common language about the matter.

Institutional Disputes and Stabilisation of Childhood and Youth in Africa

Description: A stable language of childhood and youth is necessary for actors involved in the problem area of childhood and youth. However, this language is not given. It emerges through complex processes (Aries, 1973; Turmel, 2008). The case of childhood and youth is taken because of its relevance to the present purpose. In fact, this practice was not limited to them. For example, in the colonies, these practices were widespread (e.g. phrenology and scientific racism). In pseudo-scientific ways, physical traits and abilities were measured and compared for imperial domination as well as many modern practices (Bale, 2002).

The role of the different networks of actors (scientist or not), at specific periods since colonisation, in negotiating a local and generalised stable figure of childhood and youth in Africa is of special interest to sociologists. The specific past of Africa since the colonial period make these processes particularly interesting. The interactions are opportunities of territorial maintenance and blurring between actors involved. One can analyse the sources of power of each actor.

Sources: Various sources can be used. Firstly, there are censuses. Indeed, statistics and populations studies not only provides data about patterns of social processes, but also questionnaires and other methodological tools from which

49

representations of childhood and youth can be derived. Secondly, medical textbooks, journal articles, reports and record forms are also invaluable sources for investigating biological representations. Of particular relevance are data in paediatrics and nutrition, educational and training manuals and equipment (e.g. visual). Related medical and social science sources such as textbooks and journal articles of African psychiatry, psychology, anthropologies or ethnographies are also relevant. Documents related to publicity on families, newspapers, social services reports, school manuals and administrative reports can be informative. Thirdly, judicial records and legal documents (e.g. social rights documents, labour law, family law, electoral laws, employment law, social security laws, specific benefits regulations, political parties' statutes, etc.) provide relevant data. Fourthly, when possible, interviews are important sources of information. Childhood and youth as problem areas and the expertise about them are both a source of power and vulnerability of competing occupations

Childhood and Youth Agency and Institutional Patterning of Youth in Africa

Description: As indicated in the second section, scientific knowledge as a distinctive character (Merton, 1973, Cole and Cole, 1967, Cole and Zuckerman, 1975), "the scientific is more closely connected with the real world of objects" (Elias, 1978, p. 22). Theories are kept in constant check through feedback from observation and their validity remains provisional. The dynamics of the scientific community secure this constant control (Merton, 1973). It is shown in section one that one of the characteristics of the modern state is that its operation is typically based on this regime of truth (Foucault, 2008). This means that state policies are maintained as long as they produced their expected effects. Otherwise, the observations from their implementations are fed back to the theories that

50

are used for their designing. The potential transactions involved in policy-making and the dynamics internal to scientific practices and professional dynamics increase the potential disconnection between produced knowledge or policies and the problem area on which they bear. Such vulnerability applies to knowledge and policies in Africa since the dawn of colonisation (Omobowale *et al.*, 2013, Ouedraogo, 2010, Ouedraogo and Bouda, 2011, Ouedraogo and Sall, 2010, Sawadogo, 2008). The big gap recorded between what children and young people in Africa do is an example of friction between institutional categories and social practices(De Boeck and Honwana, 2005). Sociological research may, therefore, be oriented toward the identification of these gaps, followed by the investigation of what effects they have on existing scientific knowledge and ongoing policies. In other words, one may address how these gaps lead to institutional (scientific and policy) reflexivity in Africa for more adequate knowledge and more effective action for the interests of children and young people. Potential sources, though not exhaustive, for access to the relevant data can be outlined as follows.

Sources: One way of accessing the relevant data is to explore the academic literature. Peer-reviewed journals, books and newspapers provide data about descriptive information, but also the dynamics of scientific controversies about the problem area. Judicial sources can be of significant relevance. They enable one to see the institutionalised norms and the deviations from them. Government policy review reports and reports from other interested parties, such as non-governmental organisations, are of significant value. Interviews with academics, lawyers, administrators, journalists, officials of non-governmental organisations, children and young people themselves (conditions apply).

Conclusion

In conclusion, this chapter sets an agenda for an empirical sociological research on the practices (scientific, political, and social more generally) of childhood and youth in Africa. It did not intend and has not carried such empirical research. It suggests theoretical resources for this endeavour. This is not less important, because the way research questions are asked are central in science. If the literature on childhood and youth in Africa, though rich, has revolved around some circumscribed topics and research problematics, this is because it is theoretically constrained to be so – the realities indicated throughout this paper have been always there! The suspicion about 'theory' in science may be related to its special status in philosophy. However, as Blumer (1969, p. 155) has put it "It is possible to consider the concept as an incident or an episode of scientific act and not as a detached entity". In other words "conception arises as an aid to adjustment with the insufficiency of perception; it permits new orientation and new approach; it changes and guides perception" Blumer (1969, p. 156). The aim of this paper is just that: to contribute to a new perception, an adjustment to the realities of youth in Africa whose challenge of our old conceptions is just beginning with our increasing awareness of the paradigmatic crisis. This research has shown me how difficult such an undertaking can be. Nevertheless, this was a positive difficulty, as it made me more confident than ever that the enterprise was worth the effort.

References

Abeles, M. and Collard, C., 1985. *Age, pouvoir et société en Afrique Noire*, Paris, Karthala

Amin, S. 1981. 'Underdevelopment and dependence in Black Africa – origins and contemporary forms' in L.D. Cohen, and Daniel, J., 1981, Eds. *Political economy of Africa. Selected readings*, London: Longman Group Limited

Abbott, P., 1988, *The system of professions. An essay on the division of expert labor*, Chicago: The University of Chicago

Abbott, A. D., 2001,*Chaos of disciplines*, Chicago: University of Chicago Press

Ariès, Ph., 1973, *Centuries of childhood*, London: Penguin Books

Barnes, B., 1974, *Scientific knowledge and sociological theory*, London: Routledge & Kegan Paul.

Bale, J., 2002, *Imagined Olympians: Body Culture and Colonial Representation in Rwanda*, Minneapolis: University of Minnesota Press

Barnes, B. and Bloor, D., 1982, Relativism, rationalism and sociology of knowledge, in M. Hollis and S. Lukes, eds., *Rationality and relativism*, Oxford: Blackwell

Bayart, J-F., 1993, *The state in Africa: the politics of the belly*. London: Longman

Bayart, J-F., ed, 1996, *La greffe de l'Etat*, Paris: Karthala

Bayart, J-F., Ellis, S., Hibou, B., 1999, *The criminalization of the state in Africa*, London: International African Institute

Becker, H.S., 1963, *Outsiders,* New York: Free Press

Béland, F., 1976, 'Du paradoxe professionnel: médecins et ingénieurs des années 1800', Archives européennes de Sociologie, 17, pp.306-330

Ben-David, J., 1963, Professions in the class system of present day societies, *Current Sociology*, 12, pp. 248-298

Bledstein, B. J., 1976, *The culture of professionalism*, New York: Norton

Bloor, D., 1983, *Wittgenstein: A social theory of knowledge*, New York: Columbia University Press

Ben-David, J. and Collins, R., 1966, Social factors in the origin of a new science, *American Sociological Review*, 31, pp. 451-65

Blumer, H., 1969, *Symbolic interactionism: perspective and method*, Englewood Cliffs: Prentice-Hall

Boeck, F., and Honwana, A., 2005, *Makers & breakers. Children & Youth in Postcolonial Africa*, New Jersey: Africa World Press, Inc.

Bourdieu, P., 1996, *The rules of art. Genesis and structure of the literary field*, Translated by Susan Emmanuel, Cambridge: Polity Press

Bourdieu, P.,1993, *Sociology in question, Translated by Richard Nice*, London: Sage Publications

Bourdieu, P. 2003, Participante objectivation, *The Journal of the Royal Anthropological Institute*, Vol.9, no.2, pp. 281-294

Bourdieu, P., 2004, *Science of science and reflexivity*, Translated by Richard Nice, Cambridge: Polity Press

Cain, M., 1983, The general practice lawyer and the client: towards a radical conception, in R. Dingwall and P.S.C. Lewis, eds., *The Sociology of the Professions*, London: Macmillan

Carr-Saunders, A. M., 1928, *Professions: Their organization and place in society*, Oxford: Clarendon Press

Carr-Saunders, A.M. and Wilson, P.A., 1933, *The professions*, Oxford: Clarendon Press

Chazan, N., Lewis, P., Mortier, R., Rothchild, D., and Stedman J. S., 1999, Politics and society in contemporary Africa. 3rd ed. Colorado: Lynne Rienner Publishers

Cole, S. and Cole, J.R., 1967, Scientific output and recognition: a study in the operation of the reward system in science, *American Sociological Review*, Vol.32, no.3, pp. 377-90

Cole, S. and Zuckerman, H., 1975, The emergence of a scientific speciality: the self-exemplifying case of the sociology of science, in L. A. Coser, ed., *The idea of social structure: papers in Honor of Robert K. Merton*, New York: Harcourt Brace Jovanovich

Collins, H. M., 1981, Knowledge and controversy: Studies in Modern natural science, special issue of *Social Studies of Science*, vol. 11, no. 1

Desrosières, A., 2000, *La politique des grands nombres*, Paris: La Découverte

Dingwall, R., 2008, *Essays on professions*, London: Ashgate

Dingwall, R., 1983, The sociology of the professions, London: The Macmillan Press

Diop, C.A. 2006, Articles. Yaoundé: Editions Silex

Durkheim, É. 1982, *The rules of sociological method and selected texts on sociology and its method*, London: Macmillan Education

Durkheim, E., [1947]1964, *The Division of labor in society*, New York, Free Press

Durkheim, E.,1992, *Professional ethics and civic morals*, London: Routledge

Elias, N., 1956, Problems of Involvement and Detachment, *The British Journal of Sociology*, Vol.7, no.3, pp. 226-252

Elias, N., 1956, [1939] 2000, *The civilizing process: sociogenetic and psychogenetic investigations*, Rev. ed., Oxford: Blackwell Publishers

Elias, N. 1978, *What is sociology?*, London: Hutchinson

Elias, N.,1964, 'Professions', In: Julius Gould and William L. Kolb, eds., *A dictionary of the social sciences*, New York: Free Press

Elias, N., 1983, *The court society*, Oxford: Blackwell

Elias, N., 1998, *On civilizing, power and knowledge*, Chicago: the University of Chicago Press

Elias, N., 2007, *The genesis of the naval profession*, Dublin: University College of Dublin Press

Erny, P. 1968, *L'enfant dans la pensee traditionnelle de l'Afrique Noire*, Paris: Le Livre Africain

Erny, P., 1999, *Les premiers pas dans la vie de l'enfant d'Afrique Noire. Naissance et premiere enfance*, Paris: L'Harmattan

Eschlimann, J-P, 1982, *Naître sur la terre africaine*, Paris: INADES-EDITION

Flexner, A., 1915, Is social work a profession?, In *Studies in Social Work*, no. 4, New York: New York School of Philanthropy

Freidson, E., 1970a, *Profession of medicine: a study of the sociology of applied knowledge*, New York: Dodd, Mead & Co.

Freidson, E.,1970b, *Professional dominance: the social structure of medical care*, New York: Dodd, Mead & Co.

Freidson, E., 1983, The theory of professions: state of the art, in R. Dingwall and P.S.C. Lewis, eds., *The Sociology of the Professions*, London: Macmillan

Freidson, E., 1975, *Doctoring together: A study of professional social control*, New York: Elsevier

Freidson, E., 1986, *Professional powers: A study of the institutionalization of formal knowledge*, Chicago: University of Chicago Press

Freidson, E., 1994, *Professionalism reborn*, Cambridge: Polity Press

Freidson, E., 2001, *Professionalism: the third logic*, Chicago: University of Chicago Press

Freidson, E., 1978, 'The official construction of occupation: an essay on the practical epistemology of work', paper presented at the 9th World Congress of Sociology, Uppsala, Sweden

Freidson, E.,1973, *The Professions and their Prospects*, London, SAGE Publications

Foucault, F. 2010, *The Birth of biopolotics*, New York: Palgrave Macmillan

Foucault, M., 1970, *The order of things: an archaeology of the human sciences*, London: Tavistock Publications

Foucault, M., 1971, *L'ordre du discourse*, Paris: Gallimard

Foucault, M., 1972, *The archaeology of knowledge*, Translated from the French by A.M. Sheridan Smith, London: Tavistock Publications

Gilbert, G. L. and Mulkay, M., 1984, *Opening Pandora's Box: A sociological analysis of scientists' discourse*, Cambridge: Cambridge University Press

Good, W. J., Jr., 1960, Encroachment, charlatanism, and the emerging profession: psychology, medicine and sociology. *American Sociological Review*, vol. 25, pp.1902-1914

Grmek, M. D., 1973, *Raisonnement experimental et recherches toxicologiques chez Claude Bernard*, Geneva: Droz

Halliday, C. T., 1987, *Beyond Monopoly. Lawyers, state crises, and professional empowerment*, Chicago: University of Chicago Press

Haskell, T.L., ed., 1984, *The authority of experts*, Bloomington, Indiana University Press

Holmes, F. L., 1974, *Claude Bernard and animal chemistry: The emergence of a scientist*, Cambridge, Mass; Harvard University Press

Honwana, A. & De Boeck, F., eds., 2005, *Makers and Breakers: Children & Youth in Postcolonial Africa*, Dakar: CODESRIA

Hountondji, J.P., 1992, 'Recapturing' in Mudimbe, Y.V. ed; The surreptitious speech: Présence africaine and the politics of otherness, 1947-1987, Chicago: University of Chicago Press

Hughes, C. E., 1958, *Men and their work*, New York: Free Press

Hughes, C. E., 1971, *The sociological eye: selected papers*, Chicago: Aldine

Illich, I., 1973, September 13, The professions as a form of imperialism, New Society

Illich, I., 1975, *Medical Nemesis: The expropriation of health*, London: Calder and Boyars

Johnson, J. T., 1972, *Professions and power*, London; Macmillan

Johnson, J. T., 1973a, 'Professions', in Geoffrey Hurd, ed., *Human Societies: An introduction to Sociology*, London: Routledge & Kegan Paul

Johnson, J. T., 1973b, 'Imperialism and the professions', *Sociological Review Monographs*, vol. 20, 281-309

Keita, L., 2007, 'Horton Revisited: African Traditional Thought and Western Science', *Africa Development*, Vol. XXXII, No. 4, 2007, pp.139–169

Ki-Zerbo, J., 1978, *Histoire de l'Afrique Noire*, Paris: Hathier

Knorr-Cetina, 1992, The couch, the cathedral and the laboratory: on the relationship between experiment and laboratory in science, in A. Pickering, ed., *Science as practice and as culture*, Chicago, University of Chicago Press

Kuhn, T. S., 1962, *The structure of scientific revolutions*, Chicago: University of Chicago Press

Larson, M.S., 1977, *The rise of professionalism: a sociological analysis*, London: University of California Press

Latour, B, 1987, *Science in action*, Cambridge: Harvard University Press

Latour, B and Woolgar, S., 1979, *Laboratory life: The social construction of scientific facts*, London: Sage

LY B., 1979, '*La jeunesse africaine entre la tradition et la modernité*', in UNESCO, 1979, *Jeunesse, tradition et développement en Afrique*, Unesco

LY, T. O., 1992, '*La structuration du concept de « Jeunesse » dans le discours de l'Union Soudanaise du R.D.A. (1947-1962)*', in d'ALMEIDA-TOPOR *et al.*, eds, 1992, *Les Jeunes en Afrique. T2. La politique de la ville*, Paris: L'Harmattan

Marshall, T. H., 1939, The recent history of professionalism in relation to social structure and social policy.

Medard, J-F., ed., 1991, *États d'Afrique noire, Paris*: Karthala

Medawar, P. B., 1964, Aug 1, 'Is the scientific paper fraudulent?', Saturday Review, pp. 42-43

Merton, R. K., 1973, The sociology of science: theoretical and empirical Investigations, Chicago: University of Chicago Press

Mignon, J-M., 1984, Afrique: *Jeunesses uniques, Jeunesse encadrée*, Paris: L'Harmattan

Millerson, G., 1964, *The qualifying associations*, London: Routledge

Omobowale, O.A., Sawadogo, N., Sawadogo-Compaoré, E.M.F.W., Ugbem, E.C., 2013, 'Globalization and Scholarly Publishing in West Africa. A Comparative Study of Burkina Faso and Nigeria', *International Journal of Sociology*, vol. 43, no.1, pp.8-26

Ouedraogo, J-B, 2010, *Domination impériale et limites de l'autonomie académique: enjeux épistémologiques et institutionnels de la construction d'une science multipolaire*, http://www.msh-paris.fr/fileadmin/Recherche/PDFs/RAE/101011-sciences_sociales-pouvoir-politique.pdf   [accessed 03/04/2013]

Ouedraogo, J-B and Bouda, P. 2011, 'The alchemist and the apprentice myth-hunter. Comment on social engineering in African social sciences'. In *Readings in Methodology: African Perspectives*. Edited by Jean-Bernard Ouédraogo & Carlos Cardoso. Dakar: CODESRIA

Parsons, T., 1939, The professions and social structure, *Social Forces*, 17, pp. 457-67

Parsons, T., [1951]1991, *The social system*. New York: Free Press

Parsons, T., 1971, *The system of modern societies*. Englewood Cliffs: Prentice-Hall

Parsons, T., 1968, Professions, in *International Encyclopedia of the Social Sciences*, vol. 12, pp. 536-547

Sall, I. and Ouedraogo, J-B., 2010, 'Sociology in West Africa: challenges and obstacles to academic autonomy', in S. Patel (ed), *The ISA handbook of diverse sociological traditions*. Thousand Oaks: Sage

Sawadogo, N. 2012, *A global history of the sociology of professions*, Saarbrucken: Lambert Academic Publishing

Sawadogo, N., 2008, Studying the professions in contemporary Africa. A challenge for the sociology of the professions, unpublished MA. Dissertation thesis, University of Nottingham

Simmel, G., 1971, *On individuality and social forms: selected writings*, Chicago. London: University of Chicago Press

Spencer, H., 1896, *Principles of sociology*, Vol. 3. London: Williams and Norgate

Tawney, R. H., 1920, *The acquisitive society*, New York: Harcourt, Brace

Terray, E., 1992, 'French Marxist anthropology of the 1960s and African studies: outline for an appraisal', in Mudimbe,

Y.V. ed, *The surreptitious speech: Présence africaine and the politics of otherness, 1947-1987*. Chicago: University of Chicago Press

Tönnies, F., 1955, Community and association: *Gemeinschaft und gesellschaft*, London: Routledge & K. Paul

Turmel, A., 2008, *A historical sociology of childhood*, Cambridge, Cambridge University Press

Turner, V. W., 1969, *The ritual process: structure and anti-structure*, London: Routledge & K. Paul

Turner, V. W., 1975, *Revelation and divination in Ndembu ritual*, Ithaca: Cornell University Press

UNESCO, 1979, *Jeunesse, tradition et développement en Afrique*, Unesco

UNSDRI, 1984, *L'inadaptation sociale des jeunes*, Rome: Fratelli Palombi Editori

Weber, M., 1978, Economy and society: an outline of interpretive sociology, Berkeley: University of California Press

Weber, M., 1968, *Economy and society*, [Vol.3], Bedminster Press

Weber, M., 1947, *The theory of social and economic organization: being part 1 of Wirtschaft und Gesellschaft*, London: William Hodge

Wilenski, H. L., 1964, The professionalization of everyone? *American Journal of Sociology*, 70, pp.137-58

2

New Directions in Child and Youth Research in Africa

Patricia Henderson

I begin a short set of reflections on possible new directions in child and youth research in Africa. On one level, given the diversity of the continent, the notion of a unified body of African research is problematic. In claiming a specificity for Africa in relation to research, there is the danger that we may identify too quickly forms of totalisation and therefore fail to address a sufficiently open horizon in which to reflect diversity and change. It is perhaps one of the challenges of research within Africa to demonstrate particularities through careful, detailed studies from specific regions. Yet the problem of regional studies is that locales are not cordoned off from one another or the rest of the world. Africa is a part of a global flow of ideas, imaginaries and indeed of diasporic mobile populations. Such entanglements and threads of relationship and ideas make it hard to separate Africa out from historical processes of exchange and extortion that transcend the borders of Africa as a continent. Many African children and youth have crossed vast distances, sometimes unaccompanied by adults. Such journeys include internal migration within nation-states, but also migration across country borders in pursuit of training, education, work, trade, and in flight due to political strife and civil wars in which children and remaining relatives have often been forced to reconstitute lives elsewhere, bearing the experience and fracturing of loss and exile.

On one level, Africa, in being posited as an entity in contradistinction to the rest of the world, is an ideological construct constituted through becoming an object of external scrutiny in processes of profound othering to which some scholarship, conjoined with colonisation and post colonisation, attest. Within these sets of relationships the continent is often characterised as an assemblage of problems relating to the notion of overarching lack – these are defined as social, political, economic and even human problems against which others supposedly measure their own coherence and ethical standing. Yet knowledge that attests to particularities of being, to continuities and innovation within everyday life – knowledge that may have the potential to challenge hegemonic descriptions of people's institutions and lives within Africa – often remains invisible or muted within global discourse. Histories of extraction in relations between parts of Africa and other parts of the world are occluded in these processes.

Experience of deprivation and mobility is not confined to Africa. As much contemporary research has shown, and in relation to the above points, incoherence, multiplicity, journeying, migration, improvisation, and lives lived beyond the ways they are belatedly described within academia, are increasingly experienced within so-called industrialised countries as well. Within the horizon of global capitalism, forms of incoherence and indeed the need for dexterity, improvisation, invention and code-switching – in the sense of reading and mimicking diverse requirements appropriately within heterogeneous social spaces – are common to many people's lives, including the lives of children and youth.

On a second level, precisely because of processes of othering to which the African continent and academy have been subjected, it remains of the utmost importance for African scholars to create strong networks of communication around their work and to develop critical perspectives from what is shared between them, to make discounted knowledge – what has been rendered invisible – visible within resistant spaces of the academy. This is a process to which CODESRIA admirably contributes by keeping alive a platform and a set of networks predicated on academic freedom in which scholars may engage, share their work, debate and create bonds for ongoing research. It is equally important for African scholars to create linkages with scholars along a global south-south axis, with people from India and Brazil, for example, who may share similar histories and experiences.

In relation to research in and concerning Africa, a small body of careful empirical work – dare I say ethnographic work in terms of its systematic collection of data – to do with the everyday life of children and youth exists. Little serious importance outside a small community of scholars seems to be given to the diversity in which children and youth live. Such is the case across the broader range of academic disciplines within the academy, within governments and societies more generally, and within localised communities in which social hierarchies institute certain kinds of blindness with respect to the contributions of children and youth to social life. Yet, the ways in which young people make, unmake and remake the world, to slightly reword Filip de Boeck's and Alcinda Honwana's (2005) phrase, is surely of the utmost importance. The challenge remains to impress upon our immediate countries and the international community, more broadly, the importance of research with and concerning children and youth, showing the profound ways in which young people shape society through the invention of new forms of language; a plethora of creative and often critical repertoires; their contributions to economies, to popular culture; their generation of forms of mutuality and care, and of new ways of viewing the world and their circumstances – in short, as creators of new forms of sociality in their own right.[1]

Questioning the Adequacy of Terms Within Child and Youth Studies

Many studies of children impose concepts around the figure of the child and models of childhood that do not fully reflect African realities, and that are in turn utilised sometimes uncritically by researchers in Africa who may, as intimated above, also patronise children and youth because of dominant gerontocratic ideologies in which social hierarchies are strongly marked by age. Here children's thoughts, culture and actions may be discounted.

To expand on some of the above points, beyond the academy, international non-governmental organisations (NGOs) are often responsible for the generation of narrow and sometimes shallow sets of terms through which researchers are expected to filter their empirical research – terms that, given NGOs' interventionist agendas that they consider progressive, activist, and altruistic, are often predicated on the underlying alarm and anxiety with which "the 'west' views the rest", and in particular the figure of the child. Such terms may have little long-term durability and may emerge at specific times in response to pressing concerns. The question is then: What do such terms leave out? What are we unable to see or say because we approach our research projects through their use?

Of course, the above problems highlight how knowledge is embroiled in relations of power that are not always easily shifted, especially if money for research on children is given by institutions that persist in promulgating specific ideas around the figure of the child. We are therefore called upon to carefully examine how such conceptions prescribe the limits within which we describe and approach children and their childhoods, youth and their everyday lives. By way of illustration, I will briefly explore two sets of terms that are currently well known within child research in many countries in Africa: the "AIDS orphan" and the "child soldier". Please note that in making certain critical points in the chapter I draw mainly on literature within South Africa. I do so not because I want to exclude other literatures, but because examples drawn from this region are most familiar to me. This does not detract from the ways in which the broad points I make are of relevance to research and scholarship more broadly in Africa.

The Use of the Term "AIDS Orphan"

The spectre of the AIDS orphan, as it has circulated in global discourse across many forms of media, has linked the idea of consequences of parental death to various forms of social pathology. In the most extreme cases, it is assumed that children who lose their biological parents necessarily remain without adult guidance, do not receive proper care, and are rendered homeless; that they are in danger of not being socialised appropriately, and, therefore, of demonstrating criminal and anti-social behaviour. With commentators insisting upon such forms of vulnerability, children are emptied of the knowledge and abilities they may have – the ways in which they are often embedded in and commandeer their way through larger networks of social relationship that include both young people and other adults. A narrow definition of family, namely, the nuclear family that has little reality in most parts of the world today, is imposed on communities where notions of family obligation are far broader, and where even in extreme cases of displacement, children and adults appeal to the idea of clanship, or name, or locality to forge new social ties.

The above-mentioned fears circulate around a notion of youth and children's autonomy. That children and youth should in some ways be autonomous is linked to the idea of social disintegration. Some researchers in South Africa have argued that there is no evidence that AIDS-related deaths have led to greater degrees of criminality among "unsupervised youth", or to a thorough disintegration of social worlds (Bray, 2003; Henderson, 2006; Meintjes & Giese, 2006). They have also found, contrary to the idea that as a consequence of AIDS large numbers of orphans would live without adults in their lives, that the majority of South African children who have lost one or both parents through AIDS are living with, or move between, adult persons whom they can claim as relatives in various ways (Meintjes & Giese, 2006).

Whilst not discounting the emotional trauma of children losing their parents through death, Helen Meintjes and Sonja Giese (2006), for example, point out that in a context where many South African children are marginalised due to poverty, the circumstances of poor, non-orphaned children are in some respects not dissimilar to those of children who have lost one or both parents through death. In relation to material circumstances, even when children have parents, they may often be unemployed or involved in the informal economy in uneven ways.[2] Nor is it uncommon for grandparents to contribute to the ongoing livelihoods of households and of children by supporting them with their old-age pensions irrespective of whether or not the children are orphans.

Such straightened economic realities for the majority of citizens in South Africa have led to the successful lobbying for a small Child Support Grant from the State that has recently been extended to children up to seventeen years of age. Some social service activists have argued for the importance of a basic income grant for all poor people in South Africa, an idea that has thus far been rejected by the State. The rationale for a basic income grant is that it takes into consideration a wide range of children and adults who are particularly poor, including children who have lost their parents through death to HIV/AIDS.

Conceptions around the idea of the AIDS orphan suggest that the disease is the cause of separation between parents and their children. The latter view does not recognise an understanding of antecedent forms of separation that are also embedded within societies. In particular, there is little cognisance of separations between parents and children due to legislation in, for example, apartheid South Africa, or due to patterns of migration in many different parts of Africa. Taking into account the social, economic, and political history of South Africa, parents were, and still often remain, separated for long periods of time from their children due to apartheid laws

66

and persisting patterns of migrancy related to the search for remunerated employment.

Due to pernicious influx control laws during apartheid that prevented African parents from settling permanently in urban areas, a separation between parents and children was particularly the case in rural areas where men left to seek work beyond their home areas, as did many women. South Africa's children and youth have, therefore, long been involved in fluid child-care arrangements, where not only adults, but also children have been mobile in relation to forms of fosterage (Henderson, 2003), in pursuit of schooling, work, health care and political safely. A body of ethnographic research in South Africa has highlighted the fluidity of children's lives in general and their relation to multiple care-givers over time (Jones, 1994; Henderson, 1999; Ramphele, 2002; Ross, 1995). Apart from children's mobility between caregivers before the AIDS pandemic, positive values are attached to the range of kin upon whom a child may potentially call for support (Henderson, 1999, 2006). With widespread deaths consequent upon AIDS, in the majority of cases, children continue to move within networks of kin in pursuit of everyday care. There has therefore not been a radical increase in the numbers of children living on the streets, for example, as was predicted. Nor has there been a large influx in the number of children in formal care within South Africa (Meintjes *et al*, 2007).

The above points do not mean that the long-term attrition of multiple deaths attendant upon the HIV/AIDS epidemic, particularly in southern Africa, has not had profound effects on social relations, and hence the lives of young people. Neither do they imply that children living within the presence of death do not suffer in ways that are difficult to bear and even more difficult to describe. Statistical projections of both deaths due to AIDS and to do with numbers of orphaned children are alarming, and even if inflated, are cause for concerted action and concern. However, generalised, one-dimensional conceptions of poverty and AIDS – both forms of structural violence inflected with the political – are problematic. Textures of lightness, beauty, love, strength and conviviality – often equally present in social contexts of scarcity and pain – are excluded from analysis in an attempt to depict the gravity of the epidemic. I will, therefore, argue that while not underestimating the devastating effects of HIV/AIDS on children's lives in South Africa and sub-Saharan Africa, there is a need to turn our attention to improvisation and dexterity despite fractures within social worlds in which AIDS and consequently death is prevalent.

Philosophical conceptions of orphanhood among African people, including young people with whom I have closely worked in KwaZulu-Natal, South Africa, are broader than a notion entailing the loss of biological parents. The conditions of orphanhood embrace further existential dimensions, encompassing ideas of complete destitution, alienation and a lack of belongingness. Being orphaned therefore, may accrue theoretically to a person who still has parents but who has experienced profound displacement, for example, through war. To be orphaned in this sense is to be without moorings, social support and place.

To conclude, the notion of "AIDS orphan" and the way in which it has been deployed within the context of an overwhelming AIDS epidemic, particularly in Southern Africa, has had various unforeseen outcomes. Communities have often been angry at the ways in which orphans are singled out for intervention and aid over and above other poor children. Deep-seated forms of structural violence marked by generalised poverty that have persisted over time may not be clearly recognised. Responses to an urgent crisis may therefore submerge the importance of addressing long-term relations of inequity.

Exploring Assumptions around The Notion of The "Child Soldier"

Much work of uneven quality has emerged around the unpalatable idea of the "child soldier" and child soldiering in research on Africa in the last ten years.[3] The deployment of the term predominantly positions children who become soldiers as passive victims, suggesting that they are inevitably commandeered into armies by force. This has indeed been the case in many instances, but not in all. The figure of the child soldier seems to contain adults' worst nightmares of what a child may become – in this case a young person trained to kill without compunction, who at times may have been forced to kill members of his or her own community by way of being initiated into a specific army in the context of civil war.

Many historical and literary studies of childhood show how conceptions of the figure of the child have fluctuated between two stereotypical poles, the child as the embodiment of innocence, and the "monstrous child", or the feral child, the unsocialised child, a potential figure of evil (Warner, 1994) in which normative notions within everyday moral economies have been upended. It would seem that contemporary alarm at the phenomenon of child soldiers often arises from a perception of violated innocence and horror at the idea of what children may become in undergoing war. Horror evinced at the prospect of a child soldier in some respects deflects attention away from adult responsibilities in beginning wars and in including children as combatants, often through mentally cruel and violent processes of induction that are equally processes of socialisation.

Alcinda Honwana's book (2006), *Child Soldiers in Africa*, explores the experience of girls and boys involved in armed conflict in Mozambique and Angola, mainly through a set of interviews undertaken with groups of young people in "rehabilitation camps" post conflict. She writes of the ritualistic ways in which children were inducted into armies and forced to kill; of gender differences in terms of what boys and girls respectively did and were subjected to within armies; of demobilisation strategies, including local ritual processes of healing and reincorporation of children within village life. Yet, in some respects, Honwana reinforces the stereotypes she claims to be writing against. Her ethnographic data focuses predominantly on victimisation of children in war, concentrating in an almost scopic way on the violation of girl children in relation to becoming "war wives" and on the horrors of ritual initiation into armies on the part of boys. Descriptions of longer trajectories of individual children's lives are missing from the account; histories that would enable readers to approach the ways in which children and youth may have attempted to accommodate their experience. Little detail is provided regarding the ways in which young people have re-forged social bonds in the aftermath of war and the effects of their efforts on their war experiences. Neither is there a deep sense of how war has reshaped expectations as to what it is appropriate for boys and girls to do or the ways in which worlds may be imagined. In certain respects, concentrating on forms of violation without immersion within the children's life narratives raises ethical concerns about whether a particular brand of scopic research may in itself constitute further violation.

Importantly however, Honwana notes that children have previously taken and still do take part in wars elsewhere than on the African continent. This is of significance because the stereotype of the child-soldier inevitably conjures up the image of an African child. Perhaps we need to remind ourselves that wherever there is war throughout the world, it is naïve to think that children can be excluded from its devastations. Neither can they be positioned as passive victims. Children often have strong political views. They have also been involved in many different capacities within wars, including "just wars" in the course of liberation struggles from colonialism, for example, in which their contributions have sometimes been recorded.

Their activities in such contexts have included: reporting on enemy movements, numbers and military strength; transporting goods; cooking for and feeding fighters; joining resistance efforts and sometimes serving as combatants. It must also be noted that girls and young women, although often subjected to sexual brutalisation during wars, in some cases may become combatants themselves and in doing so may experience a degree of liberation from ordinary social norms where they may have had little overt public power or opportunities to make certain kinds of decisions. The stereotype of children always being forcibly induced into armies is not necessarily an accurate portrayal of different kinds of wars and their political stakes. In some war situations, children may choose to join a particular side because of their own unfolding political convictions, after experiencing the long-term oppressive effects of the State on their families, or after witnessing the death of family members in conflict situations. Once children's communities have been disrupted, their survival may also depend on joining an armed force.

It is extremely difficult to research the realities and the imaginaries with which children live and die in periods of armed conflict. Yet researchers should not be content with a few studies referring to the inclusion of children and youth in war, thinking that these rely on a sufficient depth of data that may be generalisable. Wars take on very different characters and their specific natures and rationales affect the ways in which girls and boys become caught up in and participate in conflict and the ways in which they appropriate attempts at recovery from the effects of war. We need more careful, detailed studies of the interrelationship between adults and children in times of war, and more broadly, in relation to the social contexts that precede and emerge subsequent to war. Some fine studies spring to mind. The work of Pamela Reynolds (forthcoming, 1995a, 1995b, 2000) in South Africa and the work of Veena Das (2007, 1998) on the partition in India suggest subtle ways of tracing children's contributions to social change, as well as the depth and breadth of suffering they have endured in such processes.

To return to the context against which Reynolds' work on children and youths' political involvement hinges, the Truth and Reconciliation Commission (TRC) – a body that among other things sought to provide a record of gross human violations of individuals and of deaths and disappearances during the apartheid regime– stands out. The TRC was set up after the first South African national democratic elections in 1994 and failed in many respects to adequately document the often protracted and responsible involvement of young people in transforming society. It also underplayed the extent of the torture they endured and the sacrifices they made in confrontations with the State. The frequency with which even very young children were shot, beaten and taken into detention is an indictment of a racialised society in which the childhoods of a white minority were deemed worthy of "protection" and those of the African majority were regarded as occupying a place of exception, where acceptable standards of conduct could be abandoned.[4]

In her work, Reynolds attempts to address the lacuna of the TRC by showing how young people opposed the regime in multiple ways, including in some cases, leaving the country to join liberation movements and to receive military training. She portrays young people's involvement in the transformation of their country in ways that transcend narrow conceptions of child soldiering. Her work concentrates on carefully tracing the experience and political involvement of a group of young men from one small rural town in South Africa.

The group of young men regularly met together with Reynolds to retrace the development of their political lives and their confrontations and negotiations with the State. These collective re-tracings of the past were often painful and difficult and had to be carefully negotiated over time. Some of the young men had begun their political involvement at a very young age, drawing inspiration from older relatives or people

72

whom they knew in their neighbourhoods, and had sustained their commitment for long periods, in some instances for periods of up to fifteen years. The concerns that the young men developed in relation to their political practice were extremely sophisticated and revealed, in some cases, political maturation conjoined with ethical consideration. The young men's predominant preoccupations include: how to protect one's family from the brutality of the State given one's own political involvement; how to come to a considered understanding of the qualities of leadership through experience and time; how to take up responsible mediation between the State and one's own community; how to carry often painful secrets and knowledge about oneself and others; how to deal with betrayal, at times even with equanimity; how to attempt to prepare oneself for torture; how to shield one's family from one's own excruciating experiences of torture and, for some, how to make plans to escape the country in order to join the armed struggle; how to reconstitute community life after having returned from exile or from imprisonment, in an everyday world within a small town where it was neither unusual to encounter the men who had tortured one nor individuals who had betrayed one; and lastly, how to come to terms with the abiding inequalities and pressures of material consumption within South Africa. In my view, Reynolds' work stands out in tracing lines of political interest and involvement through time for individuals who, when very young, had to face the might of a brutal State and who were transformed in the process in often extremely painful ways and yet in ways that demonstrated wisdom and forbearance – indeed, sophisticated qualities of leadership.

Fiona Ross' (2003) work is complementary to Reynolds' study in that she has written an enriching account of young women's involvement in the struggle against the apartheid State in the same community. On one level, her work seeks to foreground the ways in which young women bore similar convictions to their male compatriots and made similar sacrifices. Neither were they exempt from the harshest treatment meted out by the South African police and military forces, including sexual violence. Reading the personal narratives to which Ross refers mitigates against gender stereotypes within the context of war. She argues for the recognition of women's and girl's contributions to the transformation of society, a recognition that is all too soon buried in official accounts of struggle.

It is ironic that in the late 1990s, with the inauguration of the first democratic South African State, the media began to emphasise the importance of the reconstitution of "normal" childhood, a return to a cordoned space of innocence (Ndebele, 1995), and called for the "moral regeneration" of the citizenry. It was a call beneath which lay discomfort at the extent of children's active involvement in the transformation of the society, and through the latter process, of the violence to which they had necessarily been exposed and in which they had sometimes taken part. Fears came to focus on young people themselves rather than on the treatment they had received under the former regime.[5] Young people were now pathologised as a problem for the new society and labeled "the lost generation", because some had sacrificed their education in order to bring about social change, and it was widely thought that their exposure to violence would necessarily lead to their own indiscriminate perpetuation of violence within the society.

Appeals for the restoration of the normative diminished the social space in which young people could publicly make a contribution to the issues of the day despite the fact that, for the first time in South Africa's history, a democratic state was emerging. The restoration of "the normative" was concerned with reinsertion of "appropriate" social hierarchies in which men, women and children resumed their "accepted" places, in particular, the return of children to a space of "safety" in which children's dependency was emphasized and in which they were infantilised. Prior to the 1994 elections, it was briefly mooted that children of fourteen years and upward be entitled to vote in acknowledgement of their contribution to the transformation of the society. This idea was quickly quashed to align the new nation-state with international definitions of childhood correlated to age. A real return to childhood would be to recognise the power of children in shaping the world and in taking seriously the call to attend to their transgressions and the critique of dominant society that they provide. As Chris Jenks (1996) has written, children are both destined and required to transgress in ways that test society, as well as social theory. This is the case because children have to submit to the violence of the existing social-historical order without having been pre-warned.

The Importance of Innovative Methods in Child and Youth Research

I would like to suggest that methods involved in conducting research with children and youth must be developed in relation to a study's particular aims and objectives. In careful anthropological research, for example, a plethora of methods may be utilised to try to capture differing dimensions of children's activities and ideas. Pamela Reynolds' ethnography (1991) on children's work in the Zambezi valley in early independent Zimbabwe is a particularly fine example in which trustworthy evidence is accrued through the use of a layering of methods in recording social life. In the book, she explores the experience, range and quantity of agricultural and domestic work undertaken by children among the Tembe-Tonga, and accomplishes this in particularly thorough and rigorous ways.

Reynolds chose a sample by mapping the area and investigating families at regular intervals across the territory along an axis. She asked children to keep diaries in which they wrote anything they thought interesting about their daily lives and compiled spot-check descriptions through observing what children were doing at regular intervals for a particular time period in and around their different homesteads. She regularly asked children and adults what children had done in the last 24 hours. Reynolds conducted interviews and open-ended discussions in which children conveyed to her the positive attributes they associated with their work in sustaining household economies. She documented different aspects of domestic and agricultural work through the changing seasons of the year and devised quantitative methods of measuring the percentage of the harvest boys and girls respectively brought in. In relation to harvesting, she was also able to compare the percentage of work undertaken by children to that carried out by adults. Because of the diversity of methods Reynolds employed in tracing children's work, she was able to demonstrate convincingly the quantity of work children undertook, something that both children and adults had underestimated, thus demonstrating the ideological ways in which children's activities were in some respects diminished. She also showed details in relation to gendered differentiation in kinds and quantities of work. She traced more subtle attributes of work in relation to feelings of pride and accomplishment, in relation to children's upbringing and interwoven with other social activities, including play.

Some examples employing participatory research methods in relation to children

I now examine a number of creative methods in relation to child research that may broadly be described as participatory. In an era of increasing importance of human rights in general, and children's rights in particular, there are attempts to render children's lives and preoccupations more visible, to ensure, as the saying goes that children's "voices" are increasingly heard in the public realm. Similarly, in the field of child research, children and youth are beginning to be viewed as co-researchers, and in some instances are called upon to design research parameters and to carry out research procedures. A

76

call for children's rights, when imposed from the outside, can often be put forward in ways that antagonise adults, by assuming that local communities have no ways of safe-guarding children or of imparting skills to them that will be useful in their daily lives. Insensitive appeals to children's rights may, at best, discount local lines of authority and culturally embedded ways of protecting and bringing up children and, at worst, render them invisible. There are precedents as to how children and adults may co-operate fruitfully on joint projects that are sensitive to local worlds but that enable a space for critique of forms of social blindness. In such examples, adults are not alienated from participation themselves in a joint process with children, a process that may simultaneously empower children with a sense of their own abilities.

Children's Knowledge of Animal Husbandry

An example from South Africa from the rural district of Msinga in KwaZulu-Natal is illustrative of such fruitful cooperation (Ewing, 2009). Deborah Ewing has conducted a form of interventionist research with young boys in which she aims to bring into the school curriculum forms of knowledge that the children already possess through their everyday care of animals. Her work marks a complex process of recognition and of appreciation of children's practical knowledge and its transmutation into knowledge that is counted as educative in relation to acquiring writing skills and the ability to record tacit knowledge made conscious and visible. In the context of South Africa, where the quality of primary education remains dire (Pendlebury, Lake & Smith, 2009) and where educational content is often alien to local worlds, the conversion of children's knowledge into a visible and prestigious knowledge through its incorporation into schooling processes, is a political act of some considerable importance. Through the latter process, legitimacy and worth are attached to ways of knowing that already exist in a community in a country where, from the

77

point of view of the dominant power, African people's abilities were derided and dismissed for many years.

Adults are also extremely interested in the project because they are concerned about the transmission of knowledge between generations in relation to their herds and agricultural pursuits more generally. Not only are these pursuits important aspects of livelihoods in the region, but they are invested with a depth of cultural meaning. In the above project, children and adults cooperate and learn from one another in ways that they feel equally excited about. This is because their sphere of activities is of common interest. In such an enabling context of communication between adults and children, not only do adults develop a respect for the knowledge children have in relation to herding and being responsible for the care of animals, but children are also able to effectively voice criticisms in relation to their everyday experience. In the exchange, adults also enjoy teaching children about specialised aspects of animal care.

A children's Radio Project

Abaqophi bas' Okhayeni Abaqinile (the strong recorders of Okhayeni) (2007) is a group of children between the ages of ten and fourteen, attending Okhayeni Primary School in the rural Ingwavuma District of KwaZulu-Natal, South Africa. Together they are involved in an innovative radio project. The area where the children live, including KwaZulu-Natal as a whole, has one of the highest rates of HIV/AIDS infection in southern Africa and indeed in the world. Many of the children have lost relatives through death. The radio project is a joint initiative of the Children's Institute of the University of Cape Town, The Zisizwe Educational Trust and Okhayeni Primary School and aims to initiate a process through which children develop the technological skills and reflexive abilities to create their own radio diaries. These are broadcast on a local community radio station. The radio diaries revolve around the children's everyday lives in a context of HIV/AIDS. Many include descriptions of place and particular events children have identified as important for them as individuals. Often relatives and friends are interviewed. Children sometimes question relatives in gentle ways as to the reasons for certain cultural practices. In one programme, for example, a child confronts her father asking why no one would answer her when she asked what had happened to her mother when she died. In this area small children were generally not informed that their parent was dead.

In local cultural repertoires, adults have been taught that confronting a child with the death of a parent will be too painful for them to bear, hence they avoid answering all questions about death that very young children ask. The radio programmes in some instances demonstrated a subtle negotiation between children and adults by showing adults the distress and pain caused by their refusal to answer children's questions as to where a deceased parent had gone when they could clearly see that they were lying there, dead. Such cultural approaches to children in times of death suggest that children's understanding of what has happened is underestimated by adults, as is their capacity to experience loss and disorientation.

The Use of Theatre and Drama in Child Research

Theatre improvisations can be usefully employed in undertaking research into children's lives. Forms of improvisation enable children to portray their everyday lives in a lively manner by mirroring the bodily comportment and speaking styles of different kinds of people within their communities. It is also a means of engaging children that they particularly enjoy. Plays that children produce about problems they have defined within their communities demonstrate that they are wry commentators on the social worlds in which they find themselves. I have also employed theatre games and workshop techniques in my own research with children in

79

Okhahlamba, South Africa (Henderson, 2006). When I was first introduced to the children who were part of an already-established intervention project, they seemed extremely shy. I was soon to learn that their initially muted responses to me and to the project facilitator, who was well known to them and who came from the same community, had to do with pronounced repertoires of respect marked through patterns of avoidance between younger and older people. I introduced a set of theatre games into the meetings with the group, as a device to encourage younger children to become more overtly expressive and communicative. The games initiated a process through which the young people eventually produced a play about problems that they had identified and defined themselves within their community.

There are two points I would like to make in reflecting on the play the young people created. The first has to do with enactment as an important distancing device through which they were able to describe painful aspects of life without skirting too closely to personal contours of pain. The fact that young people themselves brought up HIV/AIDS as a theme threading through their play suggested that in acting out parts, they were able to point to areas of pain without discomposing themselves in the company of their peers. The second point revolves around the presumed accessibility of children's voices. The habitual ways in which embodied forms of respect were re-enacted in the community in which the children lived persuaded me of the difficulties of accessing the free-floating and self-reflexive voices of children. The children's experimental, playful and critical voices were often located in unusual social spaces, for example, in the creation of the play. They also erupted spontaneously within the spaces of children's everyday work and play, including the practice of local performance genres revolving around dance and song. Similar spaces emerged between myself and the children after we had undertaken an extended journey together over time, where habitual forms of interaction were suspended and where experimental openness was achieved through mounting trust and mutual curiosity.

The Use of Art Therapy in Child Research

The Suitcase project, initiated in 2001 by researcher Glynis Clacherty in conjunction with artist Diane Welvering (Clacherty & Welvering 2006), was envisaged as art therapy, offering psycho-social support for refugee children less than eighteen years old who had found their way to an ecumenical refugee centre in Johannesburg, South Africa. Their countries of origin were the Democratic Republic of the Congo, Burundi, Rwanda, Ethiopia and Angola, although some of them had stayed for protracted periods in other countries before coming to South Africa. Some of them arrived in South Africa as unaccompanied child refugees. Clacherty recounted how they had had negative experiences of conventional counselling. She had the inspiration that suitcases as objects decorated by individual children could symbolically represent a simultaneous collage of current and former aspects of the children's selves and experience in ways that could point to survival, memory and current challenges about which they could choose to speak or to remain silent.

The young people met regularly with Clacherty and Welvering and began a process of decorating the outside of their suitcases with images of their then current lives in South Africa with the application of paint, beads and ribbons and images. They then created sets of images that recalled aspects of their past and pasted these within the suitcase interiors. When and if children wanted to approach Clacherty with some of "their stories" they could do so collectively, or privately under a tree in the courtyard of the venue where they worked. Many of the children did this in moving and sometimes drawn-out ways. The children entered into an unfolding process of creating images with which to transform their suitcases into personal reliquaries, ritual objects in which points of pain and

81

beauty in their past lives and their severance from all that had been familiar were equally marked. Aspects of their current lives and unfolding identities were also explored. The weight of the children's pain is tangible to those who read their narratives, as reported by Clacherty, and those who view the images fixed to the surfaces of the cases. There is an overwhelming sense of loss, not only of family members through death, but the dissolution of the familiar, the mourning for often rural worlds and activities that have been obliterated; there is the theme of flight, flight from immediate danger in the past and the present, flight across borders through often hostile countries, of arrival in South Africa and of the experience of being sometimes unwelcome in a stimulating yet bewildering urban environment completely different from places that had once been home.

Children Exploring Dimensions of Their Everyday Lives Through Photography

Phillip Mizzen and Yaw Ofusu-Kusi (2009, 2008, 2006) have described a photographic project carried out by children living and working on the streets of Accra, Ghana. In 1999, a similar project was published under the title *Shootback: Photos by Kids from the Nairobi Slums* (Booth-Clibborn Editions) under the guidance of Lana Wong. While this book was sold widely, in 2012 it was out of print, but a similar project endures and can be accessed at http://www.mysakenya.org/In-the-Community/photography-shootback.html. By taking seriously the idea of children as "the agents of their own enquiry", they sought to develop "collaborative and complementary research practices" with the children. Their aim was to acknowledge young people's "agency and purpose in looking to survive under circumstances not of their making, to highlight [children's] fortitude and creativity, to understand the knowledge and meanings they possess[ed], and how they act[ed] upon these understandings". To this end, children developed photographic accounts of a day spent living and working on the streets. Drawing on Reynolds, Mizzen and Ofusu-Kusi argued for the importance of "deftness and innovation of method", as I do in this paper, so as to take seriously the views and explanations of children as "a source of unofficial truth" (*ibid.* 3). In introducing the photographs, Mizzen and Ofusu-Kusi have written that they "told vividly of the environs and ecology of street life, its detail and design, fractures and strains, its palpable fragmentation" and that they shared the "physical fabric and infrastructure under stress [of Accra], and a burgeoning informal economy within and through which the children [had to] work to survive (*ibid*: 5)".

Patterns and themes, as well as repertoires of activities emerged in examining the photographs: boys pushing and carrying heavy loads through street markets; girls carrying smaller items, cooking food for sale and cleaning utensils; and the display of various merchandise the young people sold. Mizzen and Ofusu-Kusi mention the importance of details within the young people's photographs and, in particular, objects that gave a topographical dimension to a description of their lives, details that would often otherwise be missing (*ibid*: 7).

Importantly, the photographs confirmed narratives the children told about their lives, but also depicted more private and personal moments that are often inaccessible to researchers. The photographs had a strong humanising effect on perceptions of street children, because they revealed certain intimacies that overturned stereotypical conceptions of street life. They revealed the errors of type-casting street children as, for example, dirty, feral, violent, and of necessity undergoing unending hardship. Mizzen and Ofusu-Kusi were struck by the way the photographs underscored the fallibility of their existing knowledge through taking them by surprise (*ibid*: 15). Images revealed children in humorous situations displaying palpable enjoyment, posturing for the camera, and in relation to one another, compassion, tenderness and friendship (*ibid*: 9). Many of these qualities constituted "previously unobserved or unknown dimensions" of the children's lives. The above examples of creative and participatory methods in conducting research with children were all devised for particular settings and with particular goals in mind.[6] It goes without saying that methods need to be invented in relation to specific research areas of interest and cannot necessarily be applied across all research domains.

Discussing New Directions

I would suggest that a lot of hidden work, knowledge and research on children and childhood exists in Africa. Much is known about children, yet what is known remains invisible and unacknowledged in the global context and is often unshared across the continent due to configurations of knowledge and power along particular North-South axes. This may be so because such knowledge is presumed to be "inferior" or dismissed due to the deflation of local forms of knowledge in favour of an often flattening universality. In this light, it is important to bring forward the figure of the child in Africa in all its complexity and variety – something that to date has not been done. There is the necessity to search, to look afresh, to listen and to compile; to rediscover approaches to children unbounded by stereotypical ways of viewing young people and their childhoods.

Areas of research and archival retrieval need to explore everything from birth and the welcoming of the child into the world, to the shaping of the child's body; and from a consideration of children's work and creativity through to transmission of knowledge between and within generations. Different ways of upbringing need to be revisited, as well as the child's relationship with cosmologies, in particular with ancestral spirits: cosmologies encompassing the child as a figure of power connected with another world, growing into adulthood. Then too the experimental, ludic qualities attributed to the child are worthy of attention: the child in relation to laughter, music and play. As borne out in new work, particularly in relation to youth, we need to reflect on how such expressive repertoires enable children and youth to comment, often with great insight, on the social worlds in which they find themselves. Such an approach would aim at capturing the fullness of children's and youths lives, challenging us not to confine our perspectives to upholding repeated one-dimensional notions of crisis and inadequacy. There will be a sense in which such an exercise in retrieval may fracture and dislodge the manner in which African children are often uniformly portrayed with reference to notions of overarching lack. Although such a work will go some way in showing the undeniable hardships children and youth face on the continent in often imploding worlds where sociality is ripped apart and then reconfigured in the wake of scarcity, violence and loss – a condition that writers like Achille Mbembe (2003, 2001) have described as the incursion of death into life – the work will also bring to the surface some of the improvisatory repertoires children bring to bear on remaking social worlds and in journeying between diverse contexts and across borders of different sorts in often mobile and transforming ways that unsettle what we think may be the place, capacities and boundaries of childhood.

There seem to be definite gaps in contemporary studies of children and youth in Africa. Very little research is being done in relation to young children and very few studies in relation to girls and their everyday lives. An exception here is the work of Lynn Thomas in laying down the history of everyday lives of girls (Thomas *et al* 2008; 2007; 2006). At the CODESRIA conference on new directions in child and youth research, for example, only one participant spoke of her interest in documenting the lives of street children. A lot of interest is currently being shown in youth culture and young peoples' interest in music (see, for example, Drame 2009, Ntarangwi 2009a, 2009b) and in the social groups marginalised young men form in urban spaces in Africa, where they occupy ambivalent and fluid political spaces. Here, on the one hand such groups may provide stringent criticisms of the State; on the other hand, they may be called upon to give sometimes violent support to politicians in their quest for power. Many such performance genres enable a multiplicity of processes: attempts by youth to embody and reflect global trends, and the importance of local appropriations of such trends, making genres meaningful within local contexts; celebrating the ability to speak poetically through such genres; commenting on their societies in critical, amusing and important ways. Yet many of these genres are dominated by boys and young men. It is of equal importance to explore the lives and activities of young girls and young women. What social processes are they involved in? Do any social spaces exist in which they may articulate what is socially unpalatable, for example, as explored in Lila Abu-Lughod's (1999) work on poetic forms among Bedouin women in Egypt?

The question then is how to think creatively beyond the categories and conceptualisations that are habitually used in approaching descriptions of childhood and the world-making and unmaking of youth? How do we embrace risk in our conceptualisations, and even eccentricity, to ensure open-ended conceptualisations of childhood and youth that are responsive to new social and cultural developments and that draw their weight from rigorous empirical studies? We should not rely too heavily on the ongoing circulation of a narrow body of authoritative works on children and childhood in writing up our research, but seriously embrace an attempt to reflect upon, locate and bring forward new work based on finely-grained research.

I will end the chapter by exploring briefly one way in which we may refresh our approaches to the study of children and youth. I suggest that the ways in which we approach our research would benefit from an examination of the rich literary output of the African continent in which there exist autobiographical accounts of childhood or the imaginative construction of worlds by an adult taking on the voice of a child, for example as evinced in Ben Okri's prize winning novel, *The Famished Road* (Okri: 1991). As mentioned above, a predominant trope through which children and youth are described in Africa has to do with the notion of absolute lack: lack of food, of resources, of quality education, of ongoing social networks, of health, of parents, of processes of socialization.

Although Okri's book is an adult's description of life from the perspective of a child, it raises the duality of children's worlds; the importance of describing not only the lack and loss within such worlds but the creativity of children in negotiating the everyday, and its textured nature. In his book, Okri takes on the voice of Azaro, a spirit child. Spirit children in West Africa come to earth reluctantly and are drawn towards early death in order to rejoin their spirit companions in an infinitely preferable realm. However, Azaro, instead of rejoining his spirit companions, decides to live, as he cannot bear the suffering that his death will cause his mother. He takes on, therefore, the uncertainties of mortality through compassion – a compassion that he extends to his father, who at one point beats him severely. His father's cruelty is placed within a framework of understanding where he witnesses both his parents engaging in back-breaking work and various forms of humiliation to sustain their small family. Azaro is a wise child with prognostic powers. He acts as witness to the turbulent, poverty-stricken worlds in which he finds himself. These worlds are characterised by political and economic instability and the uncompromising pursuit of scarce resources on the part of the poor and unscrupulous politicians alike. The book charts physical intimidation experienced by the poor at the hands of the powerful. The ways in which life and death are closely intertwined is reflected in worlds where the living and the dead, the spirit worlds and the mundane, cross over into one another. The book describes a context of multi-sensorial fluidity and flux where cultural repertoires are shredded and reconfigured. Lines of continuity and innovation are etched. At no stage is this life viewed as pathological.

Notes

1. There exists a growing literature on child agency across a broad range of activities within social worlds. See, for example, Boyden 1990; Boyden & Holden 1991; Caputo, 1995; Donzelot 1980; Ennew & Milne, 1989; James & Prout 1990; James, 1993; Jenks 1996; Stephens 1995

2. In South Africa unemployment stands at approximately 40 %.

3. See also Nordstrom's (1997) ethnography of children and war in Mozambique. Her work contains very little solid ethnographic data on which to base her conclusions.

4. For the ways in which sovereignty is threaded through with violence reaching beyond the bounds of its own legitimation, see, for example, Agamben (1998).

5. For other writing referring to children and youths' contribution to the transformation of South African society during the struggle against apartheid see, Bundy (1987), Hyslop (1988), Carter (1991), Straker (1991), Seekings (1993), Ndebele (1995), Badat (1997), and Marks (2001).

6. For a theoretical exploration of the ways in which multi-modal teaching methods that draw on creative methods of teaching within the classroom, see Stein (2007), Newfield & Maungedzo (2006).

References

Abaqophi bas' Okhanyeni Abaqinile, Growing Up in a Time of
AIDS Children's Radio Project: CD-ROM Volume 2. 2007.
Cape Town: Children's Institute, Zisize Educational Trust
and Okhayeni Primary School.

Abu-Lughod, Lila. 1999. Veiled Sentiments: Honor Poetry in a
Bedouin Society. Berkeley: University of California Press.

Agamben, Giorgio. 1998. Homo Sacer: Sovereign Power and
Bare Life, trans. Daniel Heller-Roazen. Stanford: Stanford
University Press.

Badat, S. 1997. Black Student Politics, Higher Education and
Apartheid: from SASO to SANCO, 1968-1990. Pretoria:
Human Sciences Research Council.

Boyden, Jo. 1990. Childhood and the Policy Makers: A
Comparative Perspective on the Globalization of
Childhood. In A, James & A. Prout. Constructing and
Reconstructing Childhood, pp. 184-215. London: The
Falmer Press.

Boyden, Jo & Pat Holden 1991. Children of the Cities.
London: Zed Books.

Bray, Rachel. 2003. Predicting the Social Consequences of
Orphanhood in South Africa. Centre for Social Science
Research, University of Cape Town.

Bundy, Colin. 1987. Street Sociology and Pavement Politics:
Aspects of Youth and Student Resistance in Cape Town,
1985. Journal of Southern African Studies, 13:303-30.

Caputo, Virginia. 1995. Anthropology's Silent 'Others': A
Consideration of Some Conceptual and Methodological
Issues for the Study of Youth and Children's Cultures. In
V. Amit-talai & H. Wulff, eds., Youth Cultures: A Cross-
Cultural Perspective, pp. 19-42. London: Routledge.

Carter, Charles. 1991. Comrades and Communities: Politics
and the Construction of Hegemony in Alexandra
Township, South Africa, 1984-1987. (D. Phil Thesis.
Oxford University.)

Clacerty, Glynis and Diane Welvering. 2006. The Suitcase Stories: Refugee children reclaim their identities. Cape Town: Double Storey.

Das, Veena. 2007. Life and Words: Violence and the Descent into the Ordinary. Delhi: Sage Publications.

_____1998. Critical Events: An Anthropological Perspective on Contemporary India. Delhi: Oxford University Press.

De Boeck, Filip and Plissart, Marie-Françoise. 2004. Kinshasa: Tales of the Invisible City. Amsterdam: Royal Museum for Central Africa of Tervuren.

De Boeck, Filip and Alcinda Honwana, (eds). 2005. Makers and Breakers: Children and Youth in Postcolonial Africa. Oxford: James Currey.

Donzelot, Jaques, 1980. The Policing of Families. London: Hutchinson.

Drame, Mamadou. 2009. Le Slam, Une Nouvelle Expression de la Jeunesse a Mi-Chemin entre le Rap et la Poessie Traditionnelle. Paper presented at the CODESRIA, New Frontiers in Child and Youth Research in Africa, Douala, Cameroon 26-7 August 2009.

Ennew, Judith & Brian Milne. 1989. The Next Generation: Lives of Third World Children. London: Zed Books.

Ewing, Deborah. 2009. Children's participation: recognising and promoting agency in unequal power relations. Unpublished paper delivered at the Leverhulme theorising children's participation conference, Children's Institute, University of Cape Town.

Hecht, Tobias. 1998. At Home on the Streets: Street Children of Northeast Brazil. Cambridge: Cambridge University Press.

Henderson, Patricia, C. 1999. Living with Fragility: Children in New Crossroads. PhD thesis, Department of Social Anthropology, University of Cape Town.

_____ 2003. Questions of Fostering: an anthropological perspective. In Sandra Burman (ed.), The Fate of the Child:

Legal Decisions on Children in the New South Africa. Cape Town: Juta.

_____2006. South African AIDS orphans: Examining assumptions around vulnerability from the perspective of rural children and youth. Childhood, 13(3):303-327.

Honwana, Alcinda. 2006. Child Soldiers in Africa. Philadephia: University of Pennsylvania Press.

Hyslop, Jonathan. 1988. School Student Movements and State Education Policy: 1972-1987. In Popular Struggles in South Africa, (eds.) William Cobbett and Robin Cohen. London: James Currey.

James, Alison, & James Prout. 1990. Constructing and Reconstructing Childhood, pp. 184-215. London: The Falmer Press.

James, Alison. 1993. Childhood Identities. Edinburgh: Edinburgh University Press.

Jenks, Chris. 1996. Childhood. London: Routledge.

Marks, M. 2001. Young Warriors: Youth Politics, Identity and Violence in South Africa. Johannesburg. Witwatersrand University Press.

Mbembe, Achille. 2003. Necropolitics. Public Culture, 15(1):11-40.

_____ 2001. On the Postcolony. Berkeley: University of California Press.

Meintjes, Helen and Sonja Giese. 2006 Spinning the epidemic: The making of mythologies of orphanhood in the context of AIDS. Childhood: A global journal of child research 13(3): 407-430.

Meintjes, Helen, Sue Moses, Lizette Berry and Ruth Mampane. 2007. Home truths: The phenomenon of residential care for children in a time of AIDS. Cape Town: Children's Institute, Centre for the Study of AIDS, University of Pretoria.

Mizzen, Phillip and Ofosu-Kusi, Yaw. 2009. At Work in the Street: The Case of the 'Kubolo'. Paper presented at the

Living Rights Seminar, Institut Universitaire Kurt Bosch, Sion, Switzerland, 19-20 January 2009.

_____ 2008. Asking, Giving, Receiving: Friendship As Survival Among Accra's Street Children, unpublished paper, Department of Sociology, University of Warwick.

_____2006. Researching with, not one: using Photography in Researching Street Children in Accra, Ghana. In M. Smith (ed.), Negotiating Boundaries and Borders: Qualitative Methodology and Development Research. Oxford: Elserivier.

Ndebele, Njabulo. 1995. Children in South African National Reconstruction. In Sharon Stephens, (ed.). Children and the Politics of Culture, pp.321-33. Princeton. Princeton University Press.

Newfield, Denise, and Robert Maungedzo. 2006. Mobilising and modalising poetry in a Soweto Classroom. Unpublished article presented at the English Studies in Africa Conference, April 2006.

Ntarangwi, Mwenda. 2009a. Children's lives and children's voices: An exploration of popular music's representation of children in East Africa. Paper presented at the CODESRIA conference: New Frontiers in Child and Youth Research. Douala, Cameroon, 26-27 August 2009.

_____2009b. East African Hip Hop: Youth Culture and Globalization. Urbana IL: University of Illinois Press.

Nordstrom, Carolyn. 1997. A Different Kind of War Story. Pennsylvania: University Philadelphia of Press.

Opie, Iona and Peter Opie. 1959. The Lore and Language of Schoolchildren. Oxford: Oxford University Press.

Pendlebury, Shirley, Lori Lake & Charmain Smith (eds.). South African Child Gauge 2008/2009. Cape Town: Children's Institute.

Ramphele, Mamphela 2002. Steering by the Stars: Being Young in South Africa. Cape Town: Tafelberg Publishers.

Reynolds, Pamela, 1989. Childhood in Crossroads: Cognition and Society in South Africa (Cape Town: David Phillip Grand Rapids.

_____1991. Dance Civet Cat: Child Labour in the Zambezi Valley. London: Zed Books.

_____ 1995a. 'Not Known Because Not Looked For': Ethnographers Listening to the Young in Southern Africa. Ethnos 60(3-4): 194-221

_____1995b. The Ground of All Making: State Violence, the family and political activists. Pretoria: Human Sciences Research Council.

_____2005. Imfobe: Self-knowledge and the reach for ethics among former, young, anti-apartheid activists. Anthropology Southern Africa 28(3-4):62-72.

Ross, Fiona. 1995. Houses without Doors: Diffusing domesticity in Die Bos (Pretoria: The Human Sciences Research Council (HSRC) Programme on Marriage and Family Life.

_____2003. Bearing Witness: Women and the Truth and Reconciliation Commission in South Africa. London, Sterling: Pluto Press.

Seekings, Jeremy. 1993. Heroes or Villains? Youth Politics in the 1980s. Johannesburg: Ravan Press.

Stein, Pippa. 2007. Multimodal Pedagogies in Diverse Classrooms: Representation, Rights and Resources. London: Routledge.

_____ 2006. Fresh Stories. In Sarah Nutall (ed), Beautiful Ugly: African and Diaspora Aesthetics. Durham, London, Cape Town, The Hague: Duke University Press, Kwela Books, Prince Claus Fund for Culture and Development.

Stephens, Sharon (ed.). 1995. Children and the Politics of Culture. Princeton: Princeton University Press.

Straker, Gill. 1992. Faces in the Revolution: The Psychological Effects of Violence on Township Youth in South Africa. Cape Town: David Philip.

Thomas, Lynn, et al 2008. The Modern Girl Around the World: Consumption, Modernity, and Globalization. Duke University Press.

2007. "Gendered Reproduction: Placing Schoolgirl Pregnancies in African History." Africa After Gender: 48–62.

2006. "The Modern Girl and Racial Respectability in 1930s South Africa." The Journal of African History 47 (03): 461–490. doi:10.1017/S0021853706002131

Warner, Marina. 1994. Managing Monsters: Six Myths of Our Time. London: Vintage.

3

"It is the Common Way but not the Normal Way": Marriage, Household and Social Order in Accounts of African Youth[1]

Jeremy L. Jones

The study of "African youth", once relegated to the footnotes of African scholarship, has arguably "come of age" over the past decade. This new-found "maturity" is evidenced both by the growing conceptual depth and by the sheer diversity of investigations into the lives of young Africans. In addition to the other chapters gathered here, as well as other work published under the auspices of CODESRIA's Child and Youth Institute, any number of books and journal special editions have explicitly thematised issues of young people on the continent (e.g. Honwana and de Boeck 2005, Christiansen *et al*, 2006, Durham 2004). Even scholars studying other issues in Africa often mention the position of young people in their analysis, meaning that "youth" has entered the mainstream of intellectual discourse (e.g. Chabal and Daloz 1999).

In the process, a number of issues have come to the fore. One concerns the supposed *prolongation* of youth. "Youth", the claim begins, is no longer limited to biologically young people. Rather, as AbdouMaliq Simone (2005) puts it, "youthfulness itself is [now] re-imagined as something beyond the purview of any particular age group – something highly mobile and potentially without end" (518). This ambiguity contributes to making "youth" a potent sign of danger, whether that associated with change or that associated with violence and death (Simone, 2005). The ostensible heart of the problem is a shift in the economic fortunes of African countries: youth has been prolonged in post-structural adjustment Africa because of the dearth of employment, the drying up of "convivial" State-centric resource distribution (Mbembe 2003), and the day-to-day uncertainties of urbanisation and migration. The supposed certainties of yesteryear – be they those of "tradition", wage labour, State welfare or some combination thereof – have been replaced by rampant uncertainty and movement (Comaroff and Comaroff 2005). This produces a three-fold breach in the "normal" course of life: young people are unable to find employment, unable to marry, and unable to establish so-called "independent households". As a result, they find themselves in limbo, unable to live up to expected forms of social identity, and condemned to extended liminality.

This limbo has become axiomatic to scholarly definitions of African youth. Like violence (e.g. Cruise O'Brien, 1996), problematic sexuality (e.g. Manuel, 2008), and claims to public space (e.g. Diouf, 2003), it is a key symbol of the "crisis" of African youth (Honwana and de Boeck, 2005). My research with young Zimbabweans in urban townships, however, suggests that the axiom does not always hold. Their economic situation is no different from that of most African youth – informal economic strategies are a fact of life for most – and there is no reason to believe that they are more prone to unsafe sex and violence than young people elsewhere. Yet, almost all young township dwellers are "married" and have their own households by their late twenties (and much earlier if they are women). In short, young people are *not* failing to "graduate" (Hansen 2005) to adult status – at least insofar as marriage and household formation are taken to be key to that transition. The proviso is this: their "marriages" often begin with a form of elopement that is normatively ambiguous. It does not wholly conform to norms of proper marriage and the households that are built on it therefore persist without any official recognition (whether from families or the State).

What are we to make of this empirical fact? Far from being a mere exception to the rule, I argue that it highlights several flaws in our modeling of "prolonged youth" and African "youth" more generally. First is the notion that there is—or should be—a clear transition between "youth" and "adulthood". Why assume that is the case? Jennifer Johnson-Hanks (2002) correctly argues that this account of a life-course based on irreversible and definitive events – like marriage, employment, and household formation – obscures more than it illuminates. Not only does it hide the important fact that "African" marriage is often processual rather than event-based – and this is certainly the case in Zimbabwe – it presumes exactly what it should explain, namely, the ideological coherence of life stages like "youth" and "adulthood". In point of fact, they are not clear, hence the constant return to supposedly "natural" measures like biological age. Second is problem of mistaking moral norms for statistical ones. As Pierre Bourdieu (1977) and many after him have observed, normative "rules" should not be confused with actual practice. To quote one young Zimbabwean's seemingly contradictory description of elopement "it is the common way but not the normal way" of getting married. As scholars, we have to be able to account for the difference between the "common" and the "normal". Third are the twin assumptions that any failure to live up to normative transitions constitutes a "crisis" and that this crisis is *new*. Here we run into a methodological dilemma: "crisis" is an important category of local discourse all across Africa, and so is the idea that this crisis entails a departure from a more stable past. It is important to cater for these facts of discourse, as well as for the material context in which they exist. Still, "crisis" must be explained as a statement *about* facts rather than simply accepted as a statement *of* fact. Its invocation is hardly theoretically innocent. It should come as no surprise, for instance, that the crisis of youth is often rendered in terms of an urban/rural divide, the key binary of

97

Africa's wrought narrative of modernisation. As James Ferguson (1999) has forcefully demonstrated of Zimbabwe's northern neighbor, Zambia, that narrative is factually wrong in several key regards.

All told, these theoretical preoccupations have profound ramifications for questions of African "youth" identity. Firstly, they tend to support a notion of identity that is singular, definitive, and anchored in one's relation to the home. Social roles become a simple matter of following the rules of social institutions, in particular patriarchal institutions of kinship. These roles are then confused with lived identity. Secondly, any departure from this singular, institutional identity is cast as an historical departure, as if the rules were unproblematically followed by earlier generations of young people. There is a beguiling and self-evident truth to these claims, just as there is a beguiling truth to claims of crisis. All speak to realities on the ground, and again, most are propounded by local discourse. The scholarly emphasis on rule and ritual is not merely reflective, though: these are the key categories of positivist social science passed down to us from Durkheim (1912; 1933), and there is pressure to maintain them.[2] The problem is, maintaining such a view makes youth identity problematic, anomic, and liminal almost by definition. The logic is simple: if social order is taken to be based on each new generation taking up normative social identities, failure to do so represents a threat to that order. Youth fail to do so, therefore they are a threat: it is a conclusion that is built into our theoretical apparatus.

In exploring these issues further, I want to emphasise how they make it difficult to account the practice of elopement marriage, and with it, the true complexity of normative transitions. Elopement sits in a grey area as the "common way but not the normal way". It is deeply important for young people's plans, their interpersonal relations, and ultimately, their identity. Some of them argue that being married makes them an adult, others, more subtly, that it makes them grow up. The key is that their "marriages" and "households" are not composed by the large ceremonies or official acts or normative imagination, but by everyday actions and talk, which are variously situated with respect to such norms. Seeing the distinction is crucial, because it opens up a whole world of contestation and active, context-dependent *identification* (rather than identity *per se*). In fact, by narrowing our focus to normative failures, we both miss much of the details of youth's lives and perpetuate a theoretical framework that eviscerates identity of all complexity.

I hope what follows will begin to provide a corrective. I will start with the example of a young Shona-speaking man from Zimbabwe, and then show how his experiences constitute a blind spot in scholarly accounts of African youth. From there, I outline a normative model of "Shona" marriage and set it against the day-to-day realities of elopement and domestic life in Zimbabwean urban areas.

A Typical African Youth?

Let me begin with the story of Okocha,[3] a young Zimbabwean whom I have known since he was in grade school.

Okocha and I lived in the same house in Chitungwiza, Harare's largest "township" suburb, for several years during the late nineties and early two thousands. I shared the house with his older brother, a longtime friend and colleague, and he in turn was supporting Okocha's secondary schooling. At the time, my feelings towards Okocha were mixed. He had a bad habit of breaking into my room and stealing my already meager belongings. In 2006, Okocha and I began meeting again at a local market in Chitungwiza, where I had returned to do my dissertation research. Now a young man of about twenty, he was given to wearing a baseball cap (worn slightly askew), timberland-style boots, baggy jeans and a variety of "bling" belt-buckles. One day, we started reminiscing about old times. "You were a real *tsotsi*" [a thug, thief, dishonest or flashy person, etc.], I observed, recalling his days of petty thievery. He just laughed, "Yeah, well I was drinking a lot [of beer] those days. I liked your stuff, especially that little radio you had, but I was afraid to ask to borrow it. So, eh, uh...sorry about that."[4] Besides drinking and smoking marijuana, he admitted, he was also quite promiscuous during that period:

> When I was at school I had so many girlfriends..., at least one in each of the twelve divisions of the class....I was known for it: "that guy is a *hure* [i.e. a promiscuous person, "whore", normally a term reserved for loose women]," people said.

His "mischievous" behaviour, as he put it, saw him being shuttled between relatives, as one after another grew tired of his antics. Eventually, none wanted him around and he was forced to squat at a friend's house every night and scrounge for food. Many days, he claimed, he subsisted on nothing but beer. Having "learned a lesson", as he said, he returned to his mother's home in the rural areas (his father had died when he was a child). He quit drinking and smoking and temporarily joined an apostolic church. Visibly reformed, he returned to town, renegotiated his relationship with his brothers, and began his "A" level studies at their expense. When his key sponsor lost his formal sector job, though, he was forced to stop, and he subsequently began informal trading in earnest. He specialised in selling cell-phones that were, as he put it, "probably stolen...*but not by me!*".

By that time (2006), wage labour was increasingly looked down upon in Zimbabwe – "you pay more in bus fares than you earn in a month", Okocha observed. "Those who are a bit older", he added,

...they prepared [*vakagadzira*] their lives long ago, so that even if they don't have work, they have somewhere to start. A house, whatever. They just need to look for money for food. But our "age" [English], we have nothing to start with, nowhere to even begin. Nothing. Really.

In the months to come, though, the country's fast-expanding parallel economy exposed him (and many other young people) to unexpected possibilities. First, diamonds were discovered in an area within walking distance of his rural home, and he followed many of his friends and relatives to join in the burgeoning illegal trade. He did not dig, choosing instead to engage in an elaborate barter system whereby he would source consumer goods in town, trade them for diamonds, then immediately sell them and use the money to begin the cycle again. By late 2007, though, the diamond fields were becoming increasingly dangerous and his profits were drying up. He tried his hand at smuggling used clothes, shoes and basic commodities from Mozambique, but quickly tired of that as well. He decided to return to Chitungwiza, where he became an illegal foreign currency dealer. This trade yielded reasonable profits – though not nearly as much, he claimed, as some people thought.[5]

Like most young people in the area, Okocha was a nominal supporter of the opposition, but was not an activist. Nonetheless, in the run-up to the presidential run off in June, 2008, he was repeatedly threatened with beatings, and was robbed of nearly US$300 (his "capital") by thugs hired by the then ruling party. He was targeted because of his black-market dealings, which were repeatedly denounced by the government as a weapon of "sell-outs" seeking to effect "illegal regime change". In one encounter, he got in an argument with party member (a woman) who threatened to kick him out of his "workplace" (which was actually just a parking lot). A mêlée broke out, and a crowd beat up the woman. Concluding quite

101

reasonably that there would be police/militia retaliation, Okocha ran away to a relative's house and spent the next two weeks in hiding. When he told me the story a month later, he did so in a whisper, and furtively handed me a "diary" of events that I had asked him to keep. "After the first few days of writing, I was afraid to write anymore," he said, adding that he had hidden the papers in the roof rafters, in case somebody came to abduct and beat him up (as they had done to two of his brothers). In his diary he writes of the fight with the woman:

> How could she say that kind of shit [i.e. threaten to eject him from his "workplace"]? She thinks people like us, young as we are, would like to stand on that fucken open space, bad or good weather, carrying big satchels with heaps of cash which does not even buy a 14 inch colour TV.[6] We are just people left with nothing to do but work for food only (sic).

This is a striking distillation of the predicament of youth and blocked accumulation. In many ways, Okocha was the paradigmatic African youth we read about. Twenty-three years old, perched between desires for a better life and the hard realities of "this fucken open space", he woke up every day and set about navigating the perilous struggle for survival (cf. Vigh 2006). He smuggled goods, jumped borders, participated in the bush economy in illicit minerals, made his money from illegal foreign currency dealing, and fought in violent political battles. He had, by his own account, led a life of occasional sexual promiscuity and drunken misbehaviour. He dabbled in popular religion and had been alienated from, then reconciled with, extended family. He had gone hungry, knowing that his education would prove useless in securing a decent job. He lived hand-to-mouth at the very edge of the global economic margins.

102

One critical detail did not fit the "African youth" mold: Okocha was married, to a high-school sweetheart and he had a baby son, on whom he doted. Back in 2006, I had asked if he had given up his promiscuous ways after high school. "I have a girlfriend now", he replied, somewhat dodging the question, "and I love her. She's doing form four. I even want to marry her."

"So what's stopping you?" I asked.

"Well, maybe in a few years, when I've managed to get something."

"What do you mean?" I pressed.

"Something like money, you know. And steady work. A room of my own. And the basic things in a house. How can you get married if you don't even have your own two plate stove? Or a bed?"

I had to remind him of this plan two years later, when, while counting through a stack of worn Zimdollars, he nonchalantly informed me he had eloped with his girlfriend, who was pregnant. Although his foreign currency dealings had provided him with enough money to buy a number of household assets, he was still living with relatives, and did not plan the marriage. "Yeah, well, I knocked her up [*kumumitisa*]", he admitted, quickly adding that it was the same girl that he had always wanted to marry, so he was not too worried. "It was just fast-tracked", he joked, referencing the accelerated pace – and perhaps the barely managed chaos – of the Zimbabwean government's post-2000 "fast-track land reform". His trading partner, looking on, added: "*Marriage?* Marriage just falls on you [*zvinongokuwira*].[7] There's nothing you can do about it".

Incomplete Transitions or Incomplete Analyses?

Whether this confirms the supposed "fatalism" of African youth is difficult to say. It clearly does not confirm the claim

103

that they are failing to marry. On the contrary, marriage is just "falling" on them. This sort of *fait accompli* marriage, established in the wake of an unplanned pregnancy, is so common for township residents that it is arguably the statistical norm. In most cases it goes unremarked – many people were surprised that I should find it an interesting topic of research. Still, it is not taken as "normal". Before discussing the complicated ethnography involved, I want to note that a reading of the African youth literature certainly would not prepare one for such a reality. An extreme reading might lead to the conclusion that African youth are no longer marrying or forming independent households at all. This unmarried status, moreover, seems to be at the centre of many of their problems, and it is important to consider why this is so. To that end, I want to first briefly return to some scholarly accounts, starting with a widely cited piece written in the early 1990s, when African youth began to be the subject of intense interest. It highlights a particular set of connections between youth, marriage and household formation, and social order; connections, I argue, that persist in more recent scholarship.

In his seminal discussion of West Africa's "Lost Generation" (1996), Donald Cruise O'Brien argues that:

> There is often to be heard a contrast of today's hard times with the relatively prosperous circumstances in which one's parents grew to adulthood – and set up their independent households....

A generational contrast can thus be made between those who grew to adulthood in the first two decades of African independence (1960-1980) and their successors who see their "youth" as something which is at risk of becoming indefinitely prolonged. This contrast has its material definition: economic independence, to have enough resources to marry and set up

104

one's own family, is the fundamental aspiration of youth, in West Africa as elsewhere in the world (pp. 57, 58).

Two key themes emerge here. First is the familiar idea I noted in my introduction: namely, that the period of "youth" has been prolonged by an inability to become financially independent, to marry, and to form a household. This claim is backed by a second argument regarding a historical shift. Earlier generations, Cruise O'Brien suggests, benefited from a different set of economic and political circumstances, and therefore what was once typical (financial independence, marriage, and household formation) is no longer attainable. In Okocha's words, youth of today lack the "place to start" that youth of yesteryear had. Cruise O'Brien continues:

> With a shrinking number of viable new independent households, however, anchored in some sort of secure employment for the head of the household, one must see the future as dark enough. This would appear to be a liminal generation, on the edge of what can become a social collapse, as in Liberia and a number of other State situations where violence tears at the fabric of social relations (p. 57).

Note the rhetorical opposition between "independent" "viable", "anchored", "secure", and "future" on hand, and "dark", "liminal", "violence" and "social collapse" on the other. By this account, marriage and the creation of independent households are not merely unfulfilled desires of youth, akin to the desire for consumer goods. Rather, they hold the key to both the future of those youth and societal stability more generally. Youths' inability to fulfill normative transitions to adulthood divorces them from society and makes them a danger to themselves and others.

The idea that African youth are dangerously undersocialized informs popular rhetoric all across the continent, as well as rhetoric about Africa written from outside.

105

Robert Kaplan, for instance, infamously suggested that West African youth were "restless" and ready to "ignite", a veritable storehouse of impending anarchy (1994). Even in less alarmist accounts, it is clear that the real target of criticism is young, unmarried men. They are the "African youth" in question, and being unmarried is a crucial piece of the puzzle. When Cruise O'Brien says that "secure employment for the head of household" is needed for the household to be "viable", it is not likely that he has market women in mind. Equally, it is not unmarried young women – or women of any sort – who threaten society with violence.

Recent literature on African youth has offered a number of correctives to Cruise O'Brien's account – not to mention Kaplan's and those like it – but it has continued to emphasise both the failure to achieve normative transitions and their association with declining economic fortunes and historical change more generally (cf. Johnson-Hanks 2002). In their introduction to a collection of studies of African youth, for instance, Honwana and de Boeck (2005) state:

> A growing number of children and youth in contemporary Africa are excluded from education, healthcare, salaried jobs, and even access to an adult status, given their financial incapacity to construct a house, formally marry and raise children in turn (9)

Other writers expand further, paying special attention to local detail and differences of gender. Writing of the predicament of young men in Niger, for instance, Adeline Masquelier (2005) observes:

> There is a growing sense that today's youths are facing a crisis of unprecedented proportions. This "crisis" centres on their inability to marry and achieve full social seniority. Marriage in Mawri society is a critical *rite de passage* indexing the transition from childhood to maturity ... To become adults, both boys and

106

girls must marry: non-marriage is simply not an acceptable option ... Before a boy and girl can tie the knot, however, bridewealth...must be exchanged ... In today's circumstances of dwindling economic opportunities and ever-escalating inflation, young men without the means to marry find themselves condemned to a kind of limbo life. In this situation of prolonged immaturity, they are defined as superfluous and non-adult....
(59)

Karen Tranberg Hansen's (1992) discussion of "compound" life in Lusaka paints the same basic picture:

I suggest that...young people are not so much a "lost generation" as they are a segment of the population of whom many in fact might never become adult in a normative social and cultural sense. As in much of the rest of the southern African region, for men in Zambia, the attributes of adulthood include a job, a house or flat of one's own, and a spouse and children – in short, the ability to be in charge as household heads. Adulthood for women is differently constructed: it revolves around childbearing and is not necessarily linked to cohabitation or marriage. Thus, men remain young much longer than women.... What does it mean for the reproduction of the social order if a considerable proportion of young people remain "youth forever" (4-5)?

Jean and John Comaroff (2004) sum up the entire line of reasoning nicely:

For young Africans, the chronic unattainability of material independence means not being able to marry, to have legitimate offspring, to establish a household, to enter into the social division of labor in a manner appropriate to grown persons, to take over the mantle of authority from their parents, to connect with the ancestors. In short, to leave youth behind for

107

adulthood. And in the case of men, to arrive at full maleness (338).

One could multiply examples. They are all subtle and theoretically astute, and the argument they make seems superficially incontrovertible. The material situation of many young Africans is clearly dire, stable employment options are virtually nil and formal marriage and household formation appear to require resources that almost all young men lack. But what is at stake in making this sort of argument?

In that regard, and at the risk of gross generalisation, I want to suggest that scholarship on youth risks perpetuating three misconceptions. The first, following directly from Cruise O'Brien, involves the relation between marriage and household and the social order. In this view, independent households, formed by marriage, are taken as the source of social value, which is then encompassed and managed by a public sphere peopled by the heads of those households (i.e. husbands). In the West, this idea dates back as far as Aristotle,[8] but it also forms the kernel of capitalist ideology (Engels 1990, Rubin 1975, Collier and Yanagisako, 1987). As feminist scholars have repeatedly shown, it is both inescapably gendered in theory and distinctly non-universal in historical terms (Amadiume 1997; Collier and Yanagisako, 1987; Oyewùmí, 1997). More than that, it paints an inaccurate picture of actually existing capitalism. For instance, James Ferguson (1999) has demonstrated that colonial assumptions and anxieties about proletarian household formation in the Zambian Copper belt were misplaced. Households there, as elsewhere in Africa were rarely, if ever, made up of a nuclear family with a male breadwinner and female homemaker. In fact, the presence of a wage tended to attract a wider group of kin, effectively shifting extended family structures from rural to urban areas.

With all of this in mind, youth's supposed inability to form of "independent households" should be viewed with some

108

suspicion. Independent of what? While an independent household may lessen everyday forms of control from above, it hardly eliminates them. Nor can we assume that such control is necessarily resented. Control may just as easily be instrumentalised via patron-client relations, and the ultimate goal for young people may not be independence at all, but rather their own control over dependents. Like anyone else, African youth realise that obligation is a two-way street: if they fail to distribute their own resources to kin, they may not be able to request assistance if the need arises.

The second misconception, tied to the first, has to do with social structure. Here, I would argue that the spirit of Durkheim reigns, and with it a mythography of society as a set of enduring institutions through which new individuals and generations must continually cycle, lest the whole thing fall apart (Fortes 1970). Although the classic structural-functionalist literature on Africa is a key site for this sort of idea, there are also well-attested Marxian and structuralist variants (Meillassoux, 1981; Lévi-Strauss, 1970, see discussion of the latter in Mudimbe, 1988). The reproduction of social institutions from this perspective is "mechanical", to borrow the Durkheim's terminology (Durkheim, 1933). Society constantly acts to perpetuate itself and the social action of real live agents is ever-geared towards that end.

This approach has been endlessly critiqued, but Bourdieu's assessment (1977) is especially apposite, because it begins with marriage. The language of structure, he argues, promotes a "synchronic illusion" that effectively eliminates real duration from our accounts. Marital matters that are in practice dependent on the movement of time are made to seem "timeless" and reversible. In addition, he continues, the emphasis on socially-recognised ritual shrouds the real work of marital and kinship relations – from matchmaking to the exchange of everyday gifts, to economic interdependence. Most kinship, he asserts, is "practical" kinship, not the descent

109

and affinity structures of anthropological fame. People make kinship as much as it makes them.

The third misconception follows from the others. In it, social identity is pegged to household relations (and marriage), and in turn on the requirement to follow certain "rules" and inhabit pre-existing social "roles". Thus, if one does not follow the rules and inhabit the roles, one's very identity is put at stake. This is as fallacious a rendering of identity as its opposite, whereby it is wholly constructed by the individual concerned in line with his/her own personal interests. But youth occupies an especially problematic place in this formulation. According to the "rules", it is one phase in the linear progression of an individual life – from childhood to youth to adulthood to senescence – all of which are grounded in a particular relationship to household and kin relations, and all of which are supposedly definitive for one's identity. The peculiarity of youth, though, is that it is almost always seen to lie in the spaces *between* households: youths' own households, through marriage, and that of their parents, from which they should be exiting, even if they have not. This makes their status as "people in the process of becoming rather than being", (Honwana and de Boeck, 2005: 3) conceptually over-determined: they are "between" categorisations and therefore liminal by definition. It also makes it inevitable that young people's inability to marry and form households will be seen as a crisis: if society is taken as the reproduction of enduring institutions, with normative households at its heart, it has to be a crisis.

In point of fact, a person's identification as "married", "adult", "employed", or "head of household" hardly exhausts that person's "identity". All are what Deborah Durham has called "social shifters" (2004), because like "youth", each category is open and context-dependent. As Francis Nyamnjoh (2002) notes, drawing on his own experiences in Cameroon, rule-based ascriptive *identities* are only one ingredient in an

110

ongoing process of *identification* that is relational, polyvalent, multiple, and constantly negotiated. Aligning all of one's multiple ties into a single identity is an accomplishment, not a given. Following Paulin Hountondji, we might summarise the problem as one of "unanimism" (1996): ascribing a necessary and singular identity to people on the basis of their race, continent of birth, nationality, age, gender, household position, etc., then calling it a "crisis" when they fail to live up to that ascription.

In pointing out these misconceptions, I am not suggesting that scholars are *necessarily* wrong when they claim that African youth are failing to get married and form their own households. Depending on the context, that very well may be true. Nor am I simply highlighting an important exception. Rather, I believe that such misconceptions constitute a blind spot in our theoretical apparatus. By focusing on whether young people succeed or fail in their efforts to achieve normative adulthood, we denude marriage and household formation of any ambiguity, and miss the complex ways in which social norms and roles are actually negotiated and inhabited. A "married youth" like Okocha becomes a contradiction in terms.

The Rules of "Shona" Marriage

Let me illustrate by returning to the question of elopements in Zimbabwe. I will first describe the normative model of "Shona" marriage. Then, in the following sections, I will show this model obscures much of the everyday lives of young people – including the nature of their identity as "youth". My data will focus mostly on young men, as it is they who are supposedly unable to marry.

Accounts of "Shona" marriage proceed, first of all, as if there is some stable group called the "Shona" (Ranger, 1989), and second, as if there were ways of marrying characteristic of

111

"Shona" tradition (often termed *chivanhu* or simply *ChiShona*).[9] These categories have deep institutional roots, and spring in part from colonial efforts to create order and manage "native" populations (Mamdani, 1996). As elsewhere on the continent (Chanock 1985), "customary law" was a key site for the ideological reproduction of ethnicity and "tradition", particularly as it had to do with marriage and household. The post-colonial Zimbabwean State has not greatly altered the colonial approach; if anything it has entrenched it in institutions like the vernacular language school curriculum, which is premised on supposedly transparent links between language, a clearly demarcated population, and shared practices, i.e. a "culture" (Kuper, 1999; Bauman and Briggs, 2000; Bakare-Yusuf, 2004). People therefore learn from a very young age that there are normative forms of marriage characteristic of the particular ethnic and racial group to which they belong. Indeed, in researching elopement, I was often given "spontaneous" answers that appeared to come straight out of a vernacular textbook.

So: "Shona" marriage, ideologically rendered.[10] The Shona are organised into exogamous patrilineal descent groups marked by shared clan names (a "totem" symbolised by an animal or part thereof). Marriage (*"kuroora"*) to anyone sharing the totem of either parent is considered incest (although ritual means can be used to overcome this rule). Clans/totems do not have a political function, and marital decisions are limited to local lineage groups – often no further back than three generations, and generally limited to relatively "close" cognates. Marriage is understood as a process of "putting together kin relations" [*kubatanidza ukama*] between families, not just a couple. Wife-givers are taken to be perpetually superior to wife-takers, and are supposed to defer to any and all male in-laws (including those who are younger). Particularly strict relations hold with mothers-in-law (and their classificatory mother equivalents). In rural settings, residence is most often patrilocal, and wives are seen as perpetual strangers to the local patriline.

The normative form of marriage-by-request [*kubvunzira*] begins with a boy and girl exchanging love tokens, which may later be taken as legal proof of intent.[11] A series of deliberations mediated by other family members ensues, the father or classificatory equivalent of the prospective bride is consulted, and eventually a date is set for the exchange of bridewealth. There are a number of initial "token" payments – paying to sit, to open one's mouth, etc. – that are relatively small in value and paid in cash. Larger payments follow, though the order and composition may vary. First is *rutsambo* (the name for a type of basket). In the past, it was often composed of a hoe or some other valuable object, but payment has been monetarised for several generations (amounts of several thousand US dollars are possible). It is considered payment for conjugal rights. Next is the payment of the mother's cow (*mombe youmai*), which may be given as cash or as a real cow, depending on the wishes of the bride's mother. It is surrounded by a good deal of mystical sanction and is treated with great seriousness by all. After that comes the "*danga*" (a kraal), which is paid to the father of the bride. It is always denominated in cattle, even if payment is given in money. Amounts differ, but are generally at least five cattle, and often many times that amount. *Danga* is considered to confer rights to the children of a marriage, and as such, is rarely paid in full before there is proof of the girl's fertility. Indeed, it is rare for a son-in-law to pay all of the different aspects of bridewealth in one sitting. "One never finishes getting married" [*kuroora hakuperi*], a ChiShona proverb has it; neither does the son-in-law ever finish giving. On the contrary, he is like a fig tree, ever bearing fruit [*mukuwasha muonde, haaperi kudyiwa*]. The last major payment is *kusungira* (to tie). This involves a goat and other small payments, which are given prior to the birth of the couple's first child. It too is surrounded by mystical sanction.

113

Other recognized forms of marriage alter this central exchange process by degree. In pledge-marriage, a female child (born or unborn) is pledged to a family (not necessarily a particular man) in exchange for material support of some kind, or otherwise in order to cement an existing relationship. Service marriage, on the other hand, entails payment in kind: instead of establishing his own home or other patrifocal residence, a man moves to his father-in-law's home and works for him for a period of years before being given a wife (Jeater, 1993). Both types eliminate the need for *danga*, and oftentimes *rutsambo* payments. Then, there are two forms of elopement. The first, called *kutizisa* (causative, "make run"), involves the ritualised abduction of the girl from her home, with her consent (and often with the knowledge of her mother or aunts). Shortly afterward – one to two days – a messenger is sent by the groom to inform the girl's family of her whereabouts with a small token payment (called variously *tsvagirai kuno* – "look for her here" – and *svevedzera* or *daidzira* – to call, notify). Although the marriage may in theory be rejected, it is normally taken as *fait accompli* and the girl's family will open up negotiations that follow the pattern outlined above. The second form of elopement, called *kutizira* ("run away to") is considered an "act of desperation" on the part of the girl. Normally, she is pregnant and "runs away to" the person she considers to be the "owner" of the pregnancy [*muridzi wenhumbu*]. Again, if he accepts responsibility, he then sends a messenger with *tsvagirai kuno*, and the exchanges follow the normal request model – with the exception that he is charged "damages" (youth often use the English term) for having "broken the law" [*kupara mhosva*] and made the girl pregnant.

Zimbabwean law caters for two types of registered unions: civil and customary, the former of which can be done in a church or a court. These have different legal implications, particularly with regard to inheritance and the practice of polygyny. Nonetheless, many, if not most, marriages go entirely unregistered (Ncube 1997) and civil or church marriage plays an accessory role. Most churches, even the most fervent Pentecostals, allow or even encourage the payment of bridewealth, although they may try to regulate the form that it takes. Those churches that do not allow it (some apostolic groups, for instance) seem to only enforce the ban when both families belong to the same church. Many church marriages take place years after the customary one, even after children have grown up and left home.

Everyday Elopements

So much for the ideology. The fact is, comparatively few contemporary "Shona" marriages follow the normative model of request. This is seen to be particularly true amongst young people and in urban areas, although there is no statistical evidence to prove such claims. As one woman put it to me, "you actually get shocked [*kurohwa nehana*] if you hear of someone marrying 'properly' these days." In my long-time dealings with young township men, no more than one in five has followed the "proper" procedures of request when marrying. Those that have were likely to be avid church-goers (creating the somewhat ironic situation whereby churches are the most consistent enforcers of "tradition"). Service marriages are essentially moribund and pledge marriages are explicitly illegal (though newspapers occasionally run exposes on their continued occurrence in rural areas). Elopements, on the other hand, are quite common. Young people do not consistently distinguish between *kutizira* and *kutizisa*, and I have never heard of anyone who followed the elaborate staged kidnapping procedures that supposedly characterize the latter. The preferred terms for any elopement are *kutizira* and *kutizirana* (i.e., the reciprocal, lit. "running away to each other").

115

Reasons for *kutizira* elopements cannot be reduced to a single causative factor. Sometimes they are ascribed to star-crossed "love", other times to fate or accident. The key trope, however, is still desperation, and often the desperation is quite real. An unplanned pregnancy appears to be the trigger for the majority of elopements (as it was, for instance, with Okocha). A girl who becomes pregnant is often turned away from her parents' or guardians' home.[12] In fact, she may be chased away by male relatives if they even suspect that she has been sexually active. Thus, it is the girl who agentively "runs away to" the boy (upsetting the normal linguistic coding whereby a man marries [*kuroora*] and a woman is married [*kuroorwa*]). What follows depends a great deal on the context. If the purported father – or some other man – refuses to both accept responsibility for the pregnancy and take her in as a wife, her social status will drop considerably in many eyes. As long as she is not especially young (below 17 or 18) or on track to doing something else (particularly with regard to her education), though, the pregnancy (and marriage) may actually boost her status, as childbearing is a key tool for asserting oneself as a "real woman" (cf. Johnson-Hanks, 2002). Aside from pregnancy, women also claim that they may elope in order to escape a bad home situation, whether it is a result of poverty, sexual and physical abuse, or simply lack of space (having to share a single room with their parents and all their siblings, a common township experience).

Men also emphasise desperation as their reason for eloping. This does not mean that they necessarily feel ashamed of making someone pregnant. Particularly amongst other men, such an act attracts relatively little opprobrium. Like a young woman, a man who has a child garners a powerful rhetorical resource in arguments about his manhood. Many young men even assert that they are unlikely to agree to a marriage unless there is proof of their partner's fertility. As one young man put it:

116

If a guy marries by properly requesting, you know, paying everything then having a church wedding, people here in the 'hood laugh at him. "How could you take and pay for a woman who hasn't made a kid for you yet? What if she can't conceive? Plus, you know she's going to get half of your stuff." That's the way people actually talk.[13]

That said, many young men treat the responsibilities of fatherhood with seriousness and a fair share accept that they have a responsibility to marry in such circumstances. This is true even of very short-term relationships: several have spoken of being "run away to" mere days or weeks after having met the woman. Their acceptance of a woman may have to do with fear of her relatives, or pressure from their own family, but ultimately they have little room for maneuver. Their "desperation", then, grows from attempts to accommodate an unplanned event. As one said:

I can say most times *kutizira* just happens without you planning for it. It gets you in a real mess [*zvinokupinza pa-busy*]. So it's not good.

They may be expected to make a number of payments, or may try to do so before a pregnancy is detected in order to avoid paying "damages". Certainly if the woman is pregnant, they will be expected to provide payment for *kusungira* (again, a goat plus other food items and small payments). Because of the emphasis on family mediation of marital relations, all of this may involve multiple visits to several different relatives. In addition, they may be pressured to establish their own "household", which in the township means at least a single room with sleeping and cooking facilities.

At the same time, men's "desperation" also owes more broadly to a material context in which they claim to be unable to acquire the bulk sums necessary for a "proper" marriage. As

117

we have seen, this is a common sentiment across Africa. The difference here is that their frustration often leads them to plot an elopement (though the degree of planning varies quite dramatically). As one young man put it:

> These days eloping [*kutizira*] has become the most popular way to marry. It's because, you know, the guys don't really do very well in school, and they're just sitting at home. Only one or two have jobs. So eloping is really the only form of marriage available to them. You hear about a church wedding once in a while, whereas elopement is common.

Another added:

> The thing is, life is difficult now, and…well, for a person to gather money to pay *roora* [bridewealth], it's hard for *us* to start with that, so then you just elope.

A surprising number of men also claim to have eloped in order to keep a girl they "love" from being "stolen" by another man (particularly an older or wealthier one). This goes along with a widely held opinion that older men (in the form of sugar daddies) are responsible for "ruining" the most desirable girls before young men have a chance to court them.[14] Whatever the reason, elopement is understood as forestalling immediate bulk payments of bridewealth. "It's like *Nyore-Nyore* [literally "easy-easy", a well-known Zimbabwean purchase-hire shop]" one young man commented, "you get what you want now and pay later". What they "want" depends on the person. For some – like Okocha – it's companionship and a "partner". Others are more crass: they want a regular sexual partner and someone to cook and clean for them.

118

Ritual Exchange and Daily Care

These realities – of desperation, both real and feigned; of material strategising and "accidents" – bear a rather ambiguous relation to "tradition" and "proper" marriage. On one hand, *kutizira* counts as a "traditional" form of marriage: books record it as being such. Yet many people, including youth themselves, insist that it is neither "normal" nor "good". While it is "traditional", they add, its practice has become excessive [*kunyanya*]. To repeat one young man's paradoxical phrasing, "it is the common way here in the township for a girl to elope, but it is not the normal way to marry".[15] It is not unusual to hear someone say in one breath that the prominence of elopement shows that "our traditions are dying" [*chivanhu chedu chava kupera*], but then in the next to say that, no, elopement is a part of tradition [*chirimo muchivanhu*].

This contradiction arises in large part from the manner in which "tradition" is framed in everyday experience. As in scholarly accounts of African youth, young people often view marriage and household formation through the lens of rules and rituals. In fact, the idea of "tradition" is inseparable from a highly developed ethic and aesthetic of rule-following.[16] This is not to say that people always follow the rules; they do not. But rules do play an especially important role in their discussions, social encounters, and acts. Moreover, like organic Durkheimians, people often plot rule-breaking on a historical scale, whereby the collective consciousness of the past has deteriorated into present anomie. In a sense, the framing of tradition as rule-following makes it impossible for present practice to ever be properly traditional.

In truth, contemporary elopements do not so much do away with rules as extend them in time, putting them on perpetual hold. Where "traditional elopements" supposedly took place over the course of a few days or weeks, contemporary ones take years. In each of the five bridewealth

119

rituals I have attended, the elopement had taken place several years earlier, and in two cases the children of the marriage were already in grade school. Most elopements start with the payment of the initial token *tsvagirai kuno* fee within a few days or weeks of the event. This payment – which may be as little as a dollar – is made by an intermediary, together with a letter that details the suitor's name and address. In return, the suitor is sent a list of demands for the other components of bridewealth. Far from sitting down to pay it at one ritualised event, though, most young men either send payment in dribs and drabs, starting with the initial token fees (and the crucial *kusungira* payment, if the woman is pregnant), and put off full payment to an unknown and distant date. Sometimes the delay is intentional, but quite often it is a result of events considered to be beyond a person's control. One young man narrated it like this:

> As time goes by, the guy gathers together some money and then goes to pay *roora* [bridewealth], but it could be five, six, seven years after they eloped. He won't have paid anything, yet they will have been living as husband and wife.

Using himself as an example, he continued:

> I've tried to pay bridewealth, but my wife's mother is dead and the father married someone else and…basically we couldn't get together the right people for the ceremony. So now, her relatives say, "this son-in-law, we don't know him". Me and my wife we are happy and we get along. We don't have any problems. We're just fine, because we just understand how to deal with situations in life…but our relationship is not formalised, so that's what makes things strange. It's fine sometimes, you know – some of her relatives say "let the kids come over, we want to see them" – but you never really feel *free*, because the marriage isn't formal.

120

As it turns out, Okocha's experience was much the same. His wife's family was riven by divorce and international migration and he had difficulty figuring out whom he should inform and who should receive his payments. By the time he figured it out, he had lost his accumulated savings to the ravages of Zimbabwean hyperinflation. As a result, two years after his son was born, he had only provided a few small token payments of bridewealth and had no idea as to when the process would go forward.

This delayed and "improper" timing of payment produces an ambivalent form of recognition: in most contexts, one is recognized as married and treated as such, but lack of formalisation means that this identity is not secure. In the absence of certain payments (up to and including *rutsambo*), elopements blend in with a number of other household forms. Several scholars of Zimbabwe, for instance, have discussed the development and practice of *"mapoto"* marriage (Muzvidziwa, 2001, Barnes, 1999; Rutherford, 2001) in Zimbabwe. This term literally refers to the illegitimate use of the woman's domestic and reproductive services, i.e. her "pots". It has long been practiced in towns, commercial farms, and mining compounds. Essentially, it is a temporary marriage, where both partners enjoy the various material and intimate perks of marriage without any guarantee that the relationship will last or be officialised. Typically, no bridewealth payments at all are made, and the partners remain unknown to most of each other's kin. Oftentimes, women enter *mapoto* relations after a failed marriage or having a child outside marriage. Much the same can be said of another more recent type of union, the "small house", which is associated with urban life and the monetary economy.[17] Men with money keep "small houses", paying the rent and expenses of a [typically younger] woman, with whom they rarely live, though they may have children together. All that makes elopement different is the rather uncertain *intention* to follow the rules sometime in the future. Token payments

121

may hold open the door of full recognition, but they do not actually provide it, hence the persistence of a grey area.

For some youth, like the young man quoted above, this grey area is experienced as a space of anomie and unfreedom. He would prefer, it seems, the certainty of a clear identity vis-à-vis his in laws, even though that means playing perpetual junior to them. In fact, one of the understood goals of marriage/bridewealth ritual is to ensure that everyone in both families "knows" the other properly, thus establishing clear roles and rules for acting. This local understanding is actually in line with anthropological theories of marriage ritual: by paying bridewealth, one effects an epistemological shift, effectively bringing the whole social realm into focus (be it in terms of rights, roles, or expected trajectories) (Comaroff, 1980, 1987).

It would be wrong, however, to see this as being a necessary conclusion. As I noted above, we cannot start with the *assumption* of unified identities then call anything that deviates from such a norm a "crisis". Ambiguous relations and identities are not always experienced as negative. Muzvidziwa's (2001) evidence from *mapoto* marriages suggests that such clarity may be exactly what women (and men) in such relationships are trying to avoid. Similarly, in neighbouring Botswana, it is customary for bridewealth exchange to be delayed until the children of a marriage are themselves about to marry (Comaroff 1987). In the interim, the nature of a relationship is open by degree to negotiation and instrumentalisation in a field of power. The construction of household and kin identity is thus performative and agentive, rather than purely ascriptive and normative.

In the case of elopement marriages, much of the performative work surrounds intimate rather than ceremonial exchange. Again, following the Durkheimian tradition, the anthropological literature on exchange and in Africa has long concentrated on definitive acts of kinship, especially those involved in ritual bridewealth payments (Fortes 1969). It is not

122

as if people who have eloped wake up every day uncertain of who they are or whether or not they are married, though. The uncertainty is restricted to particular contexts. For many young people, outstanding bridewealth payments are not the object of daily concern; for all intents and purposes, they consider themselves married and proceed with their lives as if that were the case. If anything, the status of a relation is judged on more mundane transactions, like food, money, clothes, household work, and sex, to name only the most prominent.

This kind of exchange is manifest in two key areas: the negotiation of the breadwinner role and the management of household finances. Notably, young people tend to think of both in terms of *gender* rather than *affinal* relations: that is, what a man as a husband and father is supposed to do, and what a woman as wife and mother is supposed to do. For instance, men expect (and are expected) to provide all basic necessities for the home (food, clothes, hygienic items, and rents/fees), and to purchase larger assets like furniture, appliances, etc. Women, in turn, are expected to give all they have to household expenses, and to provide sexual and domestic services without question.

These roles, like "proper" marriage, are considered by most young people to be "traditional". They are demonstrably "modern", though, and derive largely from the way that wage labour was imagined in the colonial and early independence era (Ferguson 1999).[18] The breadwinner/housewife hierarchy was never an accurate representation of reality (Barnes 1999). In fact, women's market and agricultural work has always provided much of the daily "bread" of Zimbabwean households. This, when combined with the total evaporation of secure waged labour for young men over the past twenty years (Jones, 2010; cf. Simone, 2006), provides the material base for many of the conflicts youth encounter in their households. On the one hand, provision is understood as an act of love (Cole and Thomas, 2009, cf. Zelizer, 2005). Consider another entry

123

in Okocha's diary (it directly precedes the one in which he details his violent political confrontation):

> Today I'm happy becoz I've made a profit of R50.[19] It's so pleasing becoz I can now buy better food for me and my wife. I can now afford to get her hair done at the hair salon. Something she had several asked 4 but I couldn't afford (sic).

On the other hand, failure to provide can lead to any number of problems. Young women often complain that their husbands either do not make enough money, or direct it away from the household, towards alcohol use, for instance, or to kin and friends, or even to support for other girlfriends. Young men, in turn, are often deeply anxious that their wives will provide sexual favours to other men in exchange for money and material goods. The result is a deepened distrust of women's movements and handling of money – distrust that is often explicitly misogynist. For instance, one told me:

> If [your wife] hears that so and so had real tea, you know, with proper bread and margarine and milk and sugar, she's going to want that too. And if some guy says "I can get you that", she can even go with him. Those are the ones we call "real men", those ones [who can afford to buy] sausage. So that's why you can't let your wife move around too much.

Another observed:

> If I have, say, five hundred dollars, I give her two to buy vegetables and cooking oil, then I keep two, then there's another hundred that I hide because if a woman of today sees it, it's a problem. She'll say, "oh, look at my hair, oh, I need new underwear, oh face cream, oh and the one for my legs"....Today's women look too much next door. They don't have focus or vision. They only see today.

124

It is important to note that his kind of attitude, and these problems of intimate exchange more generally, are not limited to young men, or to households formed via elopements. On the contrary, they are found in "formal" marriages as well, and are often manifest in discourses about the composition and behaviour of proper "Christian" households. In short, even where the "correct" path to marriage has been followed, a normative marriage provides little more than a shared and morally sanctioned framework for the everyday work of making kinship and of negotiating identity.

Conclusion

A common Shona proverb teaches that "kinship only fills half of the cup"; the rest "is filled with food" [*ukama igasva; hunozadziswa nekudya*]. As scholars of African youth, we would do well to heed this wisdom. After all, the ambit of "practical kinship" (Bourdieu, 1990: 168) is much larger and more complex than notions of normative kinship roles and proper household formation allow, and it is constructed as much by everyday reciprocity as it is by transcendent matters of ritual and blood. True, elopement marriages like Okocha's have many negative entailments. For example, in the unfortunate event that his wife died, Okocha would probably be forced to go through the rituals and payments of bridewealth before funeral services were held – something thought to have profound spiritual consequences. Likewise, women in elopement marriages enjoy very few of the institutional protections of marriage, be it traditional or civil, and are often on the losing side of battles over divorce and inheritance. None of this means that the partners to such marriages consider themselves unmarried, though. Official recognition and proper rituals do not exhaust their identities, as "youth" and "adults", "men" and "women", "husbands" and "wives", or "fathers",

125

"mothers", and "children", etc. Rather, those forms of identity are "filled" with the day-to-day realities of intimacy.

I started this chapter by pointing to the common argument that African youth are failing to "graduate" to adult status, and that this failure owes to their inability to marry and form independent households. I then showed that, besides being empirically incorrect in the Zimbabwean case, this argument perpetuates three related conceptual errors. Each of them, I argue, prevents us from grasping the "everyday" qualities of youth identity, intimacy, and exchange.

First of all, the "failure to marry" argument confuses a description of norms with a description of realities, thus reinforcing the false idea that "tradition" was (or ever could be) stable, and occluding a fuller understanding of how people actually handle such ideal forms. "Norms" and "rules" are just one instrument, and one constraining factor, in the ongoing performance and construction of young people's lives; they should never be seen as the whole story.

Secondly, in pointing to failed transitions, scholars often make it appear as though identity depended on inhabiting a "proper" household role. Besides being a gross simplification of what it means to have an identity (or identities), this threatens to make youth identity problematic by definition. After all, youth are precisely that category of persons said to be "between" households (their parents' and their own).

Finally, the axiom of prolonged youth mistakes artifacts of its own conceptual structure for evidence of a "crisis". In many ways, contemporary rhetoric about African "youth" is akin to earlier rhetoric about the "African in town" (Ferguson, 1999): both are emblematic of transition, loss of tradition, and anomie, and in both cases, scholars have struggled to separate the facts from widespread discourses about social problems. Whereas the concern with the urban Africans depended on the idea that "African" identity was rural in nature, though, concern with youth depends on locating identity in a narrow

126

set of legal and ritual statuses – many of which, I would add, are inflected by perceived divides between urban and rural, "local" and "cosmopolitan" (Ferguson, 1999).

There is no denying that contemporary African youth face very difficult circumstances, and that these circumstances are somehow "new". Nor is the concern with prolonged youth limited to scholars; it is a profound source of existential concern for many people. Young Zimbabweans might actually agree that they are failing to marry and form independent households, just as they often complain that they are "just sitting" rather than working. But the facts tell a different story. Like Okocha, they *are* "marrying", and they *are* "working" – just not in ways they and others consider "normal" in a larger historical sense.

As a way forward, let me suggest three tasks for scholarship on African youth. Firstly, it is vital that we take cognisance of new household forms, even (or especially) where they are disavowed by those involved. This demands greater attention to the "facts on the ground", but it also requires a conceptual shift. After all, the irony in the Zimbabwean case is that only a limited set of people refuse to recognize elopement marriages (or other unofficial unions): namely, the courts, elders and religious figures set on protecting moral norms, in-laws with a material interest in denying those relationships – and scholars who continue to insist that normative transitions are *the* key to youth identity. Secondly, as scholars, we need to use the notion of "crisis" much more judiciously and critically. Crisis is not simply a matter of material facts; it also entails the discourses developed to grasp and name those facts. Those discourses are not value-free and it is crucial that our conceptual framework accounts for their construction. Thirdly and finally, following AbdouMaliq Simone (2005), I suggest that we measure our concerns with social reproduction (whether failed or successful) with much greater attention to "provisional" forms of social relations. "Provisional" may mean "temporary" or

127

"makeshift" – as in the legal/ritual status of elopement marriages. But I would point to a second sense as well, in which relations hinge less on ceremony and propriety than on *provision* – that is, the flow of everyday goods and services. That kind of provision, I venture, "fills" not just the cup of kinship, but the bubbling pot of youth identity as well.

Notes

1. Research for this chapter was generously supported by CODESRIA. My larger project in Zimbabwe was funded by a Fulbright-Hays DDRA fellowship, and by a grant from the Nordic Africa Institute. I would like to thank the convenors of the Millennial Working Group on Youth Identity, my fellow participants, as well as the reviewers and staff at CODESRIA for their assistance. All have contributed in ways large and small to my work here.

2. The literature about Africa written in a Durkheimian vein is vast. For just some of the more famous accounts, see Evans Pritchard (1940); Fortes and Evans Pritchard (1940); Radcliffe-Brown (1968); Fortes (1968); and Fortes (1970).

3. A pseudonym, though he does use a nickname from a famous African footballer.

4. Unless otherwise noted, all dialogue is translated from the original ChiShona (or more properly, a township lingua franca of Shona, English and slang). The marriage practices I will describe are also largely "Shona" (Ranger 1989) and are hegemonic in and around Harare, although a significant minority of township residents are not of "Shona" extraction (Yoshikuni, 2007).

5. He claimed that for a street-level trader like him, an outright profit of R100 (US$8) a day would be a stunning windfall. Other street traders provided similar figures. The

128

profits were substantially higher for those further up the scale of the foreign currency trade.

6. The reference, of course, is to the sheer bulk of Zimbabwean cash, which at that point was counted in "bricks" of 100 notes each. For more on Zimbabwean hyperinflation, see Chiumbu and Musemwa (2012).

7. This might also be translated as "it just happens" i.e. without you having planned for it. "Love" is often conceived in similar terms. As a much quoted proverb has it, *moyo muti; unomera paunoda* – the heart, i.e. the center of love and emotion, is like a tree; it just grows wherever it wants.

8. Aristotle's views on "natural production" and the evils of using money to make money stem from the same domestic/public divide; only the "natural" sphere of the household (whence we take our word "economy") could produce legitimate value (Bloch and Parry 1989).

9. The translation here is a bit tricky. *ChiShona chedu* might be translated as "our Shona-ness", in the abstract. ChiShona is literally the term for the language, Shona, showing the degree to which a language and a people have come to be seen as the same (Kuper 1999). *Chivanhu chedu*, or simply *chivanhu*, literally refers to a form of shared humanity (*vanhu* being the plural "people"). In everyday conversation, it is understood as referring to the ways or customs of "Shona" people (which are sometimes prefaced *tsika nemagariro*, "ways and customs"), including negative ones like witchcraft. See the development of a similar categorisation amongst Tswana speakers in Comaroff and Comaroff (1992).

10. The following account is derived from a number of anthropological sources: Holleman (1952); Gelfand (1965); Kuper *et al* (1954); and Bourdillon (1987). Several vernacular language accounts seem to draw directly from these earlier works. Meekers (1993) offers a critique of certain aspects of the received model. In addition, there are several historical accounts that show the rise of particular forms of marriage and

domesticity: Jeater (1993); Barnes (1999); West (2002); and Kaler (2003). For more on domesticity, see also Hansen (1992).

11. In using "boy" and "girl", I follow standard accounts. The reality of cross-generational marriages is patent, though, and even amongst "youth" elopements, the male tends to be older than the female.

12. According to Holleman (1952), doing so would involve mystical threat to the girl's parents, but the shame involved seems to be the source of fear for many young people.

13. The second reference is to inheritance procedures. See Ncube and Stewart (1995). A legal marriage provides the woman with a right to inheritance, whereas so-called "non-registered customary unions" tend to grant inheritance to the patriline.

14. Being "ruined" is not simply a matter of lost virginity: it also entails the very real risk of cross-generation transmission of HIV. It is widely believed that older men infected with the virus pass it to teenage girls who in turn pass it to their future husbands, who are of their generation.

15. "Common" and "normal" are in English in the original, viz "It's the common way *muline kuti muskana atizire* yet it is not normal way, *yekuroora.*

16. Elsewhere (Jones, 2010), I explore this ethic/aesthetic, as manifest in discourses of "straightness", with reference to illicit economic action.

17. The English is normally used, although the vernacular *imba diki*, a direct translation, is also used. It should be noted that an institution with the same or similar name has existed in many other places, e.g. *la casa pequeña* in Latin America (Gutmann 1996).

18. Such labour is "traditional" only in the sense that it has been a part of the Zimbabwean landscape for a hundred years or so (Raftopoulos and Yoshikuni 1999). It is clearly not timeless, though people quite often read its structure back into precolonial history.

19. Fifty (South African) rand, worth approximately US$8 at the time.

References

Amadiume, I., 1997, *Reinventing Africa: Matriarchy, Religion*, Culture, London: Zed Books.

Bakare-Yusuf, B., 2004, "Yorubas Don't Do Gender": A Critical Review of Oyèrónké Oyewùmí's *The Invention of Women: Making Sense of Western Gender Discourses*", in S. Arnfred *et al*, eds., *African Gender Scholarship: Concepts, Methodologies and Paradigms*, Dakar: CODESRIA.

Barnes, T., 1999, *"We Women Worked So Hard": Gender, Urbanization and Social Reproduction in Colonial Harare, Zimbabwe, 1930-1956*, Oxford: James Currey.

Bauman, R., and Briggs, C.L., 2000, "Language Philosophy as Language Ideology: John Locke and Johann Gottfried Herder", in P. Kroskrity, ed., *Regimes of Langauge: Ideologies, Polities, and Identities*, Oxford: James Currey.

Biaya, T., 2005, "Youth and Street Culture in Urban Africa: Addis Ababa, Dakar, and Kinshasa", In A. Honwana and F. de Boeck, eds., *Makers and Breakers, Made and Broken: Children and Youth in Postcolonial Africa*, Dakar: CODESRIA.

Bloch, M. and Parry, J., 1989, "Introduction: Money and the Morality of Exchange", in M. Bloch and J. Parry eds., *Money and the Morality of Exchange*, Cambridge: Cambridge University Press.

Bourdieu, P., 1977, *Outline of a Theory of Practice*. New York: Cambridge University Press.

————1990. *The Logic of Practice*. Stanford: Stanford University Press.

131

Bourdillon, M.F.C., 1987, *The Shona Peoples: an Ethnography of the Contemporary Shona, with Special Reference to their Religion*, Gweru [Zimbabwe]: Mambo Books.

Chabal, P., and Daloz, J.P., 1999, *Africa Works: Disorder as a Political Instrument*, Oxford: James Currey.

Chanock, M., 1985, *Law, Custom and Social Order: The Colonial Experience in Malawi and Zambia*, Cambridge: Cambridge University Press.

Chiumbu, S, and Musemwa, M, eds. 2012. *Crisis? What Crisis? The Multiple Dimensions of the Zimbabwean Crisis*. Cape Town: HSRC Press.

Christiansen, C., Utas, M., and Vigh, H., eds, 2006, *Navigating Youth Generating Adulthood: Social Becoming in an African Context*, Uppsala: Nordic Africa Institute.

Cole, J. and Thomas, L., eds., 2009, *Love in Africa*, Chicago: University of Chicago Press.

Collier, J.F. and Yanagisako, S.J., eds., 1987, *Gender and Kinship: Essays toward a Unified Analysis*, Stanford: Stanford University Press.

Comaroff, J.L. and Comaroff, J., 1991, *Of Revelation and Revolution Vol. I*, Chicago: University of Chicago Press.

———— 2005, "Reflections on Youth, from the Past to the Postcolony", In A. Honwana and F. de Boeck, eds., *Makers and Breakers, Made and Broken: Children and Youth in Postcolonial Africa*, Dakar: CODESRIA.

Comaroff, J.L., 1980, "Bridewealth and the Control of Ambiguity in a Tswana Chiefdom" In J.L. Comaroff, ed., *The Meaning of Marriage Payments*; New York: Academic Press.

————1987, "*Sui Generis*: Feminism, Kinship Theory and Structural "Domains", In J.F. Collier and S.J. Yanagisako, eds., *Gender and Kinship: Essays toward a Unified Analysis*, Stanford: Stanford University Press.

Cruise O'Brien, D., 1996, "A Lost Generation? Youth Identity and State Decay in West Africa", In R. Werbner and T.

Ranger, eds., *Postcolonial Identities in Africa*, London: Zed, pp. 55-74.

Diouf, M., 2003, "Engaging Postcolonial Cultures: African Youth and Public Space", *African Studies Review*, 46(2), pp. 1-12.

Durham, D., 2000, "Youth and the Social Imagination in Africa: Introduction", *Anthropological Quarterly* 73 (3): pp. 113-20.

————2004, "Disappearing Youth: Youth as a Social Shifter in Botswana", *American Ethnologist* 31 (4), pp. 589-605.

Durkheim, E., 1912, *The Elementary Forms of the Religious Life*. New York: Free Press.

————1933, *Division of Labor in Society*. New York: Macmillan.

Engels, F., 1990, *The Origin of the Family, Private Property and the State*, New York: International Publishers.

Evans-Pritchard, E.E., 1940, *The Nuer: a Description of the Modes of Livelihood and Political Institutions of a Nilotic People*, Oxford: Clarendon.

Ferguson, J., 1999, *Expectations of Modernity: Myths and Meanings of Urban Life on the Zambian Copperbelt*, Berkeley: University of California Press.

Fortes, M., 1969, *Kinship and the Social Order: the Legacy of Lewis Henry Morgan*, Chicago: Aldine.

————1970, *Time and Social Structure: And Other Essays*, London: Athlone Press of the University of London.

Fortes, M. and Evans-Pritchard E.E., 1940, *African Political Systems*, London: Oxford University Press.

Gelfand, M., 1965, *African Background: The Traditional Culture of the Shona-Speaking People*, Cape Town: Juta.

Gutmann, M., 1996, *The Meanings of Macho: Being a Man in Mexico City*, Berkeley: University of California Press.

Hansen, K. T., 1992, *African Encounters with Domesticity*, New Brunswick: Rutgers University Press.

————2005, "Getting Stuck in the Compound", *Africa Today*, 51 (4): 3-16.

Holleman, J.F., 1952, *Shona Customary Law, with Reference to Kinship, Marriage, Family and the Estate*, New York: Oxford University Press.

Honwana, A. and de Boeck, F., 2005, "Children and Youth in Africa: Agency, Identity and Place", in A. Honwana and F. de Boeck, eds., *Makers and Breakers: Children and Youth in Postcolonial Africa*, Dakar: CODESRIA.

Hountondji, P., 1996, *African Philosophy: Myth and Reality*, Bloomington: University of Indiana Press.

Jeater, D., 1993, *Marriage, Perversion, and Power: The Construction of Moral Discourse in Southern Rhodesia, 1894-1930*, New York: Clarendon Press.

Jones, J. L., 2010, "'Nothing is Straight in Zimbabwe': The Rise of the *Kukiya-kiya* Economy 2000-2008", *Journal of Southern African Studies*, 36 (2): pp. 285-99.

Johnson-Hanks, J., 2002, "On the Limits of Life-Stages in Ethnography: Towards a Theory of Vital Conjunctures", *American Anthropologist*, 104 (3), pp. 865-880.

Kaler, A., 2003, *Running After Pills: Politics, Gender, and Contraception in Colonial Zimbabwe*, London: Heinemann.

Kaplan, R.D., 1994, "The Coming Anarchy", *The Atlantic*, February, Available at http://www.theatlantic.com/doc/print/199402/anarchy.

Kuper, A., 1973, *Anthropologists and Anthropology: the British School 1922-1972*, London: Lane.

———1999, *Culture: The Anthropologists' Account*, Cambridge, MA: Harvard University Press.

Kuper, H., Hughes, A.B.J. and van Velsen, J., 1954, *The Shona and Ndebele of Southern Rhodesia*. London: International African Institute.

Lévi-Strauss, C., 1970, *The Elementary Structures of Kinship*, London: Tavistock.

Mamdani, Mahmood. 1996. *Citizen and Subject: Contemporary Africa and the Legacy of Late Colonialism*. London: James Currey.

Manuel, S. 2008. *Love and Desire: Concepts, Narratives, and Practices of Sex Amongst Youths in Maputo City*. Dakar: CODESRIA.

Masquelier, A., 2005, "The Scorpion's Sting: Youth, Marriage and the Struggle for Social Maturity in Niger", *Journal of the Royal Anthropological Institute*, 11 (1), pp. 59

Meekers, D., 1993, "The Noble Custom of Roora: The Marriage Practices of the Shona of Zimbabwe", *Ethnology*, 32 (1), pp. 35-54.

Meillassoux, C., 1981, *Maidens, Meal, and Money: Capitalism and the Domestic Community, Themes in the Social Sciences*, New York: Cambridge University Press.

Mbembe, A., 2001, *On the Postcolony*, Berkeley: University of California Press.

Mudimbe, V.Y., 1988, *The Invention of Africa*, Bloomington: Indiana University Press.

Muzvidziwa, V. 2001, "Marriage as a Survival Strategy: The Case of Masvingo Zimbabwe", *Zambezia* 28 (2), pp. 147-165.

Ncube, W., 1997, *Continuity & Change: The Family in Zimbabwe*, Harare: Women and Law in Southern Africa Research Project.

Ncube, W. and Stewart, J., 1995, *Widowhood, Inheritance Laws, Customs & Practices in Southern Africa*. Harare: Women and Law in Southern Africa Research Project.

Nyamnjoh, F., 2002, "A Child is One Person's Only in the Womb": Domestication, Agency and Subjectivity in the Cameroonian Grassfields", in R. Werbner, ed, Postcolonial Subjectivities in Africa, London: Zed Books, pp. 111-138.

Oyewùmí, O., 1997, *The Invention of Women: Making African Sense of Western Gender Discourse*, Minneapolis: University of Minnesota Press.

Radcliffe Brown, A.R., 1968, *Structure and Function in Primitive Society*, London: Cohen and West.

135

Raftopoulos, B., and Yoshikuni, T., eds., 1999, *Sites of Struggle: Essays in Zimbabwe's Urban History*, Harare: Weaver Press.

Ranger, T., 1989, "Missionaries, Migrants and the Manyika: The Invention of Ethnicity in Zimbabwe", In L. Vail, ed., *The Creation of Tribalism in Southern Africa*, Berkeley: University of California Press.

Rubin, G., 1975, "The Traffic in Women: Notes on the 'Political Economy' of Sex", In R. Reiter, ed, *Toward an Anthropology of Women*, New York: Monthly Review Press, pp. 157-210.

Rutherford, B., 2001, *Working on the Margins: Black Workers, White Farmers in Postcolonial Zimbabwe*. Harare: Weaver Press.

Simone, A., 2004, *For the City Yet to Come: Changing African Life in Four Cities*, Durham: Duke University Press.

———2005. "Urban Circulation and the Everyday Politics of African Urban Youth: The Case of Douala, Cameroon", *International Journal of Urban and Regional Research*, 29 (3): 516-532.

———2006, "Pirate Towns: Reworking Social and Symbolic Infrastructures in Johannesburg and Douala", *Urban Studies*, 43 (2), pp. 357-370.

Vigh, H., 2006, "Social Death and Violent Life Chances", In C. Christiansen, M. Utas, and H. Vigh, eds, *Navigating Youth Generating Adulthood: Social Becoming in an African Context*, Uppsala: Nordic Africa Institute, pp. 31-60.

West, M.O., 2002, *The Rise of an African Middle Class: Colonial Zimbabwe 1898-1965*. Bloomington: Indiana University Press.

Yoshikuni, T., 2007, *African Urban Experiences in Colonial Zimbabwe: A Social History of Harare before 1925*. Harare: Weaver Press.

Zelizer, V., 2005, *The Purchase of Intimacy*, Princeton, N.J: Princeton University Press.

4

Children's Lives and Children's Voices: An Exploration of Popular Music's Representation of Children in East Africa

Mwenda Ntarangwi

Introduction

Much research on childhood in Africa centres primarily on children as victims and passive participants in larger socio-political problems. Even a general search for literature on childhood in Africa reveals a great number of entries that are limited to health issues, vulnerability to war, malnutrition, or other rights-related issues. It is quite telling that African children are predominantly perceived in the same way the continent and its people are, as pitiful, backward and chaotic. It is an image of children as threatened by disease, hunger, civil war and lack of education. If Africa is a "dark" continent, then African children have a "dark" childhood. Without playing down the reality of Africa's and African children's very difficult social, economic, and political challenges, I want to use a slightly different approach to the reality of African childhood and its representation. I want to see how a different kind of representation, based on expressive culture, may allow us to see the complexity of childhood realities in Africa and explore new facets of child and youth studies. I am particularly interested in how childhood in Africa is caught up in the transitions to modernity; a modernity that is itself regarded as the panacea for Africa's transition from "darkness" to "light". The expectation is that when African countries modernise, then children's lives will be improved. I therefore want to ponder how modernity could itself be a hindrance to positive experiences for children and youth in Africa.

The challenge that we face in this investigation of childhood representation in Africa is to move from the ideology of children as objects to be represented by others to one where children participate in their own representation. Nonetheless, we have to be careful not to fall prey to the tyranny of participation, in which we may assume that having children and youth present in the works we engage constitutes their participation. Participation entails power relations and choices. This is particularly important. Many African cultures emphasise the view of children as inarticulate and incompetent in socio-cultural matters and thus their representation as helpless within much of the available literature is not very far from African views of children. Many African children are often "seen", not "heard", being spoken for than regarded as beings with views and opinions to contribute to and about their social worlds. They are, as anthropologist Allison James, says "silenced spectators" (2007:261) watching their world but not talking about it in any publicly accepted manner.

Indeed, as Siziba (2009) shows, much of Africa's history is predicated on the lives of adults because of the promotion of history as the accumulation of lived experiences that precludes experiences of youth. And yet competing with this common perception and regard for children as "inadequate" members of society are the realities of child soldiers, child headed households, and children engaged in productive economic activities, both in rural and urban locations in Africa. How do we reconcile these two competing scenarios? How do we represent children as helpless and still understand their critical role in demystifying their construction as victims because of their participation in economic and political activities as shown by past studies (see, for instance, Honwana and de Boeck, 2005)? More generally, how does the field of childhood studies look in general and in Africa in particular? What place does

138

popular music as an expressive genre occupy in this terrain of representations of childhood in Africa?

To respond to these questions, while pursuing this new facet of children and youth representations in popular music, I use a symbolic and interpretive approach to analyse songs as symbols and as processes of performance through which musicians and their listeners assign meanings to their experiences and address fundamental questions about children's social lives. I, therefore, see song texts, their performance, and the meanings they carry as important symbols that point to various social and cultural realities of not only children and youth within their realm of production, but also their own communities. To analyse these symbols is thus to access an important cultural repertoire that informs children's lives, perceptions of youth and childhood, and their lived experiences. For the purposes of this work, I will use the term childhood (as a social state) or children (as agents) in reference to individuals below eighteen years of age. This I do in full recognition of the reality of a possible conflation of the term children with youth whose age is often both sociological and chronological. For instance, Article 1 of the United Nations Convention on the Rights of the Child defines "children" as persons up to the age of 18 and yet the same UN defines youth as those between 15 and 24 years (http://social.un.org/index/Youth/FAQs.aspx). In Kenya a child is defined by the Constitution (2010) as any person below the age of 18, the same age used to define children in Tanzania and Uganda. These definitions have political and economic ramifications but the goal here is to identify the age parameters guiding this chapter, wherein I focus on music that is performed by children and music that is performed to represent the realities and experiences of individuals falling within this age category of children. Before I do so, I should like to provide an overview of representations of childhood and children. The song texts chosen have specific messages

139

that relate to children or have been sung by children and represent a set of similar songs that other researchers can delve into to understand how children are represented and represent themselves in and through music, especially hip hop.

Studies and Representations of Childhood: An Overview

Until recently, studies of childhood have mostly been confined to developmental issues, especially in psychology or within family studies in sociology. Within anthropology, childhood studies emerged in the 1930s in the US under the Culture and Personality School spearheaded by Margaret Mead (1928, 1935) and Ruth Benedict (1934). In the UK, anthropological work on childhood came in the 1970s through Charlotte Hardman's work in Oxford (1973, 1974). In Africa, childhood studies have predominantly been carried out by Western anthropologists, spearheaded by the work of Robert LeVine and others on childcare (Levine *et al*, 1994) and more recently by Alma Gottlieb's work on children and religion in Ivory Coast (2004). More focused studies of childhood identities by anthropologists have represented the voices of children, revealing things that are important to them, even those that adults may consider unimportant or childish (James, 2007:264).

Outside anthropology, childhood studies in Africa have been spearheaded by different research institutes, including the Council for the Development of Social Science Research in Africa (CODESRIA) and the Organization for Social Science Research in Eastern and southern Africa (OSSREA) in which scholars from various disciplines have come together to conduct studies that have challenged Western notions of childhood, based as they are on chronological age rather than social roles. In his work on children working in Zimbabwe, for instance, Victor Muzvidziwa challenges the categories of child labour that are shrouded in issues of rights and illegality and

140

asserts that children should be regarded as workers who are positive contributors to the household income and survival, irrespective of their chronological age (2000). He shows that unlike Western categorisations of children based on chronological age, many children in Zimbabwe work as a means of survival for themselves and their siblings, especially in households that have single or no parents. Pamela Reynolds's work in Zimbabwe also shows the role played by children in the liberation war as well as in religious matters (1995). Focusing on children and youth in contexts of conflict, Ibrahim Abdullah shows how anti-establishment youth culture emerged in Sierra Leone by appropriating a revolutionary language of university students to contest political power (1997, 1998, 2006). Despite this growing interest in childhood studies within and outside anthropology, there is a dearth of scholarship on how children's lives, aspirations, and realities are represented in popular music in Africa.

The realities surrounding children's inability to freely and easily enter the public realm of self-representation complicates attempts to create any representations of childhood. This is primarily due to the complexity and politics of representation, whether of children or any other groups and individuals. Cultural critic Ella Shohat has rightly stated that any representation "must be analysed, not only in terms of who represents, but also in terms of who is being represented, for what purpose, at which historical moment, for which location, using which strategies, and in what tone of address" (1995:173). Such post-modernist critiques of grand narratives in ethnographies as well as the suspicions surrounding textual representation of lived realities calls for self-reflexive approaches to any socio-cultural representation(s).

Acknowledging these challenges of representing others, and even self, I also agree with James and Prout that children are articulate social actors who have much to say about the world (James and Prout, 1990) and can, and do, articulate

141

themselves in various ways at different times. What follows from this realisation is the need to pay more attention to avenues through which children find a voice to articulate these realities and experiences. I argue that one such avenue is music, especially popular music, which has recently become widespread in East Africa with the advent of hip-hop. This music has, through various socio-economic changes, become increasingly identified with youth and children.

Conditions created by the instability of the nation-state following various global economic and political changes have been a blessing in disguise for many youth in East Africa. Such changes have led to the emergence of a hip-hop culture based on local and global sensibilities that in turn create certain political and economic opportunities for the youth. The youth have been able to insert themselves into the local and global spheres that shape national and regional political and cultural structures and destinies, by using music as a platform for self-expression and social critique. As a result, numerous opportunities availed to many youth in East Africa through hip-hop have enabled a number of them to redefine their social identities while expanding their economic opportunities.

When Hip-hop music emerged in urban locations in East Africa in the mid-1990s, it was in response to material conditions of joblessness, decline in living conditions and massive urbanisation with its attendant problems. Many youth across social and ethnic divides were facing these declining living conditions, many of them having been born in the cities to parents who emigrated from rural areas as agriculture failed to provide a stable source of livelihood. Attracted to cities by the lure of modern life, these new immigrants saw their living standards continue to decline.

In the late 80s and early 90s, hip-hop became one medium through which to make sense of and respond to these conditions of extreme poverty and political quagmire. It provided a much-needed voice and public presence to many

142

youth facing unemployment and political powerlessness. From its direct links to rap music in urban Black America to its localised versions, hip-hop music traversed the public sphere hitherto occupied by politicians, scholars and other opinion shapers, generating not only enormous popularity among young people, but also stepping into an expanding vacuum of social, political and economic commentary (Ntarangwi, 2009). Hip-hop took on another role, becoming part of the emerging global take-over of the local resources that contribute to the formation of youth identity and their creative expressions. This take-over was predicated on an overwhelming presence of Western (predominantly American) popular cultural material and expression mediated by, among others, television, the Internet, digital music, telephony and video games that aggressively compete with and subdue local cultural expressions. It was also predicated upon an already existing Western cultural dominance perpetuated by historical structures.

The emergence of Hip-hop in East Africa was influenced by the presence of Western popular culture that intensified in the 1980s through the 1990s, as well as by certain political structures propelled by colonial and neo-colonial forces and socio-economic changes that followed Structural Adjustment Programs. These political and socio-economic realities precipitated the culture of expression realised today in hip-hop. Embedded in this structural reality, however, is a culture and value system that has continued to elevate Western modernities over those that are African. Through a colonial system of education, in both public and private secondary schools (where many East African youth are socialised), for instance, Western cultural ideals often became idolised, forming a foundation for some cultural expressions mediated through music, dress, language, and other cultural sensibilities into the post-colonial period (Ntarangwi, 2003b).

This popularity of hip-hop among youth and children and their direct participation in it has led me to explore children's voice and childhood representations in popular music. In this way "giving voice to children is not simply or only about letting children speak; it is about exploring the unique contribution to our understanding of our theorizing about the social world that children's perspectives can provide" (James, 2007:262) and the media that they choose or have access to in such representation. I am primarily interested in how narratives contained in popular music in East Africa represent childhood in East Africa in ways that give voice to otherwise "voiceless" children and, by extension, how such representation confronts and reflects changes in the socio-cultural and political terrain.

Popular music, especially hip-hop, has become a medium through which youth and childhood is represented in two ways: firstly, through lyrics, artists are able to articulate critical issues on behalf of children and youth. Secondly, it is a platform that children and youth can and have used to express their creative abilities in ways that were not available to them only a few decades ago. To date, many hip-hop groups in East Africa are composed of children and youth, some of whom are below twelve years. In Tanzania, for instance, the group Xplastaz (based in Arusha) is made up of siblings who include Diana Rutta (Dineh) and Steven Rutta (Steve) who joined the group in 1997 when they were just eleven and nine years old respectively. In Kenya, the group Ukooflani Mau Mau (based in Nairobi), which is a conglomeration of many music groups, nurtured and mentored a group of thirty children and youth from Mathare and Dandora, some of whom formed two hip-hop groups – Eastlandos and Wafalme. At the time of the research carried out for this study (2011) these artists were between 12 and 17 years of age. Clearly, children are finding avenues of representation through popular music.

A number of reasons explain this phenomenon. First is the sheer expansion and popularity of hip-hop music, due to the transformed nature of music-making. Nowadays, minimal capital investment is required to record a song or songs. With the current technology that allows people to use generic sounds as background music and the ease with which a song can be recorded on CD, many young people are able to make music much more cheaply and quickly than before. Secondly, hip-hop music, and especially rap, does not require much singing expertise, as long as a person can develop rhyme and rhythm. This may explain the flooding of the East African urban scene with new hip-hop music and musicians every month. Sadly, these artists often disappear as quickly as they appear. All in all, popular music has opened up spaces for children and youth to not only represent their own realities, but also to be much more engaged in representations of them by others.

Popular Music and Social Realities in East Africa

For decades, social scientists, especially anthropologists and ethnomusicologists, have acknowledged the existence of a strong link between music and culture. Generally, music has also been used as a source of ethnographic data, leading to a better understanding of a society (cf. Askew, 2002; Cooper, 1982; Firth, 1987; Ntarangwi, 2003a; Perullo, 2005) and as an expression of discontentment with existing social and political structures (Berliner, 1993; Eyerman and Jamison, 1998; Hebdige, 1975; Pratt, 1990). More specifically, research on popular music in East Africa has also shown that music is an ideal tool through which to assess a variety of cultural realities in a given community or society. It has been regarded as a way of reasserting an erstwhile African identity (Samper, 2004), as a means of negotiating modernity (Nyairo and Ogude, 2003) and as a reflection of everyday socio-cultural youth realities (Lemelle, 2006; Ntarangwi, 2007). Some scholars have specifically looked at how gendered identity is mobilised through popular music (Nannyonga-Tamusuza, 2002;

145

Ntarangwi, 2003; Mwangi, 2004), while others have explored, in general terms, how national politics and imaginations of statehood are constructed or mobilised through popular music (Askew, 2002; Wekesa, 2004).

Specifically focusing on hip-hop, scholars have shown how music is very much linked to the politics of identity among youth in East Africa. Ssewakiryanga's (1999) work analyses the emerging youth culture in Uganda where American popular music is an important framework from which local hip-hop culture developed. He argues that while this music may have important contributions to the local hip-hop scene, it becomes localised through a process of reinterpretation and redeployment.

Perullo's (2005) work in Tanzania looks at how rap music confronts stereotypes about young people by using politically and socially relevant lyrics to reach a broader listening audience, while Samper's (2004) work on rap in Kenya shows that, rather than being mere copycats of American hip-hop music, youth use traditions of revolution associated with the anti-colonial movements such as the Mau Mau to respond to post-colonial realities of cultural colonisation. It is clear that popular music in the form of hip-hop has become an important avenue for children and youth in East Africa to represent themselves and their realities or dreams. Furthermore, many organisations working in the area of socio-cultural change have become aware of the role played by music and sought to push various social messages to the youth through music.

South Africa's popular music star, Zola (Bongi Dlamini), for instance, was appointed Goodwill Ambassador for Eastern and Southern Africa by UNICEF. His ability to connect with and capture the attention of youth and children through his music precipitated this appointment. On his first tour in Kenya in early March of 2007, he visited a primary school in Kiambu (Central Kenya) that had been ravaged by violence against children. During the school visit Zola was reduced to tears when children from the school recounted their encounters and experiences of violence. It is quite telling that the children used the medium of music to articulate their pain and despair, saying, as Chinyama and Mwabe (2007) report, that "No one cares for us, we are raped, sodomised and destroyed by people who should be protecting us; We don't know what the future holds for us, only God knows."

The fact that these atrocities are perpetrated by people who "should be protecting" the children, convinces them that "no one cares". In 2005, a nine-year-old girl was raped and killed on her way from the school and, in 2006, eight girls and four boys were sexually abused on their way from school (Chinyama and Mwabe, 2007). That little was done to punish the perpetrators traumatised the students and instilled fear in the community. It is possible that children hardly receive the necessary responses from relevant parties because, as children, they do not readily have the instruments of power that would enable them to demand attention from the public. There is some work being done to respond to this gap in the social structure and research, especially after the passing of the 2006 Sex Offence Act, with organisations such as the African Population and Health Research Centre in Nairobi documenting various sexual offences against children and youth. That realm, however, remains limited and avenues such as music, through which children express their views, experiences, and opinions become all the more important. It is also not coincidental that Zola himself grew up in the harsh slum environment of Soweto and turned to music as a way of articulating his views on social issues. The centrality of music as an important tool for representing childhood experiences is unquestionable from this perspective.

Representing Modernity and Tradition in Childhood Experiences

Besides becoming a platform for children and youth agency in East Africa, music has also slowly emerged as a medium through which to symbolically debate the representation of African cultures within a dialogic structure, brought about by the interaction between modernity and tradition. Many Africans today struggle with the dialogic structure within which their cultural practices and attitudes develop. On the one hand, African culture has been denigrated to a relic of the past and often considered a hindrance to modernity as expressed through Maendeleo (development). On the other, there is a growing move to reclaim a proud heritage of an ideal African cultural past that seeks to establish a certain cultural rootedness in the face of global cultural and politico-economic hegemony. The latter is especially articulated by Thabo Mbeki's notion of African Rennaissance.[1]

Political and cultural globalisation that was mobilised by imperial and colonial expansion prior to, and later in, the nineteenth and twentieth centuries, paved way for contemporary globalisation, now centred on economics and technology. In much of East Africa, this has become an ongoing process of cultural expression that takes on different forms and acquires different identities, especially as a consequence of the neo-liberal economic project. The process has in turn opened local markets to foreign (mostly Western) cultural products such as films, music, dress and other opportunities for cultural exchange (or dominance) through satellite television, FM radio, e-mail, the Internet, cell phones, and other forms of cultural expression.

The mixed opportunities availed by globalisation have led to multiple experiences and responses. To some, it has led to insecurity and reclusion as certain individuals and communities reinvent their cultural identities in response to the assumed

148

homogeneity brought by globalisation. Others have taken on the opportunities availed by globalisation to positively enhance themselves socially and economically, seeing it as an avenue to a proliferation of cultural options that does lead to heterogeneity. It is almost as if these two approaches bring out another cultural struggle that many societies face – the tension between tradition and modernity.

Tanzania's popular music artiste commonly known as Professor Jay (Joseph Haule) grapples with this tension between tradition and modernity in a song titled *Taifa la Kesho* (Tomorrow's Nation) in which he becomes the voice of children, castigating the neglect, apathy, and moral decadence facing children (in Tanzania, but extendable to other African communities as well). He starts the song by stating:

> I am pained when I see children vending water
> Every day you say that education is their investment
> Education is a right for every child
> The government has declared free primary education
> Imagine children paying to ride commuter buses
> Their parents have abandoned and sacrificed them.

There are, embedded in this short excerpt, certain expectations of behaviour towards and treatment of children such as children not paying to ride public transportation and vending water. It is now a truism that formal education has become the most important form of socialisation for East Africans in preparing them to successfully integrate into the modern State. This is why basic education has been recognised as a basic right for all children in East Africa. To this end, the East African governments have instituted free primary education programs, but, as Professor Jay shows, the program has not benefited all. Professor Jay's commentary here on education and children paying to ride public transportation reveals the challenges facing the provision of education in a poor nation like Tanzania, but also the struggles that exist between traditional and modern constructions of children. When the then president, Benjamin Mkapa, reintroduced compulsory free primary education, the existing infrastructure could not cope with increased enrolment (Otieno, 2002). Therefore, despite the country's declared free education programme not all children attend school, and some engage in income-generating activities such as vending water. With high numbers of pupils enrolled in primary school and few opportunities to proceed though secondary school where only about 9 per cent of all primary school children go on to secondary school (Nkosi 2005), a large number of children will end up in poor social conditions because of the role of education in social mobility. Furthermore, even as education prepares many for a life of belonging to the modern nation-state and less to their traditional cultural group, there are many challenges of clearing demarcating boundaries between the two.

As a result, expectations of who children are and what their status in society is are regulated by received traditional norms and prevailing sociocultural realities. Such constructions of children are often challenged by the ambiguity created by, on the one hand a desire to see children through traditional cultural lenses (as not yet ready for any autonomy or to be served and to be represented in all facets of life by adults) and on the other the reality of living in a fast-changing socio-cultural terrain. Indeed, any romantic cultural representation of African traditions of childhood that expects children to be invisible, speak only when spoken to, or be at the beck and call of adults, clashes conceptually with the reality of the actual lives community members live in a modern nation-state often driven by Westernised modes of modernity, especially in urban areas. The lack of control of the lives of children (as with children living and working on urban streets) makes any expectation of adult control over the lives of children difficult

150

and complex. It may also lead to a new way of seeing children, as shown here by Professor Jay in the same song when he articulates this reality:

> Who should have a seat in public transportation, the young or old?
> I think it's the child so (s)he can bring forth others
> You bring up old traditions such as those stating the old should eat steak
> While children eat the heads and hooves so that you may rejoice.

It is common in a number of African communities and beyond for children to give up seats in public transportation to those older than them as a form of respect. In such a context respect is earned and often comes with age because a person's real social worth is measured by their contribution to the common good and it is assumed children have not lived long enough to accumulate enough of the respect accorded to adults. Yet, what Professor Jay presents in this song is a cultural dilemma. Public transportation signifies the modern amenities of mobility, moving from one's locality to another, and especially to urban areas. But in the midst of engaging with this modernity, people also want to maintain certain traditional ideologies and practices that favour adults over children whom the song refers to as "leaders of tomorrow".

How can modernity be upheld while holding on to traditional ideas and practices that do not allow for such forward movement? This seems to be the question Professor Jay is indirectly asking here and, by extension, challenging the audience to reconsider such behaviour and eventually change it. This becomes even clearer when he brings in children to sing the chorus that says, "sisters, mothers, brothers, have mercy on me, brothers, fathers, mothers, have mercy on me". The call for cultural change is not demanded by children, but

151

rather framed in the language of compassion, in "have mercy", which in itself acknowledges the kind of power adults still wield over children, even outside filial relations. Quite clearly Professor Jay recognises that children's identity is tied to their relationships with others in the society. By couching their appeal in the context of mercy, the children are targeting the emotive and "soft" side of the society. It pre-empts the existence of ill treatment on the children. The underlying meaning here is that children are suffering and that if the community truly cares about them, then it will show mercy on them. This appeal is important when seen in relation to how adults have responded to an invitation to help children. Asserting adults' unwillingness to assist children, Professor Jay presents his appeal in a way that compels adults to see the importance of helping children. He turns to every adult and asks them to recognise the interconnectedness between childhood and adulthood as well as the continuity of the nation-state. He says:

> Those who are adults now were once children
> But when I ask them to help children they turn away
> Yet they daily sing that children are the leaders of tomorrow
> We are losing many of these children and others are continually suffering
> Oh God almighty please help these angels.

The irony of stated ideals and practical realities regarding children is quite evident here. As it shows, many may say that children are tomorrow's leaders but then refuse to assist them when requested. In their song about youth, a hip hop group from Kenya known as Eastlandos, comprising Shiko (Mary Wanjiku, 16), Nash (Nahashon Ng'ang'a, 17), Sam (Samantha Nyokabi, 16) and Mary (Mary Nzomo, 15), challenge this notion of children as tomorrow's leaders when they state:[2]

152

Who said that we are tomorrow's leaders? We are today's leaders!

The young generation has emerged from the ghetto and is bringing you education.

In this song, Eastlandos show that youth in Kenya may not be interested in waiting for years to take up leadership because of their age. Indeed, as of 2011, the four artists continued to perform music while maintaining their goals of acquiring an education. Wherever they made money from their music performance, they first paid their school fees, and as a result convinced their parents of the value of music. Their parents then allowed them to continue performing music while in school.[3]

As East African communities wrestle with a type of modernity that challenges their cultural practices, a number of new ideologies emerge. Composed in the first years of the twenty first century when there were many socio-political and economic changes in East Africa to match the emerging modernity, Professor Jay's *Taifa la Kesho* reveals once again the prevailing and challenging social issues of the day. One of those issues affecting children directly is that of spanking. Spanking children as a form of punishment is not only common in much of East Africa, it is also expected and accepted. Yet, as these communities change, they are confronted with new ideas regarding spanking. This is an issue that Professor Jay addresses quite forcefully, saying:

It's not necessary to spank a child when (s)he is wrong
This is where I see parents have gone astray
Does spanking teach or hurt children?
That is a fundamental question you need to ask
Because too much spanking makes children stubborn
I do not mean you should pamper the child.

153

No, first (s)he should go to school, after which (s)he can play.

It has taken many communities in East Africa a while before they could consider spanking of children as a practice that needs to be re-evaluated and even abandoned altogether. Even though formal schooling came to East Africa as part of Western modernity, spanking became accepted as a form of punishment that endured for a long time. In Kenya, it took government intervention through Legal Notice 56/2001 to ban the use of corporal punishment as a method of disciplining students in school. Yet, a 2002 survey conducted by Population Communication Africa (PCA) showed that of 1,140 students surveyed, 52.6 per cent reported being caned (Lloyd 2002).

In Uganda, Bishop Elisha Kyamugambi of the Ankole Diocese asked the government to revisit the law barring corporal punishment for children, arguing that it instils discipline (Basiime, 2002). So far, corporal punishment is still lawful in Tanzania and leaves open the process through which it can be opposed or even abandoned. It is not that Professor Jay is opposed to corporal punishment in its entirety, but to that used "unnecessarily" on school children and actually suggests harsh punishment for such crimes as rape. In a quick turn-around from condemning corporal punishment in school, Professor Jay calls for the harshest penalty for sex offenders, especially those who defile children. He argues that:

> It would be good for the public to assist the courts
> Rather than get off the boat when it's sinking
> I am shocked that an old man with grey hair can rape a child
> I advise the courts to double the punishment on such men
> Hang them or give them a life sentence, it is justified
> I am amazed humans are greedier than hyenas
> How can they rape a two-year-old child?
> These criminals don't deserve to live they should be hanged.

154

Kenya's nominated Member of Parliament Njoki Ndung'u (2003-2007) proposed a motion that would quite literally reflect Professor Jay's call for harsh punishment on rapists. In the motion, Ndung'u proposed that convicted rapists be castrated. The motion was passed unanimously but with amendments that rejected the call for castration. The motion, which became the Sexual Offences Act 2006 states in part that "A person who commits an offence of defilement with a child aged eleven years or less shall upon conviction be sentenced to imprisonment for life" (Government of Kenya, 2006). This law and Professor Jay's song lyrics reflect the extent to which violence on children in many East African communities has received greater public presence and/or incidents escalated as children make transitions to new politico-economic and social realities. Sociologists have examined the link between crime trends and social change and shown that crime rates increase as society goes through socio-economic challenges (see, for instance, Arthur, 1992). These social changes affect children as well. Professor Jay shows that when children are neglected, they turn to criminal activities. He says in the same song that:

Why do you give our children such a hard time?
Now see how this five-year-old child is already sniffing glue
He has become distressed and turned into a pickpocket
We do not even value education any more; is this the kind of nation you want?
I am not sure if you recognise the consequences of this reality
At night these children will pick up guns and come after you.

Without proper socialisation children will turn to other forms of socialisation including those mediated through criminal activities. Sniffing glue, pickpocketing, and criminal activities are very much tied to urban youth, many of whom

155

live on the streets. Research on street children in East Africa reveals that when family income decreases, members are forced to put pressure on children to work in order to support the family (Kapoka, 2000; Kilbride, Suda and Njeru, 2000; Lorraine and Barrett, 2001). These are the realities that Professor Jay highlights in this song. Yet, to consider some of these "anti-establishment" activities as only tied to social and economic challenges is to ignore the agency of youth and children as individuals who through various forms of marginalisation and exclusion from the State, community, and even filial privileges, strategically and forcefully insert themselves into these public spaces.

Many children and youth caught up in conflict and war, for instance, have often been forcibly enlisted, but there are others who find participation in conflict as avenues through which to become useful members of an otherwise exclusive social group. In the case of children in northern Uganda, however, the neglect and exclusion shown by the government of Yoweri Museveni begets a more complex analysis of the attendant historicity and ethnic dimension.

Giving Voice to the Voiceless: The Case of Children in Northern Uganda

They have been known as "night commuters" following various documentaries in Western media, but the children of Southern Uganda are more than commuters. They have been both victims and villains of the civil war that has primarily pitted the Lord's Resistance Army (LRA) against the Uganda government. The historicity of this experience is quite intriguing and sheds light on the complexity of the current conflict. During Obote's reign in the 1980s, the majority of the national army soldiers were Acholi who, together with the Langi (Obote's ethnic group), formed a formidable force against insurgency coming from the south, led by Yoweri

156

Museveni and the National Resistance Army (NRA). The Acholi/Langi coalition did not last long. After Tito Okello and Basilio Okello, two Acholi senior officers in the army, were bypassed in the appointment of Uganda's Commander-in-Chief, there was in-fighting in the army that pitted the Acholi against the Langi. The Acholi defeated the Langi and established Tito Okello as president. Tito Okello's reign was, however, short-lived. The NRA defeated Okello's army and Museveni was sworn in as president in January 1986 (Allen 1991). This succession of events led to regional groupings which saw former Acholi soldiers and others aspiring for political leadership, regroup in opposition to the Museveni government. The ethnic animosity that ensued between the Acholi and their counterparts in the South, primarily the politically powerful Baganda, has had an important role in the protracted conflict.

In 1987, the self-elected spiritual leader of the Acholi in Uganda, Alice Auma (later known as Alice Lakwena when she took on the name of the spirit that possessed her) saw her campaign to liberate the Acholi of northern Uganda militarily crumble in the hands of the NRA. Alice had in 1986 initiated a movement for the Acholi to reverse the NRA political might but failed. Joseph Kony's LRA came in almost as a continuation of the struggle initiated by Alice (Behrend, 1999) but instead of liberation, the LRA tormented and traumatised the Acholi for years. Joseph Kony's army has survived through brute force, abducting children and forcing boys to become soldiers while girls are sexually abused and turned into servants or wives of the soldiers. This went on for over two decades until there was international pressure to highlight and stop the plight of the people of northern Uganda, many of them children.

In 2001, the US Patriot Act declared the LRA a terrorist organisation; in 2004, the US Congress passed the northern Uganda Crisis Response Act; and in 2005, the International

157

Criminal Court issued arrest warrants for Joseph Kony and four of his top commanders (www.invisiblechildren.com). All this attention helped raise awareness among many Westerners of the plight of northern Uganda, but the most effective program came through three young Americans – Jason Russell, Bobby Bailey, and Laren Poole – who went to Uganda in search of some "cool" pictures and came back with a story. Their trip was visually recorded and later turned into *The Invisible Children: Rough Cut*, a movie that changed many American youth's response to children in northern Uganda. The movie was packaged in a medium that appeals to youth, with fast music, moving captions on screen, and focusing on schooling. Through this movie, a movement emerged that led to partnerships between schools in the US and Uganda, where funds were raised to aid in the everyday needs of Ugandan children. While such responses by youth in aid of other youth bring in a new way of cross-cultural interactions, connecting outsiders with locals, therein lies the danger of misrepresentation of such interactions. This became apparent in 2012 when Invisible Children produced a video titled Kony 2012 that went viral in a short time but quickly received a major backlash that led to other videos and even professional paper presentations at conferences.[4]

Locally in Uganda, a group of musicians also came together to respond to the silence that shrouded the atrocities facing northern Uganda. This silence especially increased when many families in northern Uganda were moved to internally displaced people's camps where they live in squalor. In a song entitled "No More Virgins in Gulu" the artists – Halima Namakula, Butcherman, and Ngoni Group – contextualise their representation within the prevailing politics in Uganda. The group used President Museveni's visit to Gulu in 2005 to specifically foreground their story. The song narrates the difficult circumstances in which people in northern Uganda live. It is quite instructive that the song is titled "no more virgins". Reference to virgins symbolically denotes purity and innocence that many associate with children and childhood. Yet, all this has literally been taken away from the children of northern Uganda as their fellow Ugandans and government watch. In the chorus, the song indicts the neglect that the Museveni government has shown to the people of northern Uganda who now live in Gulu. They sing:

> Dear Museveni we are happy, to receive you here in Gulu
> The education is poor, communication is poor
> There is (sic) no more virgin in Gulu, they were all raped by Kony
> The situation is poor, but all the same we are happy

The use of the phrase "but all the same we are happy" is to show that children and people of Gulu have been so neglected that hardships make them "happy" rather than bitter. How can people facing such hardships be happy? These artists are showing the sarcasm that comes from a condition where people realise that the government may not really care about their welfare. Why else would they be neglected for two decades unless they were living in conditions that make them happy?

Uganda's geographic regions reflect ethnic boundaries with the Acholi primarily occupying northern Uganda. Their neglect is not only regional but also ethnic. The perception in Uganda is that the southerners are the ones who have ruled Uganda for the longest, with the Buganda Kingdom in pre-colonial times and Museveni, who is from the south, having been president since 1986. This ethnic neglect may explain why the song goes on to say that the musicians are wondering why Ugandans are so saddened by international catastrophes, like the bombing of the Word Trade Center in New York in 2001, yet not bothered by the death and suffering of their fellow Ugandans in the

159

north. The artistes ask, "is the blood of Americans so special different from ours? Is their blood blue and ours red?".

The musicians then give an example of how all the churches in Uganda prayed for the US after the September 11, 2001 attacks but they didn't pray for Gulu. When the children of Gulu sing that they are happy despite the breakdown of infrastructure, they are responding to this cold treatment they receive from their fellow Ugandans and the government. The people in Gulu have lost all hope as the artists explain when they say: "Even when they say that they are happy to see President Museveni; they sing it with their lips, but their hearts are bleeding".

The song then urges Ugandans to pray for the people of Gulu, for the hard and sad life that they have endured for so long. They say that every day is a day of running, running in search of safety, unlike people living in the other regions of Uganda, where there is peace. The song reminds the audience of the atrocities that have been endured by the people of Gulu. Even if there has been a truce and not much fighting in Northern Uganda recently, the people, especially the children, have to live with the emotional and physical scars of war. Many of them had their noses, ears, breasts and limbs cut off for refusing to join or support the LRA. They carry those physical scars that also extend to emotional and psychological levels. Even with reduced atrocities visited on the people of Gulu, their living conditions in the camps have been terrible. This is why the song continues to narrate the challenges of living in the camps. The artists say:

> War is a very nasty experience
> People suffer and sleep in Internally Displaced Peoples
> Camps
> Parents share a single room with their six children
> When the parents are having sex in the night
> The children see or hear everything that is going on.

War has dehumanised and left them naked, robbed them of
privacy and culture
Congestion in the camps spreads diseases faster
Leading to high infant mortality, and bad general welfare

The humiliating living conditions at the camps show that
there is need for new and deliberate ways of helping people in
northern Uganda. The song highlights the shame and loss of
culture, this time not due to modernising, but due to internal
warfare. It is clear that, to understand the role played by
popular music in highlighting the plight of children and youth,
one has to pay attention both to the content of various songs
as well as the socio-cultural realities of the day. In so doing,
one can make connections between the lives of children and
youth and the challenges they face on the one hand, and the
representations of such realities on the other.

Conclusion

I have argued here that while representing children and
youth in Africa is quite a challenge for lack of ample
scholarship, popular music has emerged as an important
platform for such representation. Popular music, as a cultural
product, reveals a lot about the social structure of the society
from which it emanates. Indeed, popular songs, and culture in
general, are not only about society; they do not just reflect, but
are part of the socio-cultural fabric. They articulate and mould
life experience while becoming forms of expressing social
reality and aspirations of children and youth in a rapidly
changing context. In revealing what I would like to call the
deep structure of socio-cultural reality of East African life,
music is able to delve into the core of issues that are not
otherwise addressed by those in positions of power and that
cannot be otherwise expressed. In this way, music is a central
medium through which social experience is channelled.

In privileging music as a source of ethnographic data and a platform for representing children and youth in East Africa, I am showing that cultural activities and events are often mediated through popular culture and are worthy of independent analysis and interpretation. It is therefore my argument that songs can be viewed as "cultural texts" that hinge on the discursive, representation and contestation of the cultural whole of any community or society. Seeing music as a creative expression of a society's institutions, values, and experiences, I have shown how social issues are played out in music whose structure directly reflects social reality and ideology. Though few scholars have concentrated on the analysis of song texts as cultural texts (and in particular popular music), I have argued here that song texts are important sources of ethnographic data and can be good pointers to East Africa's changing social structure, especially as it affects children and youth.

Notes

1. See, http://www.anc.org.za/ancdocs/history/mbeki/1998/tm0813.htm accessed May 12, 2009.

2. The ages of the members of Eastlandos given here are for 2011. In February 2013 Samantha and Shiko were still part of Eastlando but Shiko was still pursuing her studies and Samantha was focused on hip hop. For more on this story please see http://www.standardmedia.co.ke/?articleID=2000076324&pageNo=2

3. I am indebted to Felix Gicharu for this information on Eastlandos.

4. The Kony 2012 controversy started with questions of representation and who has power to say what about another

162

person or group of people and then moved to Invisible Children's finances and sponsors. For more discussion see http://concernedafricascholars.org/wp-content/uploads/2012/04/Kony-React-Respond.pdf

References

Abdullah, I., 1997, "Introduction", Africa Development, Vol. XXII, Nos. 3/4.

Abdullah, I., 1998, "The Revolutionary United Front: A Revolt of the Lumpen Proletariat", in C. Clapham (ed.) African Guerrillas. Oxford: James Currey.

Abdullah, I., 2006, "Africans Do Not Live by Bread Alone: Against Greed, Not Grievance", African Review of Books, March 2006.

Allen, T., 1991, "Understand Alice: Uganda's Holy Spirit Movement in Context", Africa, Vol. 61, No. 3, pp. 370-399.

Arthur, J., 1992, "Social Change and Crime Rates in Puerto Rico", International Journal of Offender Therapy and Comparative Criminology, Vol. 36, No. 2, pp. 103-119.

Askew, K., 2002, Performing the Nation: Swahili Music and Cultural Politics in Tanzania, Chicago: University of Chicago Press.

Basiime, F., 2002, "Ankole Bishop wants Whip for Errant Kids", The Monitor, November 15, 2002. p. 5.

Behrend, H., 1999, Alice Lakwena and the Holy Spirits: War in Northern Uganda 1986-1987, Oxford: James Currey.

Benedict, R., 1934, Patterns of Culture, Boston: Houghton Mifflin.

Berliner, P., 1993, The Soul of Mbira: Music and Traditions of the Shona People of Zimbabwe, Chicago: University of Chicago Press.

Chinyama, V. and Mwabe, J., 2007, "Sexual Violence Afflicts the Lives of Children at a School in Central Kenya", (www.unicef.org/infobycountry/kenya_39054.html) accessed 23rd September 2007.

Clifford, J. and Marcus, G., eds, 1986, Writing Culture: The Poetics and Politics of Ethnography, Berkeley: University of California Press.

Cooper, B.L., 1982, Images of American Society in Popular Music, Chicago: Nelson-Hall.

Eyerman, R. and Jamison, A., 1998, Music and Social Movements: Mobilizing Traditions in the Twentieth Century, Cambridge University Press.

Firth, S., 1987, "Why Do Songs Have Words?" in A. White, ed., Lost in Music: Culture, Style and the Music Event, London and New York: Routledge and Paul. pp. 77-106.

Gottlieb, A., 2004, The Afterlife is where we Come From: Culture and Infancy in West Africa, Chicago: University of Chicago Press.

Government of Kenya, 2006, "The Sexual Offences Act, 2006", Kenya Gazette Supplement No. 52, Act No. 3, Nairobi: Government Printers.

Hardman, C., 1973, "Can There Be an Anthropology of Children?" Journal of the Anthropology Society of Oxford, Vol. 4, No. 1, pp. 85–99.

Hardman, C., 1974, "Fact and Fantasy in the Playground", New Society, Vol. 26, pp. 801–803.

Hebdige, D., 1975, Resistance through Rituals, New York: Holmes Meier Publishers Inc.

Honwana, A. and De Boeck, F., 2005, Makers and Breakers: Children and Youth I Postcolonial Africa, Dakar: CODESRIA.

James, A., 2007, "Giving Voice to Children's Voices: Practices and Problems, Pitfalls and Potentials", American Anthropologist, Vol. 109, No. 2, pp. 261–272.

164

James, A. and Prout, A., 1990, Constructing and Reconstructing Childhood, Lewes: Falmer Press.

Kapoka, P., 2000, "The Problem of Street Children in Africa: an Ignored Tragedy," Paper Presented at the International Conference on Street Children and Street Children's Health in East Africa, Dar es Salaam, Tanzania, April 19-21, 2000.

Kilbride, P., Suda, C., and Njeru, E., 2000, Street Children in Kenya: Voices of Children in Search of a Childhood, Bergin and Garvey.

Lemelle, S., 2006, "Ni Wapi Tunakwenda": Hip-hop Culture and the Children of Arusha", in D. Basu and S. Lemelle, eds., The Vinyl Ain't Final: Hip-hop and Globalization of Black Popular Culture, London: Pluto Press. pp. 209-234.

LeVine, R., Dixon, S., LeVine, S., Richman, A., Leiderman, H., Keefer, C., and Brazelton, B., 1994, Child Care and Culture: Lessons from Africa, Cambridge: Cambridge University Press.

Lloyd, N., 2002, "Caning Still Rampant in Schools", The East African Standard, May 8, 2002. p. 4.

Mead, M., 1928, Coming of Age in Samoa, New York: Morrow.

Mead, M., 1935, Sex and Temperament in Three Primitive Societies, New York: Morrow.

Merriam, A., 1964, The Anthropology of Music, Evanston: Northwestern University Press.

Muzvidziwa, V., 2000, "Child Labour or Child Work? Wither Policy", in M. Bourdillon, ed., Earning a Life: Children Working in Zimbabwe, Harare: Weaver Press. pp. 179-184.

Mwangi, E., 2004, "Masculinity and Nationalism in East African Hip-hop Music", Tydskrif vir Letterkunde, Vol. 4, No. 2, pp. 5-20.

Nannyonga-Tamusuza, S., 2002, "Gender, Ethnicity, and Politics in Kadongo-Kamu Music of Uganda: Analysing the Song Kayanda", in M. Palmberg and A. Kirkegaard, eds.,

165

Playing with Identities in Contemporary Music in Africa, Uppsala: Nordiska Afrikainstitutet. p. 143-148.

Nkosi, M., 2005, "Tanzania Looks Beyond Free Schooling", (http://news.bbc.co.uk/1/hi/wrld/africa/4687083.stm) 3rd October 2007.

Ntarangwi, M., 2003a, Gender Identity and Performance: Understanding Swahili Social Realities through Song, Trenton, NJ: Africa World Press.

Ntarangwi, M., 2003b, "The Challenges of Education and Development in Post-Colonial Kenya", Africa Development, Vol. XXVIII, Nos. 3&4, pp. 209-225.

Ntarangwi, M., 2007, "Hip-hop, Westernization, and Gender in East Africa", in K. Njogu and H. Mapeau, eds, Songs and Politics in Eastern Africa, Dar es Salaam: Mkuki na Nyota Press. pp. 37-62.

Ntarangwi, M., 2009, East African Hip-hop: Youth Culture and Globalization, Urbana, Il: University of Illinois Press.

Nyairo, J. and Ogude, J., 2003, "Popular Music and the Negotiation of Contemporary Kenyan Identity: The Example of Nairobi City Ensemble", Social Identities, Vol. 9, No. 3, pp. 383-400.

Otieno, C., 2002, "Chaos as Tanzania Provides Free Schooling", (http://news.bbc.co.uk/1/hi/world/africa/1775421.stm) 4th September 2007.

Perullo, A., 2005, "Hooligans and Heroes: Youth Identity and Hip-hop in Dar es Salaam, Tanzania", Africa Today, Vol. 51, pp. 75-101.

Pratt, R., 1990, Rhythm and Resistance: Explorations in the Political Use of Popular Music, Greenwood Press.

Reynolds, P., 1995. Traditional Healers and Childhood in Zimbabwe. Athens: Ohio University Press.

Samper, D., 2004, "Africa is Still Our Mama": Kenyan Rappers, Youth Identity, and the Revitalization of

Traditional Values", African Identities, Vol. 2, No. 1, pp. 37-51.

Siziba, G. 2009, "Redefining the Production and Reproduction of Culture in Zimbabwe's Urban Space: The Case of Urban Grooves", paper prepared for CODESRIA available at http://www.codesria.org/IMG/pdf/Gugulethu_Siziba_Zi mbabwe.pdf

Shohat, E., 1995, "The Struggle Over Representation: Casting, Coalitions, and the Politics of Identification", in R. Campa, E., Kaplan, and M. Sprinker, eds, Late Imperial Culture, London: Verso. pp. 166-178.

Spiro, M., 1996, "Postmodernist Anthropology, Subjectivity, and Science: A Modernist Critique", Comparative Studies in Society and History, Vol. 38, No. 4, pp. 759-780.

Ssewakiryanga, R., 1999, " New Kids on the Block": African-American Music and Uganda Youth", CODESRIA Bulletin, Vol. 1&2, pp. 24-28.

Wekesa, P., 2004, "The Politics of Marginal Forms: Popular Music, Cultural Identity and Political Opposition in Kenya", Africa Development, Vol. XXIX, No. 4, pp. 92-112.

Young, L., and Barrett, H., 2001, "Adapting Visual Methods: Action Research with Kampala Street Children", Area, Vol. 33, No. 2, pp. 141-152.

5

Teenage Girls, Cell Phones and Perceptions of Autonomy: Examples from Molyko Neighbourhood, South West Region, Cameroon

Flavius Mayoa Mokake

Introduction

Two things have inspired this Chapter. The first is an event witnessed in January 2003 between two freshmen of the University of Buea, returning from their December break. On this characteristically bright and sunny afternoon in Molyko, I was walking back home after lectures along the main university street, a wide and elongated space between two magnificent gates; the main gate into and from town and the second gate that leads directly into or out of the university campus. Within about 400metres of the gate, there were no trees whose branches or shadows could shield pedestrians from the scorching sun, especially in the heart of the dry season. The road is well-paved and covered with a double lane tarmac with a number of streetlights at successive intervals, adding to its beauty at night. Since 2006, the street hosts a monumental plaque to commemorate the martyrs that lost their lives during the May-June 2006 student strike (Abangma, 2009).

It was exactly at a point close to the main gate which leads one out into Molyko Town that I encountered two young girls who seemed excited at meeting each other for the first time since they had gone on their December break. Girl A had a facial expression that showed she had missed her friend as she excitedly ran across the street to meet her. This caught my attention. The other girl, as if already expecting her friend, instantly called out, "hey my friend". Interestingly, the two friends did not greet each other with the warmth that is often expected of close friends who had not seen each in a while. Rather, the first girl quickly brandished her new Samsung cell phone and paused in anticipation of her friend showing off her own cell phone. To her dismay her friend did not have a phone yet, at which the first girl commented, "my friend, don't tell me that you are still to have a phone!" It should be noted that these students had spent barely eleven weeks in the university and this period before the Christmas vacation is commonly considered as the period when most students, especially girls, undergo a social metamorphosis that is very often visible when they return in January.

It is during this period that most youth experience social life with little or no parental control, have their first intimate sexual relationships, lose their virginity and begin to enjoy the pleasures of a semi-independent life (since most students live in Residential Halls). A number of inferences could be drawn from this brief narrative: the popularity and appropriation of cell phones by youth, the social status attached to those that possess this gadget, the sacrifices youth can make to acquire a phone and the social exclusion of those that are "unconnected". The question we may be tempted to ask at this point is: how did this young, unemployed and dependent university girl acquire her brand new Samsung phone? My speculation now, as then, is that it was a present from a man-friend or from a relative living abroad.

The second thing is the popularity of cell phones among the youth in the Molyko neighbourhood, their appropriation and use, especially by young girls, and how their inception has drastically changed social relations. Cell phones have become so popular that young women will do anything to win one. In December 2010, for instance, a national newspaper Cameroon Today carried a news report of a high school girl named Erica who was publicly disgraced after stealing a phone at a Christian rally in Molyko, switching it off and hiding it under her bra. When questioned about the act Erica, blamed the devil.1 In fact, there has emerged a cell phone culture in Cameroon that is very visible and in vogue in the Molyko neighbourhood, where owning a phone and conspicuously displaying are is part of one's social identity. Curiously, little scholarly attention has been paid to this growing phenomenon of cell phones and their effect on the social attitudes of the youth in Cameroon. Nonetheless, W. G. Nkwi has examined the history of telephone in Buea in Cameroon from the colonial period through to the postcolonial period and the changing communication landscape that the introduction of cellular phone has triggered (Nkwi, 2008; 2009: 50-57).

The sociology of the cell phone in the neighbourhood is very complex. Cell phone use has generated an economy of its own, with, for the most part, previously unemployed youth benefiting from the brisk business it has generated (Nkwi, 2009: 60-66). The dynamics of this teleconomy notwithstanding, little has been said on how young women in Molyko use their handsets as tools to assert themselves within social spaces. In this chapter I attempt to fill this scholarly gap by examining the impact cell phones have had and are having on the social attitudes of teenage girls in the Molyko neighbourhood. In order to achieve this, I have found it worthwhile to adopt the following specific format:

1. Examine briefly the introduction of cell phones in the Molyko neighbourhood.
2. Assess how the inception of the cell phone has generated a sub-culture among young women in this varsity town.
3. Discuss how the persuasiveness of advertising images influences young girls' choices of phones and how the brand of phone owned determines social networks.

171

4. Discuss the various ways through which young women have appropriated the cell phone and how they are using the phone as a tool of social manipulation and control. In this regard I look at whether this could be understood as a form of agency.

Contextualizing the Study Area

Molyko is a rapidly urbanising town in the South West Region of Cameroon. It has perhaps the fastest pace of urbanisation in the country. It is a small cosmopolitan neighbourhood situated in the erstwhile colonial town of Buea. It is a rapidly urbanising neighbourhood with a heterogeneous population (Mokake, 2011). This heterogeneous population is dominated by the youth, most of whom are students in the University of Buea, secondary and high schools or professional institutions in the locality. It should be mentioned that Buea boasts the only Anglophone University in Cameroon (a country in which both English and French are official languages but French dominates) and attracts thousands of youth who either migrate into the town to obtain university education or benefit from the opportunities that the creation of the university offers (Lum and Ntangsi, 2004). The opportunities that the recent developments in the town provide have lured youth from different social and cultural backgrounds, region and level of socialisation. Most of the hotels (El Palacio, Paramount, B47 Hotels, etc.) and Guest Houses in Buea are located in this area and seem to be doing brisk business.

The gender composition of this rapidly urbanising town is also very interesting. The youthful population is dominated by girls who are in their teens or twenties. Some of the girls are students while others are school drop-outs engaged in the informal economy, *inter alia* in hair-dressing salons, tailoring workshops, as "call-box" operators, etc. Others are

172

salespersons in cell phone shops that dot the town and in the catering industry. However, some earn a living as commercial sex-workers.

Life in Molyko is as hard as it is in most towns or student communities in Cameroon and the youth tend to respond differently to social challenges posed by the society (Jua, 2003). While some have found alternative income-generating employment in the informal sector, others have resorted to "cheap" but illicit forms of earning money, *inter alia* cyber scamming and petty theft. This has challenged the social equilibrium that may have existed in the neighbourhood and as a result immensely affected social relations between and across socio-demographic categories. The introduction of the cell phone has further exacerbated these social changes.

Molyko also hosts Super Dealers (an agent who acts as liaison between the public and the phone company by providing services to the public) for two of the largest cell phone companies, MTN and Orange. MTN is the most popular network. Both networks also have regional offices in Molyko. In fact, these two regional offices are adjacent to each other. Cellular phone promotions by these two network providers often begin here before spreading into neighbouring areas. An added phenomenon linked to the phone is the increasing number of phone repairers, with over fifty repairers located in Molyko alone. The proximity of these repair shops to one another has led to the development of a highly competitive business culture. Repair shops also serve as outlets for phone accessories with a variety of items on sale, including batteries, chargers, cases/covers, USB cables, etc. In addition, they also provide other services like downloading popular ring tones into phones. This change in the socio-economic landscape of the telephone (Horst and Miller, 2006) in Buea and Molyko in particular is a recent development associated with the changing sociology of the cell phone (Geser, 2004). As Nkwi (2009) argues, it is the uncertain economy of the town

173

that is the leading logic behind the boom in cell phones in Molyko. But as economic opportunities in traditional sectors such as agriculture dwindle, new forms of work emerge and with them come new ways of socialising and doing business. It is within this social space of Molyko, presented here in a summary fashion, that I examine the impact that the cell phone has had on the social behaviour of young women.

Methodology

Data for this study were acquired through two primary procedures. The principal tool was observation, but random sampling was also conducted. The trend of cell phone use and appropriation by youth was observed within the last decade, from the time it was first introduced. It facilitated our understanding of the evolution of the communication landscape in Molyko. It was observed that this communication landscape has drastically changed within the last decade.

To obtain the perception of how cell phone affects the social behaviour of young women, opinions of randomly selected youth were gathered. Respondents ranged between the ages of 17 and 27 years and responded to such questions as why women prefer the cutest phones, the number of phones individuals possesses, how cell phones facilitate the establishment of social contacts and how the type of phone owned determines social status and relations. Fifteen male and twenty-five female informants responded to the questionnaires, with respondents representing different social and educational backgrounds. Personal information about the respondents was obtained in both private and public spaces. From the responses received, I was able to determine that young women use their phones as a tool to control their social relations and to simultaneously escape social control from parents or guardians.

The discussion in this chapter also follows from data collected through a deep reading of advertising images from the two principal cell phone network providers in Molyko. Images from various advertisements were important sources of valuable information for reading certain correlations between images of young women who used cell phones and those of the characters used in advertising cell phones. It was not lost to any observer that it was mostly women with flashy phones that were used on most of the cell phone advertisements displayed on billboards in Molyko neighbourhood. From my analysis of some of the advertisements and images they displayed, it was clear that all the images were youth-oriented and presented young women using cute phones. One of the images by MTN when the company introduced its "Me-2-U" service presented a happy young woman that had just received credit from her boyfriend. The "Me-2-U" is a service option whereby airtime can be transferred from one user to another without the receiver necessarily paying for a telephone credit card. The sender is debited 50 francs for the service. No doubt the advertisement played an important role in influencing young women to make their choice of phones, as they aspire to identify with the women on the billboard advertisements. For cross-reference purpose, available literature on the topic was also reviewed.

Youth and Cell Phones

In its present digital GSM version (Global System for Cell Communications, originally *Groupe Spécial Mobile*), the cell phone has broken communication boundaries in spectacular ways since 1995, when it was predominantly used for business purposes and possession was restricted to income earners most of whom had completed school, with no gender barrier (Geser, 2006: 2). However, by 2001, the velocity at which the technological gadget had diffused through the different social strata and countries with rather divergent levels of socio-economic development was unprecedented. With its increasing

175

diffusion over the years, certain generational cleavages were dismantled. Of interest here is the increasing popularity of the cell phone among young people. It has been argued that this phenomenal increase in cell phone appropriation could be explained by the fact the youth are more susceptible and adaptive to technological change than adults (Nkwi, 2008; Geser, 2006).

Another reason for the preference of young people for cell phones is that the globalisation of this technology creates new avenues for the youth to communicate with their social peers. Geser provides empirical evidence showing that young people are most eager to embrace new communication technologies among all demographic groups (2006: 4). As such, the cell phone has become an object of intimacy comparable to keys or wallets.

The number of youth who have a cell phone has also increased with the drop in phone prices that led to a flooding of the market with a variety in brands and the level of sophistication of phones, although this point should be considered with caution, given that most youth still go for the dearest and trendiest cell phones. New markets are sites for cheaper phones to young people, especially in developing societies. In these developing societies, the perception of the cell phone is changing, often assuming a new meaning that supersedes the utility of the telephone as a medium solely for voice communication. According to Hulme and Peters, the cell phone is increasingly perceived as a multi-purpose device (2004), allowing teenagers to define and re-define the identity of the cellular phone as a dynamic social technology. Being a symbol of identity, this technology has generated a lot of contradictions: it has created new social networks, hierarchies and insecurities.

Since the cell phone became popular among youth, social theorists have developed frames to better understand relationship between young people and cell phones. The

176

principal frame has been to look at the importance of fashion as a statement about identity in the life of teenagers (Katz and Sugiyama, 2005; Campbell, 2006) and this helps them to understand their identity. Some perceive it outside the framework of fashion (Lorente, 2002). Other studies have shown that the admiration of the cell phone evinced by young people is not even differentiated in terms of gender. Some studies show that young women are more prone to being addicted to the cell phone than boys because their movement in many social spaces is more tightly controlled than that of boys and cell phones allow them to maintain a degree of contacts at certain hours (Geser, 2006: 5-6). This access to cell phones by many has contributed, to some extent, to the levelling of gender differences as females start to have contact with friends and peers outside the traditional spaces controlled by their male relatives. I shall elucidate this point by focusing on parental control.

Girls, Cell Phones and Parental Control

Cell phones help young girls in Molyko to escape parental surveillance while providing an opportunity for parents to monitor the movement, actions, and social relations of their daughters. Unlike the fixed phone, the cell phone, allows for spatial boundaries of the home to become highly porous to discretionary communication. The category of youth described here are young women in their late teens and twenties who are unmarried, have a feeling of "self-autonomy", and that have used the cell phone as a weapon of social manoeuvring that is often outside the normal social control. Some well-to-do parents buy cell phones for their daughters for a number of cogent reasons: to maintain some control of the whereabouts of their children, for coordination and security purposes, for assuring themselves that their children are well, and for allowing them to call home whenever they are in need (Geser,

2006: 7). Because of this possibility of overcoming the spatial boundaries of the home, teenage girls in Molyko town enjoy a considerable degree of latitude to call and receive calls without the embarrassment of revealing a possible romantic liaison that would otherwise be frowned upon by parents. It also allows for the girls to make and receive calls very late at night when other family members are likely to be asleep. When the possibility of short message sending (SMS) is added to this cell phone culture, it becomes clear that these young girls are provided with a level of autonomy that was never possible in the era before cell phones. They are not only physically outside of their parents' constant surveillance, but also able to communicate freely with people outside of the parents' social space and control.

The introduction of late-night calls almost for free and free SMS in the months of May 2009, for instance, provided an opportunity for young women to communicate freely late into the night. In fact, when late-night calls were introduced, it took just a charged battery and at most 100 francs to make calls all night communicate with a friend could therefore last for as long as the battery permitted. In late 2009, this service was reviewed and given a maximum of eight minutes for 100 francs. Despite the restrictions, this calling plan is far cheaper than standard calling rates set for use during the day that are as high as 180 francs per minute within the same network and higher if the call is to a subscriber of a different network. As Francis Nyamnjoh shows, most people are forced to purchase dual-SIM phones or swap SIM in a single SIM phone because the two principal networks hardly work simultaneously (2009: 5).

Within the social context of Molyko, girls have exploited this service, for good or ill. Through this service, for instance, students are able to share assignments tips, brief friends of their location and the "breaking news" in town. As some of the girls surveyed stated, cell phones have also been useful for safety purposes, especially at a time when insecurity is a major concern to the local authorities. These young women that have to be out late at night stated that they could contact a male friend or relative to escort them home or, in case of an assault or difficulties, even communicate with their parents. In addition, this service allowed some women to communicate freely without the supervision of their parents and to establish a social network with their peers that was outside their parents' social control.

The phone can also be used as a tool to manipulate parents and other family members. Most of the girls confessed that they sometimes use this communication gadget to extort money from their parents. These items are of great importance to these girls as they help in establishing a social identity and status. They often claim to be in dire straits that normally attract the sympathy of others, from which they reap monetary benefits. Some respondents mentioned that they would send a message about being in a desperate situation and ask for some airtime or money from their phone contacts.

With the cellular phone, the girls in Molyko perceived a degree of autonomy and resistance to control. Some switch off, ignore calls or give misleading information about their location or activity. In this way their safety and well-being are disconnected from their actual physicality. Given that most of these young girls are pseudo-independent from their parents, they have the latitude to go wherever they desire, attend parties late into the night and hang out with whoever they choose. Their choice of peers is determined by their level of connectivity and degree of socialisation. This kind of autonomy provided by cell phones can lead to a number of interesting discussion questions: do parents now regard their daughters differently because they are able to make certain social decisions outside of the parent's surveillance? Do parents regard their daughters as less dependent on them now that they have cell phones? Do members of the society regard these girls in a different light given their ability to make contact with people within and outside their immediate locales? Let us look at some possible answers to these questions as we explore how cell phones allow for different ways of engaging in social life.

Cellular Phones, Connectivity and Social Life

If anything the cell phone has given teenage girls in the neighbourhood the ability to connect to the wider world, to access new social spaces and to control their social life/relations. In the preceding section we discussed the reasons why parents purchase phones for their children. In this section our concern is to examine the ways through which young girls in Molyko assert a degree of independence and in turn manipulate their social ties and lifestyle. This will be examined in terms of the level of connectivity, types and/or number of phones and how these bear on their social network.

The first point to examine here is the issue of connectivity. This communication concept is very complex, especially in a discourse concerning teenage girls in Molyko. Molyko's girls perceive connectivity beyond just being hooked up by a technological device to one's peers within a given social space and as a phenomenon whereby one can benefit from being connected. This sense of connectivity is intricately linked to the social life of these youth. With this complex sense of connectivity, they will stop at nothing to get connected in order to become beneficiaries of this process. Thus, it is very common for these youth to possess more than one phone or number. Some have up to three cell networks: CAMTEL, MTN and Orange. The number of phone numbers a person has shown how connected the person is in relation to others as well as their socioeconomic standing. Having three different networks guarantees constant connectivity irrespective of location or time, especially given that the three networks do not have connectivity across the country. Also the high rates of calling across networks require calling within the same networks than risking the high cost of calling across networks.

As one girl stated in the survey, having three networks was just being strategic. The more numbers a person has, the higher the social network. It is also an opportunity for young women to decide whom she wants to be in contact with and at what time, since she rarely provides all her phone numbers to a single individual. Special numbers are given to "special people" with the latitude to contact them at all times, while others have restricted access. As mentioned above, the number of phones one has reveals a person's social status, which in turn influences the person's social ties. With these multiple contacts, girls are able to schedule and reschedule appointments, side-lining those they do not want to contact at a given time.

The content of phone calls is often very revealing of many social issues. To Horst and Miller, it is an avenue to interpret a person's social network, both hidden and overt (2005). One unique characteristic among the girls in Molyko that I studied is that the storage capacity that is allocated to contacts and messages in their phones is often nearly full to capacity because of the multiple contacts they have. Of the five phones whose phonebooks were perused (with the consent of the owners) during the research, two thirds of the contacts were men, most of whom were not of the same age group as these girls. These were mostly well-positioned married men (Mbomas) residing out of town and frequently visit Molyko during weekends for assignations with girls, some of the young enough to be their daughters. It should be noted that most of the girls refused to share the content of their phones with the researcher because they are/were uncomfortable with somebody perusing their phones. The text messages in the phones could reveal deeply private aspects of the girls' lives, with messages of a sexual nature.

Another issue that has accompanied the use of cell phones among young girls in Molyko is the "beeping" or "flashing" culture. Beeping or flashing involves dialling another cell number and letting it ring once or twice before disconnecting. The person on the other side sees a missed call and the caller's identity. This is often done to send a coded message, especially when sent to a male friend. When a girl beeps or flashes a male friend, he can interpret it in one of three ways: the girl is "around" and may be available to socialise in the evening; she wants him to call back; or she wants him to transfer airtime to her so she can make phone calls. While the cell phone culture may be giving some autonomy to girls it is interesting to note that my research revealed that girls rarely make phone calls even if they have credit, instead, they prefer to be called. This re-establishes the social dynamic of courtship and dating with the expectation that the man will make the move and channel the direction of the relationship even though such norms are constantly being challenged.

Men are therefore expected to call, arrange a date, and then leave it up to the girl to attend if she so desires. If she wishes not to honour the request, she merely puts off her phone and switches to her other contact number. At times a delay in arrival at the scheduled venue may attract one or several phone calls from the impatient male friend who may often get an ambiguous reply regarding the actual location of the girl and thus, allowing for the phone to be used to excuse the girl's mismanagement of time. Clearly the ability of the girl to decide, via the phone, whether or not to honour a request for a date by a man may signal certain levels of autonomy not present in a face-to-face encounter that is often dominated by the man. However, because men continue to have some economic advantages over these girls, it is still possible for men to use their material advantage to exert their masculine authority over these girls. All in all it is not lost to the keen observer that cell phones allow for these girls to start exercising certain levels of autonomy and choice that were not possible a generation ago.

Conclusion

The introduction of the cell phone has affected the lives of many in urban spaces, but the focus of this study has been to examine the multiple ways through which young women in Molyko have appropriated this technology and are using it in different ways to negotiate their positions in society. It shows how young girls use their cell phone not only to escape parental surveillance but as a tool to get money from them and other members of their social networks. This has led to a new feeling of power and perception of autonomy to their social lives. The study has argued that young girls are more addicted to the cell phone than their male counterparts because traditionally girls have been under more strict social surveillance than boys. As a result these girls use the cell phone for different purposes, including negotiating with friends. Advertising images also play a role in this process of socialisation as persuasive images have not only produced certain images of what it is to be a young person and young people's perceptions of a phone. Further study needs to be carried out to find out how much of personal autonomy these cell phones provide for girls in other areas of Africa to provide a comparative analysis of the role of new media in African social life.

Notes

1. See story at http://news.cameroon-today.com/?p=2559, retrieved February 20, 2011.

References

Abangma, J. Arrey, "Governance in the University and Students' Crises in Cameroon," in T. N. Fonchingong and J. B. Gemandze, Cameroon: The Stakes and Challenges of Governance and Development, pp. 75-110.

Berg, S., A. S. Taylor & R. Harper, "Mobile Phones for the Next Generation: Device Designs for Teenagers," pp. 1-9. Available online at http://www.dwrc.surrey.ac.uk/portals/0/chi2003.pdf.

Campbell, Rachel. 2006. "Teenage Girls and Cellular Phones: Discourses of Independence, Safety and 'Rebellion'", Journal of Youth Studies, Vol. 9, No. 2, pp. 195-212.

Geser, H., 2004. "Towards a Sociological Theory of the Mobile Phone," in Sociology in Switzerland: Sociology of the Mobile Phone. Online Publications. Zurich. Available online at http://socio.ch/mobile/t_geser1.pdf.

------- 2006a. "Pre-teen Cell Phone Adoption: Consequences for Later Patterns of Phone Usage and Involvement," in Sociology in Switzerland: Sociology of the Mobile Phone. Online Publications. Zurich. Available online at http://socio.ch/mobile/t_geser2.pdf.

------- 2006b. "Are Girls (Even) More Addicted? Some Gender Patterns of Cell Phone Usage," in Sociology in Switzerland: Sociology of the Mobile Phone. Online Publications. Zurich. Available online at http://socio.ch/mobile/t_geser3.pdf.

Haugen, G. D. M., 2005. 'Relation between Money and Love in Post-Divorce Families: Children's Perspectives', Childhood: A Journal of Child Research, Vol. 12, No. 4, pp. 507-526.

Horst, A. & D. Miller, 2006. The Cell Phone: An Anthropology of Communication, Oxford: Oxford University Press.

184

Hulme, M. & S. Peters, "Me, My Phone and I: The Role of the Mobile Phone." pp. 1-4. Available online at http://imgs.obviousmag.org/archives/uploads/2004/Hul mePeters.pdf

Jua, Nantang, "Differential Responses to Disappearing Transitional Pathways: Redefining Possibility among Cameroonian Youth," African Studies Review, (Sept., 2003): pp. 13-36.

Katz, J. E. & S. Sugiyama, 2005. "Mobile Phones as Fashion Statements: The Co-creation of Mobile Communication's Public Meaning," pp. 63-82. Available online at http://comminfo.rutgers.edu/ci/cmcs/publications/article s/mobilephones as fashion statements.pdf.

Ling, R., 2001. "Adolescent Girls and Young Adult Men: Two Sub-Cultures of Mobile Telephone," Telenor R & D Report, 34, pp.1-16. Available online at http://www.telenor.com/rd/pub/rep01/R 34_2001.pdf.

Lorente, S., 2002. "Youth and Cell Phones: Something More than a Fashion," *Revista de Estudios de Juventud*, No. 57, pp. 9-24.

Lum, S. A. & Max Ntangsi. 2004. "The Impact of the Creation of the University of Buea on the Socio-Economic Life of Molyko", Journal of Applied Social Sciences, Vol.4, No. 2, pp. 148-161.

Mokake, F. M., 2011. "Youth, Globalisation and Lumpen Culture in the Molyko Neighbourhood of Buea, Cameroon," Kaliao, Vol. 3, No. 6. Pp. 5-21.

Nkwi, W. G., 2008. "The Voice of the Voiceless: Telephone and Telephone Operators in Anglophone Cameroon," Epasa Moto, Vol. 3, No.2, pp. 187-206.

------- 2009. "From the Elitist to the Commonality of Voice Communication: The History of the Telephone in Buea, Cameroon," in F. Nyamnjoh, M. de Bruijn and V. Dijk, Mobile Phones: The New Talking Drums of Everyday Africa, pp. 50-68. Bamenda: Langaa RPCIG.
185

6

Street Dialogue Spaces: Youth and the Reshaping of Public Political Process in Côte d'Ivoire

Silué Oumar

Introduction

One April morning in 1990, Abidjan's inhabitants were awakened by hordes of young people booing the President of the Republic and chanting "Houphouët thief! Houphouët thief!" In primary schools, younger students followed close on the heels of their older colleagues holding up slates with this message: "Houphouët thief! No school! We are hungry!" (Baulin, 2000:136). The same year, Zouglou established itself across Côte d'Ivoire as challenging protest music. In 2002, a group led by Guillaume Kigbofori Soro of the Côte d'Ivoire Patriotic Movement (MPCI) staged a rebellion in northern Côte d'Ivoire. Soro, who was deemed by many Ivorian socio-political observers as too young to assume such responsibility, defied expectations by becoming the head of the Ivorian Government in 2007. In Abidjan, Douk Saga and his friends from the Jet Set launched in 2003 what they termed the "*Coupé-décalé*" meant to "Save Côte d'Ivoire".

These were the harbingers of the growing influence of youth in the Ivorian public space over the past few years. The purpose of this chapter is to determine the ways in which Ivorian youth are involved in politics. Through observation and interviews by the author in addition to existing studies on youth street corner sub-cultures in francophone West Africa, this study explores youth participation in politics with specific reference to Street Dialogue Spaces (SDSs) that emerged in

187

Côte d'Ivoire in the 1980s. Fieldwork in these SDSs has been ongoing since 2005. The study covers all active political spaces on either side of the border, separating the government-controlled and rebel-controlled zones. It should be recalled that the military and political conflict that erupted on 19 September 2002 split the country into two: the south, controlled by loyalist forces or Defence and Security Forces (FDS), and the north, held by the rebellion or Armed Forces of the New Forces (FAFN).

Youth in Ivorian Politics

Ivorian public space is gradually brought to life by a new category of actors: the youth of street dialogue spaces. Who are they? Where do you find them and why? The Ivorian Youth, Education and Sports Ministry defined youth as anybody between the ages of 18 to 35 years (INS, 1998), which is considered a period half-way between childhood and adulthood. According to some authors, in terms of chronological age, youth is limited to all individuals under 25 years (Wrzesiñka, 1995:65), while others believe that it is difficult to set limits based on rigid chronological criteria since youth also fall under political, economic, social and cultural considerations (Mbembe, 1991; Comaroff, 2000). While the definition of youth is complex, I use the term here to refer to individuals around 25 to 40 years of age, expressly for the purposes of this study. In fact, people of less than 25 years of age are rare in the SDSs considered in this study.

Street dialogue spaces are where young individuals meet to take a critical look at the latest political developments. These debates, as they are described, most often take place near public spaces and involve actors who have an impact on the Ivorian socio-political life. In these spaces, where opinions are expressed and formed, they read about events through the prism of their conflicting convictions. In most cases, the

188

debates are led by jobless and unmarried young men living in the popular suburbs of Abidjan, especially Yopougon, Abobo, and Koumassi. These gatherings are locally referred to as "agoras and parliament" and "Grins". On the one hand "agoras and parliaments" take the form of political meetings led by orators who attract audiences in the hundreds and even thousands. On the other hand, "Grins" are groups (discreet and more limited in number) of people who assemble around a tea pot boiling on a charcoal stove and the tea party is very often accompanied by the consumption of meat and peanuts.

Street Dialogue Spaces

SDSs surfaced in Côte d'Ivoire in the 80s. The first one to be formally identified is the "Sorbonne", located in the Plateau district of Abidjan. To determine how Sorbonne been imagined historically is tantamount to being interested in the public space concept in Côte d'Ivoire. To Leimdorfer, the concept refers to both a physical and symbolic space shared by a variety of actors and whose access and multifarious uses are guaranteed by a power (State, President, ministries, municipalities, ethnic communities) (Leimdorfer, 1999:53). From a Habermasian perspective, public space is this intermediate sphere, this half-way between the State and the Civil Society, which was formed during the *Lumières* era and in which public opinion is built through dialogue (Habermas, 1997:38-40). But in Wolton's view, public space cannot be proclaimed (Wolton, 2000:222). Opening public space to different expressions of opinions does not suffice to create a public space. Aghi Bahi sees the "Sorbonne" as one of the non-bourgeois places of birth of public space (Bahi, 2003:7). This public space is where different religious, economic, social, cultural and political actors aggregate, although mutually opposed by historically situated values.

189

Bourdieu developed his space theory to explain attitude diversity and mobility. He divided space into "fields". These fields are, for example, art, sport, literature, politics, etc. with a hierarchical relationship (Bourdieu 1980). Space building is the way hierarchical structures are represented between different fields, especially within politics. Space is not granted. It is the product of a construction based on a multitude of objective power relations forced upon all actors involved in a field, regardless of their mutual perceptions and intentions. Power relations are forged according to different categories and quantities of power or "capital". Thus, SDSs has representatives of economic capital (in its different forms), social capital (social networks, connections), cultural capital (education, vocational and general training, taste, sensation, music, etc.) and symbolic capital (prestige, reputation, fame, honours, etc.). The political field includes all political institutions, that is, the State, other public communities and several actors who are hard to identify (Maugenest, 2005).

In these places, the political field is combative in form to ensure a legitimate perception of the social world. The purpose here is to conquer – through space reconstruction – the power to form groups or categories, with their inherent characteristics and properties, whether good or bad. The effective production of social groups (re)categorised by these actors is aimed at maintaining or modifying hierarchical positions between fields – political, economic, cultural, social, etc., denying access to certain groups (stigmatised ones), certain fields and/or restricting to certain groups the potential benefits that certain fields might generate. Even though, by their activities, SDSs are interested in culture and sport, they have focused more on the political field where they have captured much attention.

If people of less than 25 years of age are rare in the SDSs, so are women. Students completing their studies, those looking for employment opportunities, or jobless youth are the ones who mainly animate these spaces. Their ages vary between 25 and 38. Young men in their 40s are found in the SDSs. The political field in Côte d'Ivoire has been rather violent since the 1990s which does not make for the integration of women into such spaces. Although since the September 2002 crisis, more women have been actively involved in the public realm, they are still under-represented in the political field.

In Crises Maelstrom: Inventing Street Dialogue Spaces

SDSs appeared in a context of deep social changes, as socio-professional mobility narrowed for the youth. Between 1980 and 1990, Côte d'Ivoire plunged into a cycle of economic recession, the causes of which are linked to both external and internal factors. The key causes of the crisis were falling prices of raw materials on international markets, oil shocks, drought, over-indebtedness resulting from state investments (some for prestige and unprofitable)[1] and the mismanagement of public finances.

The Ivorian economy, which mostly relies on exports of cash crops, was destabilised by the deteriorating terms of trade for raw materials. Recourse to foreign investments, overly limited internal savings and insufficient crop diversification are some of the factors which made Côte d'Ivoire unable to resist the collapse of coffee and cocoa prices as from 1978. Subsequently, external debt increased fourfold between 1975 and 1979. Adding to this huge debt were balance of payment and budgetary deficits which represented 17.4 per cent and 11.9 per cent of GDP respectively. Côte d'Ivoire had no choice but to turn to the Bretton-Woods institutions for a first Structural Adjustment Programme (SAP), which was implemented from 198 to 1983, followed by two other SAPs in 1983 and 1986 (Akindès, 2000). With these programmes, the country was required to reduce spending and raise earnings, conditionalities that mostly affected city dwellers and

191

particularly the youth, a vulnerable component of the population, people with low capital.

The SAPs led to an increase in urban transport fares, fuel prices, water and electricity bills as well as food commodity prices. Prices soared while there was a freeze on civil service salaries and many public corporations were shut down. Concurrently, between 1980 and 1984, per capita GDP plummeted by 26.2 per cent. In 1984, civil service recruitments were reduced, restricting young graduates' access to employment in this sector or in State-owned companies while also reducing the number of scholarships granted to university and secondary school students. The hardships of daily life reflected by this set of indicators resulted in the emergence of what Ivorians termed "*conjoncture*" (current economic situation) to describe the country's deteriorating economic situation in comparison to the previous era.

It was in the context of the economic crisis of the 1980s that the Abidjan-based "Sorbonne" came into being. Old "Philo"[2] and other Ivorian job seekers used to meet in the public squares of Abidjan business centre to "kill time" and criticise President Houphouët Boigny's management of the country until they could find a job. Their political polarisation occurred in parallel with the development of political and regional conflicts and upheavals in Côte d'Ivoire. In 2002, it was not until dissent appeared between the "Sorbonne" leaders that this space split into 3 blocs. The first bloc, made up of "Agoras and Parliaments", was close to the ruling party, the Ivorian Popular Front (FPI), party of President Laurent Gbagbo; the second bloc was led by young followers who identified with the opposition, notably the Rally of the Republicans (RDR)party of former Prime Minister Alassane Dramane Ouattara (Théroux-Bénoni and Bahi, 2005:9-12); and the third and most recently created bloc captured the spaces of the rebellion-controlled zone which identified with its ideology (Silué, 2006). The most famous of them is the "*Sénat*" (Senate)

192

based in Bouaké, a city hosting the main administrative services of the Ivorian rebellion. The Senate's members are both youth close to Alsassane Ouattara's RDR and youth who sided with the rebels. The latter were subsumed into the movement that supported Soro Guillaume. Nowadays (2012), some of these youths are being incorporated in the civil service.

Street dialogue spaces have rallied behind political parties or organisations whose ultimate goal is to rule the country. Beyond what may be described as rapprochement or inter-connection with the political sphere, the youth of these spaces have (re)invented a new culture. The table below illustrates the various affiliations.

SDS	Region of concentration	Assumed affiliation with political parties	Roots	Comments
Sorbonne Agora *Parlement* *Congrès*	South	FPI/Gbagbo	Affiliation with FESCI (Students federation), from "Sorbonne" street university	In 2011, FESCI agreed to participate in the "Reconciliation and reconstruction"
Grins	North	RDR/Ouattara	Informal groups of youth, tea and food sharing and hierarchical structure	
Sénat	Center (Bouaké)	Rebel groups (Mouvement pour le soutien de Soro Guillaume) & RDR		Are being integrated in the administration as civil servants

Youth's Game-playing in Politics

SDSs are close to political parties or their affiliated organisations. These spaces have enriched public discourse by inventing new practices. SDSs have contributed to a general street culture, emerging in spaces forsaken to structural violence. Erupting at the borderline of this multi-faceted violence (Biaya, 2000), new forms of social practices have become to be known as "standing parliaments" in Kinshasa, DRC and "Grins" in Mali, Burkina Faso and other sub-Saharan countries (Kieffer, 2006). Long disappointed by the failed promises made by their leaders, young people have invented ways of externalising their feelings and frustrations somewhere in between the boundaries of legality and illegality, of what is allowed and forbidden.

SDSs have appeared in this context as alternative places for education and training. The names they give themselves are revealing of this educational project. "Grins" is one of the names covered by a generic term like "University of Free Time" (UTL)[3] while "Agoras and Parliaments" are referred to as "Open Sky University" with a faculty of political science (Bahi, 2003:4). Here, identity-building is reflected in a symbolic way that turns streets into lecture halls where "teachers" give classes to students, with key "Lab work".[4] The orators of "Agoras and Parliaments" and the "Senate", called professors, display their knowledge and language skills in front of audiences who sometimes come with pens and writing pads to take notes.

"Grins" are modelled on African traditional societies and operate on the principles of respect for elders, abnegation and discipline that govern relationships between older and younger generations. The most visible roles in these gatherings, including *Kôrô* (elder) and *Dôgô* (younger brother), have not been formally systematised in a written document, but they have become established with time. Failure to abide by this organisation model carries sanctions ranging from fines to

194

chores or in the worst cases banishment from the gathering. "*Kôrô* is an incarnation of wisdom. He is morally irreproachable. He is a model of good behaviour that everyone admires" (Silué, 2006). The *Dôgô* have the task of preparing and serving tea. Of course, they are also in charge of buying sugar and tea.

SDSs are alternative education places offering the youth new possibilities for knowledge building. The documents on sale in the "Agoras and Parliaments" and the "Senate" contribute to their intellectual enrichment and prepare them for accessing the political city-state. This political socialisation also trains the youth in oral (public speaking), discussion and debating skills. Not surprisingly the "Sorbonne" slogan is "words of mouth, words of mouth only" while the "Grins" slogan is *akilisso* (temple of knowledge), emphasising the major role of discourse practices in these spaces.

Civil commitment has also been strongly inculcated into the actors of SDSs. Unfolding alongside the republican values preached are debates allowing citizens to reflect, in their own way, on the future of their country. This commitment is at times the basis for expressing nationalist sentiment or collective fears against a real or imaginary enemy. "Agoras and Parliaments" accuse France and the United Nations (UNO of instigating the September 19, 2002 war in Côte d'Ivoire (Banégas, 2006; Marshall, 2005). The "Grins" and the "Senate" do not trust the ruling party and its affiliated press (Théroux-Bénoni and Bahi, 2005; Silué, 2006).

A Safety Net: Inventing New Solidarity Ties

SDSs have emerged as places for building solidarity ties. In an environment where people have to be resourceful, these spaces fill the gap left by institutions with weak integration, such as the family, whereby politics and economic hardships have led to fewer opportunities for social cohesion. SDSs have, therefore, become part of the social organisation of the suburbs. Initially a meeting-place for young, secondary school goers or drop-outs, SDSs have gradually turned into a place of social refuge as members grow older. The community is a foster family where members are educated. Street dialogue space is a place for socialisation or a continuation of the traditional organisation model founded on the principles governing intergenerational relationship (Kieffer, 2006:70). The new structure, reproduced along family lines, relies on values such as brotherhood and solidarity. All the members know one another, to the extent that individual qualities, defects and tastes are no secret to anyone of them. Members' union ties are also strengthened through sports and other socio-cultural activities.

During protests, this solidarity can quickly turn into a herd instinct, not only between individuals, but between organisations as well. Thus, when a structure organises an activity, other structures throw their energies into it to make the project a success. This solidarity operates between blocs. For instance, when the "Powerful Abobo Conference" (TPCA) organises a meeting, the orators of other spaces like the "Sorbonne" provide support either by taking the floor or adding to the human resources. The vitality of the solidarity tie is the best life insurance in Ivorian politics because it is indicative of mobilisation capacity. The rapprochement between political leaders and street dialogue spaces can be explained in part by the latter's capacity to mobilise large crowds during inter-party power tests.

Presumably, it was the saturation of the solidarity tie between SDS members as they came into contact with the political world that turned them into a militia in the Duverger sense, that is to say, organisations with military attributes ("security" services or departments, salutes, uniforms, drills and military languages) or in some cases, creation of armed militia. This is currently the case for pastor Gammi, head of

Western Côte d'Ivoire Liberation Movement (MILOCI) and orator at the Abidjan-based "Sorbonne". Others like Maguy le Tocard, orator at the "Sorbonne", also operate a militia. Willy Djimi, orator at one of the Parliaments of the popular suburb of Yopougon and a registered sociology graduate student at the University of Cocody in Abidjan, is also a chief militiaman. Trained in commando techniques, these men are mobilised to provide security during "Agoras and Parliaments" demonstrations. The "Grins" and the "Senate" also have their security operatives who are deployed to "protect" members of the parties with which they are affiliated.

Street Dialogue Spaces as Instruments for the Dissemination of Political Ideology

The history of street dialogue spaces in Côte d'Ivoire has clearly shown that at a given time of their evolution, they succumbed to political temptation. Originally, the first space known as the "Sorbonne" showed interest in all topical subjects (economics, health, agriculture, etc.); the process of political exploitation actually started in 1999 under President Robert Guéi's administration. The outbreak of war in 2002 led to the birth of blocs and inter-bloc war. Aware of the advantage they could reap from SDSs, political leaders moved closer to them. As an immediate consequence, SDSs were transformed into media for the dissemination of political ideology (FIDH, LIDHO, and MIDH 2013).

The actors of SDSs are in some ways political actors. They take far-reaching political decisions and make their voices heard by those who have been officially proclaimed political leaders. As such, their political legitimacy has been acknowledged and accepted by all. Based on this legitimacy, they can take positions regarding the events taking place on the Ivorian political scene. On the other hand, although they have no official recognition as political organisations, SDSs operate on the basis of their self-proclaimed autonomy. This is because these organisations position themselves at the heart of the political game, especially through their close ties to political parties. With the eruption of the war, the National Congress of Resistance for Democracy (CNRD), a coalition of all political parties with close ties to the presidential movement, has a membership including the National Federation of Ivorian Agoras and Parliaments (FENAAPCI) and the National Federation of Orators of Ivorian Parliaments and Agoras (FENOPACI). Ideology is propagated in three ways. Young people open their spaces to politicians for meetings. To remain active, the spaces in turn approach politicians. Other factors facilitating ideology propagation include actors' mobility (through the communes), especially orators, emotion-building and speech-writing for political leaders (Silué, 2007). Finally, youth's interconnections with political actors, development and exchange based on their social capital, pave the way for them to convert political capital into socio-economic capital.

At the Heart of the Political Game: Between Resourcefulness and Vote-catching

Since 1990, Côte d'Ivoire has witnessed the extreme politicisation of individual relations. Any event quickly takes a public and political turn. Company workers' strikes and student movements, for instance, are all turned into a "presidential matter". Political parties are increasing in number and their influence over the management of public affairs grows. In this game, SDS youth, most of whom are jobless, exchange their political capital for advantages and services from political leaders. Indeed:

> In this country, the only people who do not feel the impact of economic crisis are the politicians; they have access to all

services. If you want to be successful, you'd better get closer to them.[5]

Young SDS actors are keenly aware that they are using their political positioning to bargain for their socio-professional integration. There is a flow of services and gifts between the youth and political leaders. Youth are responsible for resource mobilisation, which covers organisation of meetings between the political party youth and their leaders. The youth help prepare (through bus seeking, distribution and sale of t-shirts, flyers and other activist gadgets, etc.) the audiences for the leaders by preceding them to highly strategic spots, warming up meetings and carrying out power tests (punitive operations against turncoats or opponents, marches or picket lines, intimidation, etc.) In exchange for these services, SDSs youth have access to privileges that include conservation of their spaces, obtaining cash or privileges or getting a job. The FENAAPCI President is a student in tax administration at the *Ecole Nationale d'Administration* (ENA) and many of the "Parliament" orators have been employed since 2008 by the Abidjan Port Authority (PAA). Many others have entered the police training school and other departments of public administration. In its June 17, 2005 issue, the *Courrier d'Abidjan* newspaper wrote in connection with the relationship that:

> The President of Ivoirian Popular Front (FPI), Pascal Affi N'Guessan, was about to offer a lot of equipment to the National Federation of Ivorian Agoras and Parliament (FENAAPCI), led by Idriss Ouattara (…). According to our sources, the FPI president's support to Agoras and Parliaments – fifty in number – located across the entire Ivorian territory, will consist in donating practical equipment. That is to say tools that "Parliamentarians" need to perform their activities. These include many megaphones, loudspeakers, complete sound equipment, benches, marquees, etc., which orators and the

199

public need during debates. (…) In fact, the FPI president's tour to explain the crisis in the Agoras and Parliaments of Abidjan at the peak of the crisis was in response to the grievances of these places leadership.[6]

In the "Grins" and the "Senate", underlying the political struggle is economic logic. When people join a dialogue space, their purpose is to tap any economic resources that are likely to improve their difficult social condition. Thus, for a member:

> With the on-going crisis, the Grin generates hope for economic integration because it allows you to build a small network of relations, and when you are in perfect control, you can then win bids, contracts or get a small job [K. 15 September, 2006].

The oratorical contest market is favourable to "Parliaments" and "Senate" orators, particularly as it tends to become professionalised. At the "Sorbonne", these orators make 15,000 to 20,000 CFAF daily, not to mention the small "occasional treats" which they receive from those who invited them. These are meals with a menu made of grilled fish or meat, a spicy soup and attiéké served with beverages. This festive atmosphere has been palpable since the announcement of future presidential elections for 29 November 2009. The counterpart for exchanging with the youth is their mobilisation capacity, enhanced by new information and communication technologies (NICTs).

Space Domination Through Control of NICTs

NICTs have profoundly modified the operation of SDSs. Between 1980 and 2009, SDSs re-appropriated the modern communication media appearing in Côte d'Ivoire. Traditional media like radios were mobilised according to their political inclination. In Parliaments and Agoras, the opposition press and international media are perceived as "collaborators" of the Rebellion. *Radio France Internationale* (RFI) fell victim of this suspicious feeling to the extent that it was called Radio Rubbish International. On the other hand, in the "Grins" and the "Senate", international media such as RFI, the British Broadcasting Corporation (BBC), Africa No. 1 and Voice of America (VOA) were praised because they were deemed more credible and impartial.

Web resources top the list of instruments used to prepare speeches for SDS actors. Information on topical issues is tapped from the web. Hours are spent in cybercafés downloading onto DVDs and flash drives a database on issues of interest to them. The freedom to communicate can confer advantages. The coup d'état of 24 December 1999 was coordinated by cell phone (Kieffer, 2000:28). The young insurgents used their cell phones to convey orders on the management of this military action. Guillaume Kigbafori Soro used a satellite phone to coordinate the coup d'état of 19 September 2002 (Soro, 2005:85) and Charles Blé Goudé, leader of COJEP, also used his cell phone during the November 2004 events (Blé, 2006:110).

Cell phone are used to mobilise collective action. They allow fast and secure communication of watchwords. One official of this space explained to us how messages are circulated through the cell phone:

> When there is an urgent message to convey, General Blé Goudé calls Richard. At times they are not together. Now, he is the one calling officials to convey watchwords to the different Parliaments and Agoras of Côte d'Ivoire. Thus, when you reach an individual, you are in touch with the whole structure. Anyway, the cell phone is an essential tool for us [G. 6 May, 2006].

While those surveyed were unable to exactly quantify the number of message dispatches, texting has, however, become fully integrated in the communication mechanism of SDSs. And yet, the frequency of texting varies according to what is happening on the political scene. In a crisis, texting is used more intensively:

> We regularly exchange messages. But when there is a movement, that is to say, when political activity is intense, texting is used more frequently. When you have a 1,000 CFAF credit recharge, it may be exhausted in less than an hour. The credit recharge is quickly exhausted but texting is also done more quickly [K., member of Sorbonne, May 6, 2006].

Texting also acts as a security device for the young people because the parties involved can discreetly send and receive messages (Martin, 2007:107; Journet, 2007:28). This feature is particularly appreciated as it allows them to communicate rapidly in crisis situations without drawing the attention of people around them. The concern for security by those involved justifies the coded language used in communicational transactions. At one point, a form of writing only known to and shared by members of these spaces was even devised. The language was created and maintained in order to protect the identity of some people and the confidential nature of some so-called strategic pieces of information. The confidential nature of messages led them to create a "sacred" form of writing, only known to a few. Texting uses a language level which very often does not follow the writing standards of the French language.

In the 1980s, the NICTs invasion of Africa (Chénau-Loquay, 2003:122) brought the Ivorian youth under the influence of video clubs.[7] When CDs, VCDs and DVDs emerged on the market in 2000, political actors finally had an opportunity to go into film production. Because not all political leaders' speeches could reach the population, as the population could not accompany them in their tours, CDs and CD-ROMs were recorded by SDSs, notably the "Sorbonne", and other leaders of the patriotic galaxy. These media were then sold at the "Sorbonne" at a discount (between 500 and 1000 CFAF).

Space control through NICTs deployment is indicative of the youth's attempt to control the future. They ultimately see NICTs as a way of projecting themselves into a bright future in which they have full control over current threats and opportunities. Space here is plural, fragmented, informal and deregulated, with little weights allocated to time management and content. The manipulations derived from the use of cell phones, ipods and computers have given birth to *homo electrus*, gifted with such skills as will allow him/her to dominate his/her space and subject it through his/her imposition of standards. When the space produced by the youth tries to become formalised, to establish its identity and standard, social elders view it with circumspection. It becomes suspicious. Elders see through the visible cracks left by the youth what they suspect to be an invention of a new protean sub-culture and a new idea-generating order, the confusing and defuse outlines of which are both fascinating and frightening.

Reinventing Youth Culture

SDSs mirror a microcosm of Ivorian political circles. They are the forewarning signs of the emergence of new forms of sociability. SDSs contribute to the process of city state production by the youth. Between resourcefulness and violence, they have invented new forms of sociability to circumvent or break the rules preventing them from expressing themselves. The youth's use of violence in politics is a way of giving vent to the resentments linked to the structural violence (unemployment, dysfunctional schools, weak social networks, etc.) with which they have to contend daily. One of their

203

answers to the situation is another form of violence through mass protest, pirating intellectual property, marches, strikes, physical and/or oral confrontations between these spaces and the armed forces (police, gendarmes, etc.) on the one hand, and between the spaces themselves, on the other. When cornered after dialogue failed with their elder city state managers, they then use force out of anger. Thus, nowadays when the youth want to be heard, there are outbreaks of violence that operate as a collective catharsis through which they can externalise their long-contained frustrations.

Violence further appears as a resource, a tool with which the youth can acquire political power. By the use of force, they make their way to power by penetrating the entire social fabric. The emerging new political figures are reinforcing this feeling of self-development and self-assertion. Guillaume Kigbafori Soro, Charles Blé Goudé and Karamoko Yayoro are the new figures of success. Many young people are making their way into politics alongside several football players who have settled in the wastelands of Abidjan and other cities in the countryside.

The youth have many integration options: business creation or enrolling as a member of a political leader support club or a political party, a militia or rebellion member and, in the case of educated youth, as an activist of the Ivorian Student Federation (FESCI); each of the rebellion and "Senate" youth wants to become a Ouattara Issiaka, nicknamed "Wattao", a rebel leader adulated by the youth. The dream of almost all FESCI members[8] is to follow a similar path to most of their elders who now hold influential positions on the Ivorian political stage. The life story of their elders is quite revealing from this perspective. From the first FESCI secretary general (Martial Ahipeaud, who later became a teacher and scholar at the Department of History of the University of Bouaké) to the latest official (Serges Koffi), all former members of this movement have created organisations with close ties to political leaders or have been directly employed by them. In this connection, Damana Adia Pikas, former No. 2 of FESCI from 1995 to 1998 and current special adviser to FPI president Affi N'Guessan, in charge of political matters and a Ministry of Home Affairs official, who works as a civil administrator, an assistant to the managing director of Local Decentralisation and Development (DGDDL) thundered:

> The Côte d'Ivoire of tomorrow will be led by the FESCI generation. (…) It's a question of the Fascist spirit and system and not of individuals.[9]

All the former union leaders have a life story which directly or indirectly fascinates the youth. According to the youth, these successes are the result of their own personal efforts. Thus:

> Contrary to the independence generation, which came of age during the one-party one thought-of-the-day system, today while sons bear their fathers' name, they are also and mostly the ones who now reveal their parents, make them known to the public at large. (…) From a generation of "Daddies' sons", Côte d'Ivoire has shifted to "Sons' daddies". (…) Our generation is one of young women and men who are forging their own destiny and who, like a river, are making their own bed. A generation of self-made men who do not wait for their choices and tastes to be dictated to them; they know that *"no hay camino, se hace camino al andar"*: there is no road, the road is made by walking (Blé, 2009: 50-51).

Juvenile sub-culture (re)production is a reflection of self-destructive, self-reproducing and self-reinventing body politics that exist in a conflicting environment. Bodies appear as a field where consensual and sometimes conflicting logics crisscross. The result of these divergences is to turn those bodies into a battlefield, an arena in which young people fight not only each other but also their elders. But the space created through these

205

public interactions becomes a tool for thought and action as well as a means of control and domination (Lefebvre, 2000:35). It is also a body-producing place that allows this new "envelope" to become a tool for building new identities that are likely to facilitate integration into new spaces.

Turned into a Foucauldian bio power, the youth body is the seat of delivery of power. This power should be understood to mean the ability, in the face of constraint and domination, to transform one's body into socio-economic capital. This capital is transferred to places where the capacity to tilt towards the youth can be demonstrated. The struggle for power conquest abolishes moral and educational limits and opts instead for body techniques by learning specific and even violent practices. The individual reinvents himself/herself by giving new meaning to the use of his/her body and, hence, to reproduction techniques as a whole (Mauss, 1950:383). The body is also a mediating vehicle for integration, success and fame. Youth movements across different socio-cultural contexts are part of a vast body techniques "project" which aggregates several imaginations embedded in often conflicting social-economic dynamics.

High-Tech Generation

The current generation of SDSs members is a cross-section of the Ivorian youth as a whole. An increasing number of them own a cell phone, communicate through the Web, play CDs and DVDs. More recently, ipods have become part of SDSs' practices. These devices are used as vehicles for broadcasting ideologies and have given birth to new practices, notably by creating new communication codes. A new way of communicating which is not respectful of traditional writing standards has come into being through texting, "beeping" (or "flashing") and "MMS".

This language infringement is a creation in Michel de Certeau's sense (1990) since these young people have invented a new use not provided for in the cell phone operators' project. This diversion of use hinges on the flexibility of a concise writing mode which, contrary to Desjeux's argument (2005), is not that simple. The writing named SMS is all the more complex as it reflects the emergence of new juvenile identities in a technology-saturated consumer society. The appropriation inroads made through texting, Bluetooth and beeping are the harbingers of new ways of reappropriating these new objects that participate in the creation of youth lifestyle.

Informality Persists

All the measures taken to end CD and DVD sales in these spaces and notably in their matrix, the "Sorbonne", failed. To some extent, the installation and development of informal transactions in the trade, cultural and pharmaceutical sectors have been facilitated by these spaces. Medication and pirated music CDs are displayed side by side for sale. Worse still, everyone goes shopping in those places: the police, gendarmes, the military, priests, nuns, pastors, civil servants, the jobless, pupils, students, senior citizens, etc. Cybercrime is encouraged through acts of CD piracy. Between May and June, 2009, there was the case of "a secretary who was sleeping with her boss in the Plateau district which, once again, prompted debate on piracy at the "Sorbonne". A porn video of about 15 minutes purportedly featuring a woman and her head of department hit newspaper headlines in Côte d'Ivoire and the CD was on sale at the "Sorbonne" for 1000 CFAF or was accessible via Bluetooth on cell phones at a cost of 500 CFAF. The scandal was devastating and made the population uncomfortable, as they felt compassion for the woman whose face, unlike that of her partner, could be seen on the footage.

In order to end the spiralling distribution of the video, the police carried out a sting operation at the "Sorbonne" to seize and destroy the embarrassing CDs. But, as always, this video continues to be sold at the "Sorbonne"; multiple forms of informal activity are thus encouraged by this space, which also resists the conventional economy by evading all controls.

The development of the informal sector is also facilitated through the exploitation of the spaces hosting SDSs. Their illegal settling on private and state-owned spaces is also cause for dispute with the municipal authorities. Some crises were also linked to the commercial activities taking place there. Public space is acquired through the imposition of trademarks and counter-trademarks followed by appropriation; public space is thus no longer a shared space because stakes are involved; it then becomes more of a territory to be conquered or defended.

The way the "Sorbonne" occupies and conserves the space where "Sorbonnards" perform their activities resulted in some power tests between the "Sorbonne", the Plateau Municipality and the Ivorian Copyrights Office (BURIDA). The wasteland where the TPCA conference participants[10] meet is disputed with two entities: a businessperson and the municipality. Between June and July 2004, a dispute erupted between conference participants and this businessperson, resulting in the destruction of the building being constructed on this space.

The mode of space acquisition and conservation is indicative of a redefinition of street uses by the actors. These are territories whose appropriation, control and defence constitute socio-political stakes. They are also highly reactive and mobilising spaces in which forms of approval or protest can erupt. The latent or violent clashes linked to the management of SDSs are part of the general difficulties posed by urban space management in Côte d'Ivoire. Very strong pressures are exerted on urban real estate, followed by extreme land speculation; yet, not so long ago, land was a nontransferable good. Housing projects for civil servants, private sector employees or simply privately-built homes soon turn urban space into a Gruyere cheese at the mercy of greedy new urbanites caught in the spiral of an poorly-controlled land development.

Street Dialogue Spaces as an Alternative Exchange Mechanism

SDSs are an alternative means of communication between the people and the authorities but also between the people themselves. The debates initiated in these spaces at times forces leaders to express their positions on burning issues. They act here as polling stations established not only to sound out or "listen to" the street but also and mostly to provide answers to the questions and fears of an audience under various influences. The challenge is to test a person's opinion on unfolding events (Champagne, 1990:215). The populations encourage dialogue in order to have good visibility and perfect legibility of current political affairs thereby encouraging a kind of "bottom-up" politics. The individual, notably a youngster originating from a popular suburb can, through those spaces, speak directly or indirectly to the authorities who were previously inaccessible by virtue their origins and functions.

Also, SDSs allow citizens to engage in dialogue among themselves on matters of the city state. Despite the threat of a single thought pattern in these spaces and their replication in different blocs, the truth is that SDSs operate as windows through which individuals can express themselves in the public space. However, in the face of political censorship, rumour-mongering offers the population an opportunity to exchange information on the ruling power. The emergence and propagation of rumours create a game space to challenge the ruling order and contribute to the strategies deployed by social actors for adjusting forms of expressions of claims and discontent. The SDSs phenomenon is one of these spontaneous and popular modes of intervention in politics in Côte d'Ivoire and some African countries. Information comes to satisfy a need for information and training (Nyamnjoh, 2005:218).

Conclusion

At the initiative of the youth, SDSs appeared in Côte d'Ivoire in 1980, in the context of a socio-economic crisis. Appearing initially in a general format as the "Sorbonne", they operate today as three different blocs. SDSs have interconnections with political spheres. As a result, the intrigues taking place in those spheres are taken over by the streets. Agoras and Parliaments bring together young people with close ties to the ruling party, the FPI. The "Grins" identify with the RDR's message while the "Senate" subscribes to the rebellion's ideology.

Integrated in the communication mechanism of parties and political organisations to which they have ties, SDSs contribute to the building and activity of public space in general and the political sphere in particular. They participate in the propagation of the political ideologies of the parties they support. They open their spaces for the organisation of public meetings or debates and jointly prepare speeches with politicians while moving from one space to another "campaigning" for their candidates.

SDSs operate as alternative means of communication with the social fabric as a whole. By their practice of violence, NICTs re-appropriation, strategies implemented to facilitate their integration in the job market based on their political positioning and building of new identities, SDSs represent alternative places of expression. Behind the wall of occasional deviant behaviours, new forms of political participation, a different world vision filled with technological applications, are being foreshadowed. Politics is an instrument, a means of social positioning (Tessy, 1992:259; Coulibaly, 2002) in a public space where mobility is restricted for most of the younger population. They are "places of resistance" where there are opportunities for citizens from the poorest social strata or the so called "lower than low" to force exchange with the leaders or so called "top of the top" on the management of the city state's affairs. For, while decision-making is, for leaders, a game in which they can make mistakes and make "adjustments" later on, here they are putting human lives on the line. And in the vanguard of these new forms of resistance and expression are the youth with new ideas, acting as vehicles for complex new ideologies. As they resist being confined to a social thinking mould, these ideas have given rise to suspicion.

Notes

1.The cocoa rice paid to the producer decreased from 400 CFAF per kg to 250 CFAF, then to 200 CFAF in 1990.

2. He is said to be the no.1 orator at the Abidjan-based "Sorbonne".

3. *Fraternité-Matin* newspaper No. 13293, Tuesday 3 March 2009.

4. "Lab work" refers to the practical exercises given to students.

5. Statement by Mrs Constance Yaï, former minister and women's rights activist in Côte d'Ivoire.

6. newspaper, 17 June 2005.

7. *Fraternité Matin* no. 9371, 10 January 1996.

8. Name given to FESCI militants.

9. *L'Inter* newspaper no. 3013, Friday 30 May 2008.

10. Name given to all those who are active in the space: orators, traders, curious bystanders, etc.

References

Akindès, F., 2000, *"Inégalités sociales et régulation politique en Côte d'Ivoire. La paupérisation est-elle réversible?"* in *Politique Africaine*, no. 78, pp. 126-141.

Bahi, A.A., *"La 'Sorbonne' d'Abidjan: rêve de démocratie ou naissance d'un espace public"*, in *Revue Africaine de Sociologie*, Vol. 7, No. 1, pp. 1-18.

Banégas, R., 2006, *"La France et l'ONU devant le 'parlement' de Yopougon"* in *Politique Africaine*, No. 104, pp. 141-158, Paris: Karthala.

Bayart, J.-F., *et al.* 1992, *"Le politique par le bas en Afrique noir"*, Karthala: Paris.

Biaya, T.K., 2000, *"Jeunes et culture de la rue en Afrique urbaine (Addis-Abeba, Dakar et Kinshasa)"* in *Politique Africaine*, No. 80, pp. 12-75, Paris: Karthala.

Blé, G-C., 2006, *"Crise ivoirienne. Ma part de vérité"*, Abidjan: Leaders' team associated and Frat Mat éditions.

Blé, G-C., 2009, *"D'un stade à un autre"*, Abidjan: Leaders' team associated et Frat mat éditions.

Baulin, J., 2000, *"La succession d'Houphouët-Boigny"*, Paris: Karthala.

Bourdieu, P., 1984, *"Questions de sociologies"*, Paris: Minuit.

Champagne, P., 1990, *"Faire l'opinion: le nouveau jeu politique"*, Paris: Minuit.

Chénau-Loquay, A., 2003, *"NTIC: fracture ou développement?"* in i, No. 1, pp. 121-140, Paris: Karthala.

Comaroff, J., Comaroff, J., 2000, *"i"* in *Politique Africaine*, No. 80, pp. 90-110, Paris: Karthala.

Coulibaly, A.A., 2002, *"Le système politique ivoirien. De la colonie à la IIè République"*, Paris: L'Harmattan.

FIDH, LHDO, and MIDH, 2013, Ivory Coast: *"The Fight Against Impunity at a Crossroad"*, available at www.fidh.org/IMG/pdf/cotedivoire617uk2013basdef.pdf, accessed June 10, 2015.

212

Foucault, M., 1976, "*La volonté de savoir*", Paris: Gallimard.

Habermas, J., 1997, "*L'espace public. Archéologie de la publicité comme dimension constitutive de la société bourgeoise*", Paris: Karthala.

Journet, N., 2007, "*La culture du mobile*" in *Sciences Humaines*, No. 185, pp. 24-28.

Lefebvre, H., 2000, "Dessein de l'ouvrage," in H. Lefebvre, La production de l'espace. Paris 2000 (1974), pp. 7–82).

Calhoun, C. 1993, (ed.), Habermas and the Public Sphere. MIT Press.

Leimdorfer, F., 1999, "*Enjeux et imaginaires de l'espace public à Abidjan*" in *Politique Africaine*, No. 74, pp. 51-74, Paris: Karthala.

Kieffer, G-A., 2000, "*Armée ivoirienne: le refus du déclassement*" in i, No. 78, pp. 26-44, Paris: Karthala.

Kieffer, J., 2006, "*Les jeunes des 'grins' de thé et la campagne électorale de Ouagadougou*" in *Politique Africaine*, No. 101, pp. 63-82, Paris: Karthala.

Marshall, R., 2005, "*La France en Côte d'Ivoire: l'interventionnisme à l'épreuve des faits*" in Politique Africaine, No. 98, pp. 21-41, Paris: Karthala.

Martin, C., 2007, "*Le téléphone portable et nous. En famille, entre amis, au travail*", Paris: L'Harmattan.

Maugenest, D., 2005, "*Gouverner la violence. Société civile et société politique*", Abidjan: CERAP.

Mauss, M., 1950, "*Sociologie et anthropologie*", Paris, PUF.

Mbembe, A., 1991, "*Les jeunes et l'ordre politique en Afrique noire*", Paris: L'Harmattan.

Nyamnjoh, F.B., 2005, "Africa's Media, Democracy and the Policy of Belonging", Pretoria, London and New York: Zed Books.

Silué, N O., 2007, "*Les espaces de discussions de rues. Instruments de diffusion des idéologies politiques pendant le conflit en Côte d'Ivoire*" Contribution to the MASA Roundtable. Abidjan and Yamoussoukro: Chaire UNESCO/University of Cocody.

Silué, N O., 2006, *"Médiatisation des idéologies politiques dans les espaces de discussions de rues: le cas du discours politique sur l'identité nationale au cours des audiences foraines de 2006"*. Contribution to the *"Conflits en Côte d'Ivoire: dynamiques et représentations"'*", Abidjan: CERAP/IDDH.

Soro, G., 2005, *"Pourquoi je suis devenu un rebelle. La Côte d'Ivoire au bord du gouffre"*, Paris: Hachette Littératures.

Tessy, B., 1992, *"La démocratie par le haut en Côte d'Ivoire"*, Paris: L'Harmattan.

Théroux-Benoni, L., and Bahi, A., 2006, "i" in *Les frontières de la citoyenneté et la violence politique en Côte d'Ivoire*. E. Sall and J.-B. Ouédraogo, eds. Dakar: CODESRIA.

Wolton, D., 2000, *"Internet, et puis après ? Une théorie critique des nouveaux médias"*, Paris: Flammarion.

Wrzesiñka, A., 1995, *"La jeunesse africaine et les transformations socio-culturelles en Afrique noire (le cas du Zaïre)"*, in Africana Bulletin, No. 43, pp. 43-72.

7

The City Production Process: Ouagadougou Youth, Street Culture and New Forms of Engaging with Burkina Faso's Political Sphere

Ollo Pépin Hien

Introduction

The production of a "street culture" undoubtedly reveals the tragic socioeconomic conditions and structural violence experienced by young people in working-class neighbourhoods in the city of Ouagadougou. In a social context strongly marked by urban violence, economic crisis and the difficult construction of the nation-state, the younger generations, which are increasingly marginalised, have invented new forms of sociability tinged with violence known as *"grins de thé"* (tea clubs). *Grins de thé,* which openly abound in the streets of the city, are places where young people – mainly young men – often unmarried and without steady employment, meet on a daily basis to "kill time" by drinking tea.

Imported by students from western Burkina Faso (Bobo-Dioulasso) and neighbouring Mali (largely from the Mandingo cultural area), these tea clubs are part of a general movement of street culture development that is producing new lifestyles and new social and political practices among young people. These "hardscrabble worlds" are also spaces where social standards and representations are produced, often in defiance of the dominant collective consciousness. Despite the reductionist stereotypes and clichés weighing heavily on these youths in the street, *grins de thé* constitute a prime target for politicians. In light of this, reflecting on the *grins de thé* that fill the streets of

Ouagadougou affords us an opportunity to examine the social bond that provides information about how social configurations are formed in a changing context of urban cross-fertilisation. We are also called upon to examine the multifaceted processes of production of representations of the social world in these new emerging configurations. Accordingly, we will attempt to describe the position of these young people in their current social and political universes. Through a phenomenological approach to *grins de thé*, we intend to look objectively at the subjective processes that build the social world shared by the youth of Ouagadougou.

This chapter is based on fieldwork carried out in two neighbourhoods of Ouagadougou, Zogona (Sector 13) and Wemtenga (Sector 29). Twenty individual semi-structured interviews were carried out with youth from different *grins de thé*. Informal interviews were recorded and analysed. The author regularly frequented different clubs allowing for some participant observation used in data collected for the chapter.

Urban Dynamics and Decompartmentalisation of Established Social Structures

The process of formation of the city of Ouagadougou created upheaval in the established order; it caused a slow, progressive and irreversible social implosion, inevitably leading to the decompartmentalisation of its structures and the destruction of established social affiliations. The urban population gradually integrated into new social configurations. These new configurations are revelatory of the fragmentation of the modern social space, with the emergence of new social roles and statuses, considerable new inequalities and the introduction of new values pertaining to modern society. Thus, the "decline of the community gave way to extreme egoism and an inducement to isolationism imposed by pressing market constraints" (Ouédraogo, 2005).

216

Indeed, the former world, founded on community and therefore on a different spatial scale, was governed by different cooperative and hierarchical principles and particular emotional states and these principles were "traditional". The process of formation of the city brought about the destruction of the traditional social morphology that existed prior to the urbanisation phenomenon that brought forth Ouagadougou. The changes transformed the urban personality; urban men's and women's relations to others were redefined. In the city, the absence of traditional frameworks for social integration led to a fragmented urban fabric and an almost total loosening of traditional social ties ensuing from the very principles of modernity. This fragmentation has generated new social relationships typified by broad indifference, a blasé attitude, calculation, freedom, individuality and new communities. The gain in individual freedom has caused a drop in moral density; the subsequent disintegration of the old social bond has gradually led to "anomie", to borrow Durkheim's expression.

Analysis of an urban fabric such as that of Ouagadougou reveals a high degree of depersonalisation of social relationships, a decline in participation in the recognized, normative social world, an erosion of the moral order and growing social problems such as the drop in social status of youth. Thus, the structural forms of urban exclusion typical of the city create a mass of vulnerable outcasts in the urban world. It can be noted that "under such conditions, the poorest members of society are marginalised, kept at a distance from the most common means of accumulation; excluded from the circuits of distribution of common goods and the wealth produced for society as a whole. The breaking of the 'egalitarian bond' has become the dominant rule of social life" (Ouédraogo, 2005). By disrupting the old social structure, the city claimed to put an end to social inequalities, but instead created new ones.

The rending of the old social fabric that we imagine and experience is the result of a multitude of material and symbolic breaks that generate banal and generalised exclusion. The current prevalence of this exclusion is a visible mark of the "human drought" being experienced in this city. The great majority of urban young people are unable to participate effectively in the general material and symbolic exchange, i.e. in the market of production and consumption. They are ejected from what modern society holds most dear: the sphere of economic goods and privileges. This form of exclusion comprises a break in the economic bond that faithfully or normatively ties these young people to a model of society. According to one youth: "It's tough in Ouaga. It's really hell. There's no work; no support either. Even if you bust your butt, you need some money to start up any economic activity. Life is really hard in Ouaga" (Soul, known as "the Malagasy", Sector 13, Zogona). Although they form a demographic majority, most young people in the city of Ouagadougou are rejected by the economic sphere. The poverty and unemployment in which they live is experienced as a form of exclusion. These troubled youths both reject school and fail in it, thereby entrenching their exclusion from normal education. Cast out by the very institutions supposed to integrate them into society (schools, the market, family relationships, etc.) and intended to create bonds between the members of an imagined society, these young people sometimes resort to irony, denouncing the illusion of the ideal society, which is the dominant representation. Indeed, traditional society is gone and modern society is not what it claims to be.

The exclusion of the juvenile category from the economic sphere inevitably leads to other forms of social failure in which young people are unable to gain access to the models conveyed by dominant representations. The most shocking forms of the process whereby young people become outcasts in the urban dynamics lie in their ousting from the normative representations of modern society. They do not seem to be allowed to participate in the normative models of their society, i.e. in what is "beautiful", "good" or "proper"; they largely have no wage jobs, and when they do, such jobs are badly paid or are irregular informal jobs; no proper housing or family space; difficulty in setting up a modern family with proper space, children and partner; difficult access to the formal political sphere and debates, etc. This failure to achieve normality is synonymous with a break in the social bond, but also with the symbolic and ideological bond that should normally attach these young people to their society. In this context of exclusion of youth, they manage to reconstitute a community-type social bond of sorts through their *"grins de thé"*.

Reconstituting a Social Bond: The Emergence of the *"grins de thé"*

The cross-fertilisation prevailing in the urban fabric creates dynamics of flexible social groups which disintegrate and are reformed. Faced with the erosion of the traditional foundations of solidarity, youthful outcasts reconstitute a moral order based on their own form of solidarity through their *grins de thé*. It can be readily observed that, in this city that produces an excluding anomic violence, the recreation of a social bond by young people on the margin of society obliges us to conclude that community relationships coexist with the societal order of relationships. In this case, *grins de thé* form a sub-group and a sub-culture within the overall society. The particular linguistic practices common in *grins de thé* reflect this sub-culture; in the *grins* the members use a mixture of French, Mooré, Dioula and Nushi, a slang produced in Abidjan and disseminated throughout the cities of Burkina Faso.

219

There is a need to analyse the social morphology and physiology of these informal youth groups, and examine their social function.

The disastrous socio-economic conditions and structural violence experienced by young people in working-class neighbourhoods generate the production of a street culture through *grins de thé*. A *grin* begins when young people gather in a part of the street, in front of the wall of a compound, due to their relationships as neighbours, relatives, friends, or classmates. "Young people drink tea, talk, listen to music, play games or gamble to kill time" (Kieffer, 2006). The young people who hang out in the streets to drink tea and kill time are generally unmarried, may or may not hold degrees, and make their living from the "hardscrabble economy", i.e. small-scale trade, "deals", and occasional jobs as handlers or craftsmen. These informal groups may present several characteristics: *grins* may be made up of young people, in their vast majority, males, indistinctively Christians or Muslims, employed in the informal sector, students, or young public or private sector workers who are former classmates. In Ouagadougou, contrary to what is observed in Bobo-Dioulasso, young women seldom participate in *grins*. If they do, they accompany either their brother or boyfriend. In fact, young women are rather apprehensive of the *grins* which they see as male groups in which they (women) are the objects of discussion. This brings to the fore the masculine characteristic of those peer groups. Young women gather in hair salons, called *"Instituts de beauté"*, where they have discussions with female peers. Young women seem little involved in political activism, whereas organised older women are more and more active in the political sphere.

The grins are also known as "HQ" (headquarters – "QG" in French) and have names that evoke the real or imaginary references and understandings of their young members. One young man explained: "our HQ is called "the base" because that's a military name. Our HQ is also called "Torabora". We

220

were thinking of the Torabora mountains where Bin Laden took refuge to escape the Americans. Besides, the landscape is rocky around here" (Robert, known as "Souka", Sector 13, Zogona). Young people who have broken ties with their families find a refuge in their *grin*, a sort of "second family". The organization of the grins is based on the model of ancient community institutions founded on the seniority principle: "there is a hierarchy within the *grin*. The tea is shared by order of "*kôrôcracy*" (seniority principle). Even if there is a decision to be taken, the younger ones wait for the "*kôrôs*" (big brothers) to arrive before taking any decisions. Younger representatives to the authorities of the base hold an intermediary position. And the youngest ones are at the bottom of the heap; it's organised by age range. It works like democratic centralism. When the "*kôrôs*" take decisions, the others carry them out. The youngest members are apprentices" (Yassia, Sector No. 13, Zogona). Each of the members of the group occupies a clearly defined position.

Several recurring patterns emerge from the *grins*: "the "*fakir*", the "*dôgôs*", the youngest members of the group who regularly make the tea; the "errand boys" who are also younger members in charge of buying cigarettes for the "*kôrôs*" and the tea, fetching water and making the fire to prepare the tea; the "storekeeper" is responsible for handling the stores and equipment of the *grin* (Ben, Sector 13, Zogona). A *grin* is also a space for socialising the younger members of the group. They listen to the advice of their "*kôrôs*" on how to behave. It is a genuine "school of life".

A grin presents itself as an institution that produces its own norms, codes of conduct and obligations: "if there are happy or sad events, we pool funds to help the person. At noon, we share a meal. Those who have money buy food and everyone eats. But where "*gos*" (young women) are concerned, there's not too much solidarity. If somebody wants to romance a "*go*", we don't make a coalition to go see the "*go*" and plead in your

221

favour. The guys wait for you to fail and then they make fun of you" (Yassia, Sector 13, Zogona). A *grin* is a world of mutual assistance, sharing and reciprocal support, both emotional and material. Reciprocity is the foundation for exchanges between group members. Sociality is forged within the group thanks to a unifying social practice. By "acting together" the members of the group build their solidarity: "in this difficult situation, the grins play a major role. Mutual support, psychological support, advice, raising awareness. We support each other a bit through solidarity. Otherwise, without that, it would be even harder for us all" (Hien, Sector 13, Zogona).

The overall de-socialisation of the city has been accompanied by its re-socialisation in small groups such as the *grins de thé*. New social forms are organised based on a typical and traditional model of the social bond. The dissolution of the social bond has given rise to new strategies of innovation or survival, such as collective resistance by youth movements against the advance of social pathologies arising from the deterioration of the urban social fabric. Thus, two social, societal and community orders coexist in the urban structure, each occupying a diametrically opposite position. These different social orders reflect conflicting or even contradictory values or collective representations within the urban space.

There is also another form of *grin*, or youth group, more stigmatised, considered as deviant, more heavily marked by violence, social destitution, unemployment, alcohol, petty trade or services, and drugs. These are known as "ghettos". Ghettos appear to be formed by young people sharing a specific style, e.g. rastafarians and rappers and are prone to social stigmatisation. Although they represent the underprivileged areas of the city and are made up of young people in conflict with broader society, the distinction between *grins* and ghettos is to be seen on a continuum more or less indexed by external, symbolic markers and supposed or assumed marginal, condemned practices relating to a general conception of the

222

law. The expression "ghetto", as it is used by the youths of the grins, refers to an image popularised by television, movie and musical products imported from the United States: "there are hood HQs too. You have to make a distinction, there are HQs, *grins de thé*, and ghettos. Ghettos are where kids meet up to smoke drugs. In the ghettos, they just meet for 2 hours at a time, that's all, and at a specific time. Whereas in a *grin* you can show up any time and there'll be someone. In a ghetto, it's the power relationship that counts. There's no respect between them, when somebody has more power, then they are the one who decides. There's no "*kôrô*", no hierarchy. When they talk, it's only to do wrong. Older people can't tell the difference between ghettos and HQs. That's why many of them don't like *grins*" (Soul, known as "the Malagasy", Sector 13, Zogona).

Young people in Ouagadougou's "ghettos" prefer to wallow in artificial antagonisms and imitations of morality, as they lack the cohesion that produces belief in stable, shared values, fed in turn by recognition of and participation in institutions. The inadmissibility of their ideas or lifestyles is above all a symptom of a value conflict that often implies forms of exclusion. The hostile social practices of these youths, who are "outcasts within" (Xibérras, 2000) their society further deteriorate the fabric of their social relationships and compromise their futures. The situation is indicative of a real crisis affecting the social bond which can be seen in the rise of incivility, acts of delinquency and a growing sense of insecurity. The "social bond crisis" indubitably attests to the fact that, in the urban space, social mechanisms for learning and legitimising self-control and mutual respect are in a state of crisis. The uncivil behaviours of this "uncivil society" take on a subjective meaning that is deeply anchored in social contradictions and the change in relationships to values, norms and simple rules of community living. This behaviour causes disruptions in the civil order that threaten the very idea of

223

citizenship or at least show that citizenship has become problematical and conflictual.

In an urban context of cultural liberalism, demands for personal fulfillment and independence and rejection of the beliefs and social representations handed down by their parents' generation are skyrocketing among the young people of the ghettos. The ghettos are part of a more open cultural order that is more permeable to foreign influences. In an urban environment marked by structural violence, the economic crisis casts these young people out of the spaces held by people who are integrated into the dominant political system and economy. The "new generations have invented forms of expression more violent than those used by their elders, and have drawn inspiration from foreign imagery in building their identity" (Kiefer, 2006). References to media images are typical of young people inserting themselves into the transnational, de-territorialised world to which they aspire. Signs written in chalk or charcoal and stuck on walls, telephone or electricity poles, bridge posts, etc., refer to foreign imagery such as American rap stars, to take one example. This form of appropriation of the urban space, of the street, is a decisive factor in the life of the ghettos. They use it to produce their own system of reference, values and forms of "street culture" and to claim ownership over their territory in their own way. The "street stops being a mere sphere of administrative and religious control and becomes a space for activities, creation and recreation" (Biaya, 2000). This means of controlling their territory is based on the delineation of a physical space and the definition of its usages. Their acts take on meaning and signification, within this defined territory, in the framework of a street culture in conflict with all local cultural trends and legacies.

The exclusion of these young people linked to manifestations of "petty crime" plunges them into a sort of identity malaise that culminates in a clear will to build their

224

personal identity with benchmarks and references they forge for themselves. This subjectivation leads them to deride the norms and codes of the dominant society by forming a new value system and a new world view. Thus, practices of rejection and identity-building processes lead young people to reconstruct a new, alternative social order for themselves, which is not easily perceived by outsiders. These urban youths assert their identities in a counter-culture or counter-society that allows them to cultivate their differences. Faced with this identity challenge, ghetto youth engage in a process of identity deconstruction-reconstruction. Drugs, through their effects, become simultaneously a mirror, a therapy, a tool for adaptation and, more generally, a metaphor that allows them to raise the issue of unequal relations and contest the social order that brands them outcasts.

These young people are not merely deprived of material wealth: "People analyse the *grins* from a distance. They don't get close to the *grins* to find out what is going on there. They call us lazy, unemployed people who spend all our time drinking tea and smoking cigarettes. People like that refuse to open up to the *grins*. They have no philosophy in life. But when there is a funeral like that in the neighbourhood, they come and ask us to go dig the grave in the cemetery. That is when people see how important we are" (Ben, Sector 13, Zogona). In the process of symbolic exclusion, young people are relegated to the margin as much as they put themselves there by "people", "they" and "people like that". The social majority casts considerable aspersions on *grins de thé* and ghettos: "our neighbour the lieutenant who was here just now, he's not from the same generation as us. He said that he would come and haul us in one day, because we don't work and yet we pay for tea to drink every day. The day he found out there was a young doctor in our HQ, he was surprised" (Yassia, Sector 13, Zogona). To combat their isolation, young people develop their own mode of organisation and blame society for not showing them more recognition. Yet, despite the stigma surrounding *grins*, they are paradoxically a major political resource for political entrepreneurs.

Grins and Politics: Between the Heresy of the Dominated and the Orthodoxy of the Dominators

The *grins de thé* and ghettos that abound in the streets of the city of Ouagadougou are informal public spaces where conversations among members generally focus on a wide range of subjects: sports, politics, music, leisure activities, denunciation of social inequalities, etc. According to one young woman: "when I come to the *grin* here, I come to discuss national and international news" (Florence, Sector 13, Zogona). These informal public spaces contribute to the emergence of new political imaginings among young people. Their relationships with the political sphere are a continuation of their social practices, characterised by hardscrabble tactics, i.e. doing what it takes to get by every day, sarcastic attitudes, and a taste for paradoxes.

Electoral campaigns are prime times for meetings between the political parties and ordinary citizens. They offer opportunities for politicians to reactivate their social ties and political resources. They also provide a space where the competition between the political parties in the running generates political products: problems, programmes, analyses, commentaries, concepts, events, and promises, amongst which ordinary citizens, given the status of consumers, must choose. The unfolding of these electoral campaigns takes on a festive air with their rallies, night-time sessions, and distributions of items: gadgets, t-shirts, wraps and caps, all accompanied by big popular events enhanced by music. Electoral campaigns operate like markets: an encounter of giving and receiving between political entrepreneurs and ordinary citizens called upon to make political choices. At such times, the political

226

parties deploy a variety of mobilisation strategies aimed at youths. Politicians who ignored the street and made detours to avoid *grins de thé* suddenly reappear in these places, which become one of their prime targets, an "essential cog in the wheel of the electoral campaign" despite the persistent, indelible stigma attached to the *grins*. This statement illustrates the situation: "our HQ is one of the neighbourhood HQs that bring together a lot of people, so all the politicians come to us. Politicians start visiting us when electoral campaigns draw near" (Hien, Sector 13, Zogona).

The grins receive tea and sugar and visits from political leaders. During electoral campaigns, young people are integrated into the "general exchange of services". They enter into clientelistic relationships with politicians to "play the game" of reproduction of the dominant system by mobilising to gain economic advantages from the political manna. They view it as an opportunity to get fat off the money of politicians and their political preferences are reduced to economic realism. The partisan engagement of these young people is bought and sold. Their goal is not to win a victory for the ideas of a political party or its political programme, or an ideology based on values: "me, when I take part in a campaign, I get paid. We bargain up front; it's like a contract. For me to mobilise people, there is a contract. But I don't go for promises. If I do that for you, I want my share. For instance, I could ask for 100,000 francs and, at each rally, if I have to travel, I ask for money (…). They can ask you for a list of guys you mobilised for a rally. They look at the list and pay you 1000 francs for each person" (Oumar Dassasgo, quoted by Kieffer, 2006). Far from being political activists, these young people only join a party for the duration of the electoral campaign and are temporarily mobilised to achieve limited and immediate goals. Politics becomes a "deal" like any other, in fact, a booming business. Instead of traditional forms of party membership with cards and dues, they prefer a partial, temporary, circumstantial and reversible commitment.

Motivated by instrumental rationality, these young people are quick to make the most of the exchange-based relationship specific to the electoral period before it ends. In the climate of electoral transactions, *grins* are metamorphosed into party cells that offer their services to any political party that calls on them in order to accumulate the most resources possible, which will be used for the operating expenses of the *grin*. Election time marks the triumph of ruse in the game of political haggling. Politicians are aware they are entering into a fool's bargain, but they have to "play the game". The reciprocal relationship that politicians seek to establish through electoral gifts is derided by young people who are mostly not even enrolled on the voting list. This explains the electoral abstentionism or protest votes that can be observed among the young.

The presence of a political imagination among young people that puts the accent on ruse, dispassionate engagement and instrumentality of political parties can be explained in part by the disillusionment with the world that can be perceived in their general discourse when they describe and denounce social inequalities and injustice, the moral economy of the corruption of the "system" that makes the political arena a derisory parade of politicians. One young man explained the reasons for their resentment: "young people suffer while big, fancy cars drive around in Ouaga. There are people buying cars worth 80 million, when most of the population is poor. Those people don't think about the hereafter. It isn't normal for somebody to eat enough food for 40 people, just for himself" (Soul, known as "the Malagasy", Sector. 13, Zogona). In their tea clubs, young people denounce the growing polarisation of the social space, divided between a minority of 'haves' and a majority of increasingly destitute 'have-nots'. Contestation of the political elite, combined with experience of the social inequalities characterising the reigning social order, reveals a

228

sarcastic attitude among youths in relation to the national social world. In addition, the politicians' false electoral promises form the foundation for the depoliticisation of young people and their distrust of all political speeches and speakers: "politicians are real phoneys. There's nobody phonier than a politician. They'll never keep their word" (Soul, known as "the Malagasy", Sector 13, Zogona). Thus, political parties are depreciated, set aside in favour of more "concrete" action.

Political parties lose their legitimacy in the eyes of young people and their identity is confused because the "causes" they defend are not at all in phase with their inner aspirations.

Clientelistic distributions during electoral campaigns pervert the electoral system and induce political disaffiliation in young people, causing a crisis in youth activism. The decline of "traditional activism" (Dubar, 2000) due to a regular drop in youth participation in party politics can be measured by the number of membership cards issued by the political parties and the trends in electoral scores. New forms of conditional and temporary political engagement and participation in a context of commodification of the vote have led to the collapse and confusion of political references and the fragmentation of ideological references. The great ideological confrontations of the past and the purely verbal sparring matches of the educated youth formerly determined the "normal" form of activism, involving strong internalisation of collective values and effective participation in public affairs. The republican and democratic form of commitment to party politics among young people would be to express, affirm and defend their opinions and ensure victory for their party's cause, which also becomes their own "cause".

The multiple forms of electoral exchanges in which young members of *grins de thé* are involved create a link between young people and politicians. The politicians constitute social capital that the youths mobilise to deal with various day-to-day hardships they constantly face: "the young people who aren't

229

struggling, here, they're the ones running after the guys from the C.D.P.[1] They're the ones organising C.D.P. events and they take advantage of them to run their own deals on the side. Then, when, from time to time, they have problems, they go and see the guys there to get help. That's all they get. But they're not getting any more status in the neighbourhood. They haven't changed" (Ibrahim, Sector 13, Zogona). Some of the young members of the grins adopt a strategy of collaboration with politicians to benefit from their favours.

As "plebeian" informal public spheres in the Habermasian sense of the term, certain *grins de thé* and ghettos show a variety of forms of expression of social criticism against the "system", suspending immediate adhesion to political orthodoxy. The ghettos have become major centres for the hip hop and Rastafarian movements, which speak out and take ethical and political stances in the public arena. The reference to the ghetto mobilised by young members of *grins de thé* and ghettos is a way of contesting the authorities. In their speech, they denounce the difficult living conditions experienced by the inhabitants of working-class neighbourhoods of the city of Ouagadougou. Many of the rap and reggae artists in the current star system come from "ghettos". According to Z and Ali: "rap gives you a chance to denounce certain things" (Julien Kieffer, 2006). The titles of one compilation are revealing: *"la caravane des justiciers"* (the caravan of righters of wrongs); *"ils ne pensent qu'à eux. Nous on doit penser à ceux qui viendront après nous"* (they only think of themselves. We have to think about those who will come after us) (Ali Ouidi, quoted by Julien Kieffer, 2006).

These rap artists call for greater awareness of social injustice, and they solemnly proclaim that "the revolution of those whose voices are not heard will come" (quoted by Kieffer, 2006). These cultural borrowings promoted by transnationalism and globalization come from African-American diaspora cultural movements that denounce social injustice and inequalities. The construction of a popular urban

230

street culture bears witness to the will of young urbanites to create their own standards, references and identities. The formation and emergence of a new urban identity is expressed through violent claims as they seek to build their legitimacy in the public sphere.

Another fraction of the young people in the *grins de thé*/ghettos joins forces with intellectuals in an ethical and political front conceived as a form of popular resistance in the pragmatic register of concrete action. These young people are deeply involved in a process of collective mobilisation against the unbearable turpitude of the dominant class: "alone, there is nothing I can do to fight and change the situation. That is why I fight alongside the union organisations to make things change" (Hien, Sector 13, Zogona). Young members of *grins de thé* organise popular resistance against the dominant social model through individual, then collective reactions to the violence induced by the insecurity affecting young people: "at the 'grassroots' level, we often participate in protest marches against the high cost of living, against the ruling system. Through these marches, we fight for better living conditions for the people of Burkina Faso and for ourselves" (Romaric, Sector 13, Zogona).

The horrible assassination of journalist Norbert Zongo in December 1998, was a strong moment of social and political turmoil that prompted young members of *grins de thé* to launch a powerful movement of popular contestation of the established order. In this case, we are obliged to question the conditions of social performance of the educated, academic discourse. The existence of synergy between intellectual criticism and the popular thinking of the *grins de thé* can be seen in the social genealogy of the contesting discourse arising from the same protest dynamics that grew out of the current social tensions. This social criticism is only the objective emanation of a collective effort to develop a political discourse of

231

resistance against a "plutocratic system" born of the structural adjustment programme.

Satirical journalist Norbert Zongo amplified radical social criticism of the "essence of liberalism" which met with favourable echoes among young members of *grins de thé* and ghettos. The youth took on his political claim as their own and wielded his contesting arguments like symbolic weapons against the dominant political order. The political claim was founded on popular elaboration of protest arguments which young people have turned into their own symbolic weapon against the repeated assaults of the dominant political order: "this social criticism whose homogeneity must always be questioned is both a will to negate the current social world and, based on this negation, a proposal for its subversion with a view to laying the foundations for a new order stripped of the unbearable aspects of today's world" (Ouédraogo, 2005).

The journalist crystallised popular awareness of latent opinions or attitudes. By formalising latent predispositions into opinions, then effective behaviour, he amplified them and accelerated their evolution and exercised a massive dynamogenic influence on young people, who have a psychological predisposition to fight to satisfy their needs and expectations. The political movement deployed after the murder of journalist Norbert Zongo was structured very early on around a coalition of "mass democratic organizations and political parties" otherwise known as the *"mouvement trop c'est trop!"* (enough is enough movement). Since then, other social movements appeared based on youth and mainly students' initiatives such as *"la vie chère"* - "the expensive life" (Hagberg 2010). The young members of *grins de thé* who are active participants in such movements are taken in hand by a front of social forces for change, within which youths point an accusing finger at those who dominate the "system": "it's the system in place. It's because of mismanagement by the authorities of the country. They have monopolised all of our nation's wealth.

There is also the frequency of misappropriation of public funds. And then the young people are the victims because they need resources to live, too" (Hien, Sector 13, Zogona). It is a call for greater justice through a radical denunciation of leaders accused of using the government as their principal source of accumulation. These "*nouveaux riches*" are on the lookout for any opportunities afforded by their dominant position in the social hierarchy.

The intensity of the protest has drawn these young people into urban political violence as a new form of radical indictment of the established order. Obeying a watchword of "active resistance" laid down by the leadership of the social front, young people continue to regularly take to the streets and engage in violent confrontations with the "forces of law and order", physically destroying public property as a symbol of the government, setting up barricades and burning tires on the main thoroughfares of the city. The members of this "shock division" of the social front that expresses itself in the street through violent political action have been described by journalists as "urban guerrillas" (Hien 2004).

Conclusion

Young people are producing and disseminating new values within postcolonial social formations they are reinventing for themselves. The street takes on a considerable cultural dimension that gives rise to new popular figures through body images, attitudes and practices tinged with universalism. Thus, *grins de thé* appear as one of the ways of negotiating the means of social existence for young people faced with the rise of extreme insecurity and the dissolution of the social bond in the pervading context of blind, arrogant and dominating economism. The market economy that governs the new terms of relationships with others has led to growing and unequal

233

polarisation of social groups, generating social tensions that run throughout the urban fabric.

Analysis of the theme should therefore be part of the genesis of a local historic experience that informs social ties, defines criteria of belonging, and redefines the often invisible social boundaries and the stakes of social competition leading to urban violence. The gradual amplification of urban political violence may be interpreted as the outcome of a process rooted in the endless institutional violence experienced by the youths of the *grins de thé* and ghettos, which can be seen in their rhetoric on the social world and whose final stage takes place in the street in a violent confrontation with the "forces of law and order" that defend the established political orthodoxy and act as legitimate representatives of the government and its monopoly over social control.

The production of street culture in the margins of society marks a break from the cultures inherited from the colonial project. The postcolonial urban dynamics characterised by deinstitutionalisation is driven by new urban logics based on identity rejection and reinvention, new forms of sociability, a particular mode of management of urban territories, and new modes of popular action and expression in urban youth. The construction of an urban street culture reveals the dynamics of change in a postcolonial context caught up in its own contradictions. Beyond the forms of exclusion produced by the accelerated monetisation of social relations lies a deep-seated crisis of a nation-state in gestation, or a specific mode of governance (Hagberg 2010: 295). Indeed, as the supreme authority of social regulation, standardisation and homogenisation, and guarantor of society, the nation-state seems to have been taken hostage by hegemonic social groups that use and abuse their dominant position in government spheres to accumulate a maximum of common resources whose unequal redistribution reinforces social divides, creates often irreconcilable antagonisms and generates sarcastic

234

distance among the dominated as well as specific popular political movements and activities actually creating specific urban topographies and social spaces of debates, opinion, solidarity and identity building. The *grins* and ghettos are such spaces. Besides their political dimensions, the *grins* as flexible social spaces, appear as a nexus, a creative answer, in the management of the numerous paradoxes and gaps underlined in the daily lives of young people in Ouagadougou. This is achieved through particular cultural practices and/or styles (language, music, tea drinking, even smoking, etc.), reciprocal relations based on non-monetised exchanges, exchanges of information, services, connections, and a strong insertion in a network where social age and status are determinant.

Politically, it can be posited that the social control mechanisms of the nation-state have failed. There is an urgent need to promote and strengthen the intermediary bodies referred to by Durkheim in order to gradually reintegrate socially dominated and ostracised groups into the network of ordinary relations.

Notes

1. C.D.P.: *Congrès pour la Démocratie et le Progrès* (congress for democracy and progress), the presidential majority party.

Bibliography

Berger, Peter & Thomas Luckmann. 1966. The Social Construction of Reality: A Treatise to the Sociology of Knowledge. Garden City, New York: Anchor Books.

Biaya, Thikala, K. 2000. *"Jeunes et culture de la rue en Afrique urbaine (Addis-Abeba, Dakar et Kinshasa)"*. *Politique Africaine*, No. 80 – December 2000

Bourdieu, Pierre. 2000. *Propos sur le champ politique* Lyon: Presses universitaires de Lyon, 2000.

Dubar, Claude, 2000. *La crise des identités. L'interprétation d'une mutation* Paris: PUF, 2000.

Elias Norbert, 1997. *Logiques de l'exclusion* Paris: Fayard, 1997.

Hagberg, Stan, 2010. *"Démocratie à double façade"*, in Hilgers M. and Mazzocchetti J. (eds.) *Révoltes et oppositions dans un régime semi-autoritaire. Le cas du Burkina-Faso.* Paris: Karthala, pp.295-306

Hien Ollo Pepin, 2004, "Individus et Participation à l'espace public en pays Lobi: De la révolution à la démocratie". Mémoire de maîtrise en sociologie, Université de Ouagadougou, Département de Sociologie.

Kieffer, Julien, 2006. *"Si tu as les feuilles, tu fais la loi". Représentations et pratiques des jeunes ouagalais pendant la campagne présidentielle de 2005 (Burkina Faso)*, Ouagadougou, Etude Récit, No. 13, September 2006.

Kologo, Oumarou. 2007. *"Enjeux des dons dans le jeu électoral au Burkina Faso: analyse sociopolitique des comportements électoraux dans la ville de Ouagadougou"*. DEA Political Science thesis, UFR/SJP, University of Ouagadougou, Burkina Faso, 2006-2007.

Ouedraogo, Jean-Bernard, 2005. *"N'an laara an saara. Critique sociale et arguments de révolte populaire au Burkina Faso"*, in du Tertre E., Ouédraogo J-B. & Trivière F-X. (eds.), *Exercices sociologiques autour de Roger Cornu. Dans le chaudron de la sorcière.* Paris: L'Harmattan.

Xiberras, Martine. 2000. *Les théories de l'exclusion.* Paris: Armand Colin, 2000.

Index

Depoliticisation 229
Durham, Deborah 6, 110
Durkheim 8, 44, 98, 109, 235

Elopement 96-99, 112, 114, 115,118-128
Ethnography 88, 104
Exclusion 156, 170, 217-219, 223-225, 234

Freedom 10, 63, 201, 217

Gbagbo, Laurent 192
Ghetto 153, 223, 225, 230
Globalisation 148, 176
Governmentality 16, 36

Habitus 38
Hip hop 18, 140-146, 152, 230
Honwana, Alcinda 2, 3, 7, 11, 22, 51, 70, 106, 138
Identity 5, 14, 20, 21, 24, 27, 96, 99, 110, 111, 122-126
    African 98
    Social 96, 171, 179

    Urban 231, 179, 223, 231, 233

Ideology 11, 15, 108, 115, 138, 162, 192, 197, 198, 210, 227

Informal economy 66, 83, 172
Insecurity 148
Institutionalisation 21, 37
Internet 143, 148

Justice 233
Kony, Joseph 157, 159
    2012 158, 163
Kuhn 39

Lakwena, Alice 157
Liminality 96
LRA (Lords Resistance Army) 156, 157, 160

Market economy 233
Marriage 16, 26, 96-99, 103-131
Mau Mau 146
Methods 4, 10, 13, 17, 18, 33, 75, 76, 84
Migration 61, 62, 66, 96, 121
Modernity 42, 137, 138, 145, 148-154, 217
Museveni, Yoweri 156-160

O'Brien, Cruise 104-106
Order, social 8, 12, 14, 25, 41-44, 95, 98, 104, 107, 108, 225, 228
Orphan 25, 64-68
Orphanhood 68

239

www.ingramcontent.com/pod-product-compliance
Lightning Source LLC
Chambersburg PA
CBHW050640280326
41932CB00015B/2720